T0301678

PRICING CREDIT PRODUCTS

# PRICING CREDIT PRODUCTS

ROBERT L. PHILLIPS

STANFORD BUSINESS BOOKS

*An Imprint of Stanford University Press*
*Stanford, California*

Stanford University Press
Stanford, California

Special discounts for bulk quantities of Stanford Business Books are available to corporations, professional associations, and other organizations. For details and discount information, contact the special sales department of Stanford University Press. Tel: (650) 725-0820, Fax: (650) 725-3457

Printed and bound by CPI Group (UK) Ltd,Croydon, CR0 4YY

Library of Congress Cataloging-in-Publication Data

Names: Phillips, Robert L. (Robert Lewis), 1955– author.
Title: Pricing credit products / Robert L. Phillips.
Description: Stanford, California : Stanford Business Books, an imprint of Stanford University Press, 2018. |
    Includes bibliographical references and index.
Identifiers: LCCN 2018004663 (print) | LCCN 2018006506 (ebook) | ISBN 9781503605657 (e-book) |
    ISBN 9780804787208 (cloth : alk. paper)
Subjects: LCSH: Consumer credit. | Loans. | Credit. | Pricing.
Classification: LCC HG3755 (e-book) | LCC HG3755 .P46 2018 (print) | DDC 332.7/43—dc23
LC record available at https://lccn.loc.gov/2018004663

Typeset by Newgen in 10/13.5 Minion

# CONTENTS

# FIGURES

# TABLES

PRICING CREDIT PRODUCTS

# INTRODUCTION

The 2007–2008 financial crisis brought the previously esoteric topic of consumer loan pricing to the front page of every newspaper in the world. As in previous financial crises, in 2007 and 2008 global credit markets "seized up," which makes it sound as if the pistons of a giant engine had jammed in place.[1] What really happened was a failure of pricing—lenders lost faith in their ability to price loans to their customers and the institutions that bought bundles of loans from lenders lost faith in their ability to evaluate those bundles. As a result loans and loan derivatives were unavailable at any price. The result was the most prolonged and damaging economic recession in the West since the Great Depression of the 1920s.

While the causes of the 2007–2008 financial crisis have been widely debated in both academic books and in the popular press, it is universally agreed that one of the major contributors (some would argue *the* major contributor) to the collapse of the financial system was feckless consumer lending. Lenders in the United States, the United Kingdom, and elsewhere made too many foolish loans to customers who should never have gotten a loan in the first place. Other loans were offered at prices that did not reflect the true risk of the loan. Why lenders felt it was a good idea to issue so many foolish loans and why the systems were not in place to protect the global economy from the consequences of their foolishness are topics for another book. The topic of this book is the more tactical question of how lenders should price their loans to best achieve their business goals while also controlling risk. The approach described in the book is called *price optimization*. Price optimization involves creating mathematical models of how customers respond to prices and calculating how prices influence the profitability and risk of different loans. Once these steps are complete, optimization algorithms can be used to find the prices that best balance demand and profitability to meet corporate goals. Adopting price optimization enables lenders to improve profitability and control risk; ideally, it will keep them from issuing too many unsound loans and offering them at foolish prices.

Price optimization was first used by passenger airlines under the name *revenue management* to set and update their prices following deregulation.[2] Passenger airlines use their rich information about customers to vary prices dynamically in order to balance demand

and supply and to maximize profitability. Following its widespread (and widely heralded) success in the passenger airline industry, the idea of using mathematical analysis to vary prices dynamically in response to market changes spread to many other industries. Online retailers have become particularly adept at the practice.

For lenders, price optimization means applying statistical analysis (aka *machine learning*) to customer data in order to estimate how future applicants will respond to different prices for different types of loans. (For a loan, the primary element of price is the interest rate; however, various fees and other charges may also contribute to the price.) These estimates of price response are used by an optimization model that sets the prices for all loans to all customer types through all channels in order to maximize profitability while also controlling risk.

Lenders have four advantages relative to other retailers when it comes to price optimization:

1. Lenders have access to a vast amount of information about every loan applicant, and that information is of a depth and richness that is the envy of most other retailers. Lenders have available to them all the information they receive with the loan application as well as the information in the applicant's credit file. Even online retailers such as Amazon do not have access to such in-depth information about their customers.

2. Consumer lenders, unlike many retailers, do not need to worry too much about arbitrage. Consumers who are issued a loan at an attractive price are unlikely to use that as an opportunity to become a lender themselves.

3. Most lenders have already established complex pricing structures that require periodically setting and updating thousands or tens of thousands of prices. For example, a large home-equity lender in the United States varies prices on the basis of size of loan, term, resident state of applicant, loan-to-value ratio (LTV), combined loan-to-value ratio (CLTV), and risk band. When all the combinations of dimensions are counted, the lender is setting tens of thousands of loan prices. This is both a challenge and an opportunity. It is a challenge to set and manage so many prices. It is an opportunity because the large number of prices enables the lender to target pricing specifically to the needs and characteristics of different customers.

4. Many lenders have sophisticated analytical groups in-house and have both the personnel and infrastructure to implement price optimization.

Despite these advantages, the retail lending industry has been slow to adopt price optimization—much slower than most other retailers, many of whom have adopted highly sophisticated systems for dynamic pricing. For example, Figure INT.1 shows the price that Amazon displayed on its website for a randomly chosen product (a 50-pack of velvet suit hangers) for a 6-month period.[3] Over this period, Amazon varied the price from a low of $14.43 to a high of $39.99. Amazon's computerized pricing algorithms continually adjust the prices of tens of thousands of items for sale online in response to changes in cost, competitive actions, inventory levels, and overall market demand. In addition, Amazon periodically performs price tests to gauge the price sensitivity of their customers to different products. The result is prices that can change very frequently—as with the pack of hangers in Figure INT.1, for which the price changed 44 times in three months, or about once every other day. This frequency of change is not atypical; Amazon, for example, changes the prices of some items many times daily. Many other online retailers, including those that sell through Amazon's platform, also utilize computerized algorithms to set and update prices. In most cases, these companies would consider their ability to adjust prices intelligently over time to be a critical factor in their ability to compete.

Most retail lenders are nowhere near Amazon's level of pricing sophistication. It is reasonable to ask why—given the advantages enumerated above—retail lenders have been laggards in adopting price optimization. One reason seems to be the fact that, for most of history, pricing was an afterthought for most lenders. Until well into the 1980s, most banks offered a single consumer-lending product—mortgages—at a single rate. Mortgage prices were set to recoup costs, including expected losses, plus a margin. Prices needed to be updated only when the cost of capital changed. It has been said that loan pricing in this era was based on the *three-six-three rule*: "Borrow at 3%, lend at 6%, on the golf course by 3:00." While facetious, this reflects the fact that retail loan pricing was for a long time extremely simple and required little sophistication.

Another reason lenders have been slow to adopt price optimization may be the natural conservatism of the industry. As one bank executive put it, "No bank wants to be first to adopt a new technology and no bank wants to be third." Lenders may also be concerned

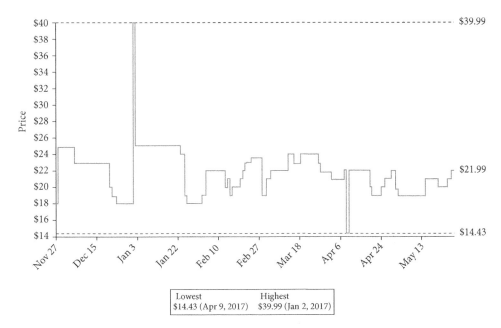

| Lowest | Highest |
|---|---|
| $14.43 (Apr 9, 2017) | $39.99 (Jan 2, 2017) |

**Figure INT.1**   Price displayed on Amazon.com for a 50-pack of velvet suit hangers from Amazon Basics from November 27, 2016, through May 16, 2017

SOURCE: Camelcamelcamel.com.

that adoption of price optimization will bring unwanted regulatory attention. This should not be a major concern: as long as proper constraints are applied, the results of price optimization can always be brought into compliance with regulation; price optimization is a way of improving on what a lender would otherwise be doing manually. Nonetheless, the concern persists: not surprisingly, these concerns appear to be the strongest in countries with the most active financial regulatory agencies such as the United States.

Although the industry lags online retail, large lenders have begun to adopt price optimization. For competitive reasons, banks are understandably reluctant to publicize their use of price optimization. However, at least 20 leading retail lenders worldwide have adopted some form of price optimization. For example, a Canadian bank reported that it realized $33 million in additional net interest margin on its unsecured loan portfolio as a result of price optimization.[4]

This book serves as a practical introduction for a lender considering the possibility of price optimization or for a researcher interested in how price optimization applies to lending. It provides an introduction to the basic concepts of price optimization, including consumer demand modeling, segmentation, and optimization. It also covers topics specific to lending—in particular risk and the calculation of loan profitability. Most of these topics have been covered elsewhere, but this book brings them together in a single place to show how a lender can use data that it has available (or can easily acquire) in a process that enables it to maximize profitability or meet other business goals.

## ORGANIZATION OF THE BOOK

The following two chapters of the book provide some background on the retail lending industry and the critical concept of risk. Chapter 1 presents an overview of the consumer-lending market, beginning with a brief history of consumer credit, followed by a discussion of the primary sources and forms of consumer credit in use today as well as the most common processes by which consumer credit is priced and prices are communicated to customers. Chapter 2 describes the sources and types of risk involved in a loan and shows how this risk can be quantified and estimated using historical data from credit scores. The final section of Chapter 2 describes a model of price-dependent risk. Much of the material in these two chapters—with the exception of the section on price-dependent risk—is likely to be familiar to those with experience in the industry.

Optimizing the price of a loan requires understanding two fundamental relationships: how the profitability of the loan changes as a function of its price and how demand for the loan depends on its price. Chapter 3 addresses the first relationship, detailing how the profitability of a loan can be calculated as a function of its price and other factors such as size and term. It also discusses the relationship of risk and loan price and why a lender with a large portfolio of loans should act "risk-neutral" in pricing an incremental loan. While determining the profitability of a loan requires somewhat tedious calculations, the underlying idea that price optimization is based on *incremental* revenue and cost is extremely important.

Understanding how the demand for a loan will change as a function of its price is the topic of Chapters 4–6. Chapter 4 describes the basics of price sensitivity and how (and why) the number of people who will take up a loan at different prices can be captured in a price-response curve. Chapter 5 discusses different methods for estimating price sensitivity. The primary focus of this chapter is describing how logistic regression can be used to fit a price-response function to historical loan demand data; however, it also discusses the use of other machine-learning approaches. Chapter 6 discusses how customer, loan, and channel attributes influence price sensitivity and how differences in price sensitivity along those dimensions can be used to segment customers. Taken together, the three chapters provide a self-contained primer on price sensitivity, starting with the basic concepts and proceeding through techniques for estimating price sensitivity and for segmenting loan transactions.

Chapter 7 is something of a capstone: it shows how the calculations of incremental profit and price response can be combined to find optimal prices. It starts with the case of finding the optimal price for a simple loan with price-dependent risk. It proceeds to cover how prices for a large set of different loans being offered to different customer segments through different channels can be optimized in the presence of multiple business constraints. Finally, it discusses how an efficient frontier can be used to illustrate the trade-off between two different objective functions, for example, maximizing profit versus maximizing lending balances.

The models of consumer price response developed in Chapters 4–6 and utilized in optimization in Chapter 7 are based on the assumption that consumers make decisions in an economically rational fashion. Research in behavioral economics has shown that this is a simplistic view of the world and that consumers consistently deviate from the assumptions of rationality. Chapter 8 discusses these deviations and how they might influence loan pricing, as well as their implications for regulators.

Appendix A presents some basic mathematical results on series and discounting that are used in the book, and Appendix B derives some of the basic properties of a simple loan. Appendix C presents an overview of consumer-choice theory and how it implies the existence of a price-response function. This theory underlies the mathematics of price sensitivity in Chapter 4 and underlies the definition of "consumer rationality" used in Chapter 8.

Price optimization for lending is quite a broad topic, and as a result, this book draws from several different fields, including statistical inference and machine learning, price theory, economics, optimization, risk analysis, and management accounting. Each of these fields is the subject of a vast and varied literature of its own; I have presented only the material that is relevant to price optimization. The notes provide references to other works for readers who would like to dig deeper into a particular topic. This book assumes familiarity with mathematics at the level typically required for an MBA, including basic calculus and some probability theory. For ease of reading, I have kept the number of notes to a minimum and have used in-text references only for direct quotations. Additional references, clarifications, and elaborations can be found in the endnotes to each chapter.

For clarity, I call anyone who is offering a loan a *lender* and anyone who is considering taking a loan a *customer*. This seems less clumsy than the more accurate term *prospective borrower.* If a customer takes a loan, she becomes a *borrower.* I use the term *consumer* in a broader sense to refer to individuals as economic decision makers with no specific reference to loans. For clarity, I refer to lenders using male pronouns and customers and borrowers using female pronouns.

This book has an accompanying data set—the "e-Car Data Set"—which can be accessed at http://www.sup.org/pricingcreditproducts or https://info.nomissolutions.com/pricing_credit_products as an Excel file. The data set includes the results of 50,000 loan offers extended by an online lender over a 2-year period to a variety of types of customer. It should enable a reader to replicate the price-sensitivity results in Chapter 5 and to explore alternative approaches to estimating price sensitivity.

## ACKNOWLEDGMENTS

Much of this book was written while I was a professor at the Columbia Business School, and it benefited from discussions with many of my colleagues at Columbia, including Guillermo Gallego, Costis Maglaras, Stephan Meier, Serdar Simsek, and Garrett van Ryzin, among others. Much of my thinking on price optimization for lending was developed through my work at Nomis Solutions and my collaboration with many colleagues there, including Prashant Balepur, Hollis Fishelson-Holstein, Matt Kuckuk, Shyue-Ming Loh, and Robin Raffard. Extensive comments on individual chapters were provided by Brenda Barnes, Greg Campbell, Frank Rohde, Mohammad Moghadasi, Eric Wells, and Kai Yin. Additional support and valuable discussion, especially regarding consumers' liquidity preferences, were provided by other colleagues, including Peter Bagshaw, Virginia McVeigh, Michael Eldredge, Brian Keyser, Megan Lazar, Özalp Özer, Frank Quilty, and Lacy Wagner.

I am grateful to the Stanford Business School for providing me a position as visiting scholar during which I was able to complete much of the book. Thanks also are due to Stanford University Press and to my editor, Margo Beth Fleming. I am especially grateful to Simon Caufield, who was my partner in crime in founding Nomis Solutions with the idea of bringing price-optimization techniques to the financial services industry. And, of course, Doria's support is critical to anything I do.

## NOTES

1. For example, the *New York Times* reported on November 11, 2008, "The credit markets seized up as confidence in the nation's financial system ebbed" (Bajaj and Healy 2008).

2. For the history of price optimization (known as *revenue management*) and its application in the airline industry, see Barnes (2012) and Phillips (2005).

3. The price track in Figure INT.1 is from the website Camelcamelcamel.com, which provides price tracking for any item sold on Amazon. For a discussion of the pricing algorithms used by sellers on Amazon, see Chen, Mislove, and Wilson (2016).

4. The Canadian unsecured personal lending benefits can be found on the Nomis Solutions website at https://view.highspot.com/viewer/59382bd7b91988384358ffb4.

# 1   THE CONSUMER CREDIT MARKET

Credit is offered to consumers and businesses in a wide variety of forms, by a wide variety of entities, under a wide variety of terms. This chapter provides an overview of consumer credit, how it evolved, and how it is provided today. Some understanding of the history of consumer credit is helpful for understanding why such a wide variety of loans are offered today and why the predominant terms under which loans are offered vary from country to country. Following a brief survey of the history of consumer credit, we describe the major categories of consumer credit and the various processes by which loans are priced and the prices communicated to customers. Finally, we discuss the different types of regulation that apply to consumer lending and how they influence pricing.

## BRIEF HISTORY

Debt and credit are older than recorded history—no one will ever be able to pinpoint the date at which one *Homo sapiens* (or was it *Homo neanderthalensis?*) provided another with something desired in that moment in return for future consideration. Anthropologists and sociologists remind us that our current concept of a loan—a sum of money received right now in return for a promise of future payments—is only a special case of the web of debts and obligations, both monetary and nonmonetary, that pervade any society.[1] But even the more restricted idea of lending money at interest is ancient—a group of Babylonian tablets dating from 1800–1600 BC describe algorithms for computing compound interest, and in later centuries lending at interest was also a common practice in ancient Greece and Rome.

The early Christian church prohibited lending (but not borrowing) money at interest, a prohibition that was upheld by the Roman Catholic Church throughout the Middle Ages. As a result, for many centuries Jewish lenders were the primary source of loans to the nobility and great merchant houses. The formal prohibition against usury, or *usuria* (the Latin word for lending at interest), began to break down in England in the early sixteenth century, when Henry VIII broke from the Catholic Church, and on the European continent following the Protestant Reformation.

Notwithstanding this long history, in Europe up until the sixteenth century, borrowing and lending were the purview of kings, nobles, and merchants: there was little consumer credit, not to mention precious few consumers in the modern sense of the word. The only credit generally available to commoners was extended by tradespeople and shopkeepers who allowed their customers to run up purchase accounts. In England, records of trade debt date back to the first decades of the sixteenth century. Account books show that many of the debts were tiny—denominated in pennies—and were regularly paid off. However, the wealthy and the nobility were often allowed to amass substantial debts. In the eighteenth century disputes among tradespeople and debtors were common, and an elaborate infrastructure of debt courts and debtors' prisons was established that lasted well into the nineteenth century. Defaults on shop credit were not uncommon; for example, Charles Dickens's father was thrown into Marshalsea debtors' prison for his inability to pay off a £40 debt to a local baker.[2]

Shop credit was typically interest-free: the borrower was expected to pay only the cumulative cost of purchased goods rather than as a source of profit itself. And, of course, merchants extended credit primarily as a way to move their goods. The first form of consumer credit to be offered by specialized institutional lenders in England was the mortgage. In the United States, mortgages were available from the late eighteenth century. However, well into the nineteenth century, the preferred method for buying a house was to save up for it, which meant a wait of ten years or more for the average wage earner. Following the Civil War, independent lenders and cooperative societies arose to provide mortgages to individuals. In this case, a typical approach to funding a house was for a prospective home owner to make a 50% down payment and borrow the rest from a savings bank, a building and loan association, or a private mortgage dealer. The borrower made interest payments semiannually for the following three to eight years, then paid the principal in a lump sum at the end of the term. Modern amortized loans—in which both principal and interest are paid off with equal monthly payments over the term of the loan—did not become popular until the 1920s.[3]

The late nineteenth century saw the rise of installment credit in the United States as a means to enable families to purchase the increasing number of expensive goods being brought to market. The first innovation to be widely sold on installment was the reaping machine. A new reaping machine enabled farmers to increase their productivity tenfold, but most farmers could not afford to purchase one. The industrialist Cyrus McCormick is credited with introducing an installment plan, and competing manufacturers quickly followed his lead. Many farming families were willing to take on the resulting debt in order to enjoy the benefits of increased productivity.

Urban families did not want reapers, but they did want sewing machines, which were marketed on a national scale starting in the 1850s. Like reapers, sewing machines were expensive, and installment sales were necessary to put them within reach of the average family. Unlike shop credit, installment sales of sewing machines usually involved an additional charge. In 1900 a Singer machine could be purchased for $30 cash up front or $40 on an installment plan. The additional charge was justified to the purchaser through the convenience of installment payments, but it also provided Singer with the opportunity to cover losses from defaults as well as the forgone returns from the capital advanced.

The first two decades of the twentieth century saw an explosion of installment credit in the United States. Mass production, mass marketing, and a growing middle class combined to create both supply and demand for an array of goods that many households could not afford to purchase from ready cash. Carriages, bicycles, pianos, furniture—even clothing—could all be purchased on installment during the early years of the twentieth century. But it was the arrival of the automobile that really initiated American consumers into the world of credit. In 1924 General Motors established the General Motors Acceptance Corporation (GMAC) to provide loans to help consumers purchase GM cars; the program was wildly successful and was soon imitated by other manufacturers. By 1929, 76% of new cars in the United States were sold on credit.

Commercial bankers were latecomers to consumer lending: banks began to establish consumer-lending departments only in the 1920s. The primary reason banks did not venture into personal lending earlier was the traditional sanctity of deposits—bankers were terrified that a large number of depositors would simultaneously demand their money, which they would be unable to supply because it was out on loan. (This is, of course, exactly what happened in 1929.) A secondary reason bankers were reluctant to extend credit to consumers was the common belief that consumer loans were highly risky. Bankers felt that business loans were "productive"—the money would be invested in ways that would generate income to repay the loan. In contrast, consumer loans were primarily for consumption, and there was no guarantee that a borrower would feel obligated (or have the wherewithal) to repay the loan after using the money for purchases. Furthermore, businesses—unlike many consumers—typically had valuable assets that could be seized if the loan was not repaid.

Banks had begun to experiment with consumer lending in the 1920s, but consumer-lending departments did not become commonplace until the mid-1930s. Perhaps surprisingly, it was the Great Depression that hastened the spread of consumer lending from a handful of urban banks in 1928 to a standard offering by 1939. During the Great Depression, the market for business loans essentially evaporated and bankers were forced to overcome their initial aversion and embrace consumer lending if they were to survive at all and, of course, many didn't survive.

The most important innovation in consumer credit following World War II was the credit card. Although a few banks in the United States had issued charge cards that allowed favored customers to charge purchases directly to the bank as early as the 1930s, the first multipurpose credit card was issued by Diners Club in 1950. In the next few years Carte Blanche and American Express followed suit. Similar to today's credit cards, these cards enabled revolving credit, but they were not backed by a bank and were accepted by only a few merchants. In 1958, Bank of America launched the BankAmericard (later known as Visa), the first widely accepted modern credit card. The first credit card introduced outside the United States was Barclaycard, which launched in the United Kingdom in 1966. Credit cards enjoyed explosive growth and are today one of the most important forms of consumer credit—and certainly the source of most credit transactions—around the world.

Throughout its history consumer lending has been characterized by spurts of innovation, such as securitized mortgage lending, installment purchases, auto lending, bank lending, and credit cards. In every case, each new innovation was able to take root and grow without entirely displacing previous forms. The most recent innovation in consumer credit is peer-to-peer lending, in which platforms such as Zopa in the United Kingdom and LendingClub in the United States connect borrowers and lenders on the Internet. Whether or not this new form of lending will thrive, and if so, the extent to which it will displace other forms, is yet to be determined. In any case, this history of innovation without complete displacement of earlier forms is a major reason so many different varieties of consumer credit are available from so many different sources.

History also explains why the most popular forms of loans and pricing processes vary from country to country. For example, the 30-year fixed-rate mortgage is the most popular form of mortgage in the United States, but it is relatively rare in other countries. In Canada the most popular mortgage has a 5-year term and a 20-year amortization period. The prevalence of the 30-year fixed-rate mortgage in the American market can be traced to the efforts of the Federal Housing Administration (FHA) to stimulate housing sales during the Great Depression. The FHA simplified the mortgage market by establishing a standardized system with 25- and 30-year amortized mortgages that required a down payment of 10 percent based on a standardized appraisal. This system, which was created to support and encourage home ownership during the Great Depression, set the template for mortgages that has persisted to this day.[4]

Consumer debt has been growing across the United States and the developed world for more than a century. Figure 1.1 shows the levels of debt per household in the United States from 1920 to 2010. While the general trend has been upward, three periods of particularly rapid growth are apparent. The first, during the 1920s, coincided with the increasing popularity of installment sales (including auto loans) and the entry of banks into the consumer credit market. This phase of growth came to an end with the onset of the Great Depression:

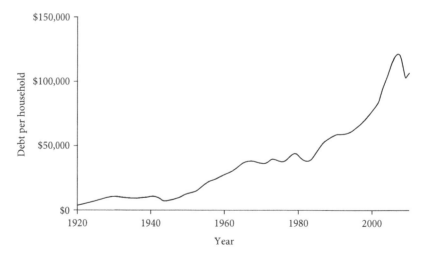

**Figure 1.1**    Real debt per household in the United States from 1920 through 2010
SOURCE: Federal Reserve Bank of New York (2017).

household debt did not increase again until after World War II. Post–World War II debt growth was fueled primarily by rapidly expanding home ownership, encouraged by government programs such as the Veterans Administration and the creation of Fannie Mae and Freddie Mac. This phase of growth came to an end in the 1970s when the growth of debt was tempered by both recession and high interest rates: the prime rate hit its all-time high of 21.5% in December 1980. Household debt began to grow again with the return of economic growth in the 1980s and grew rapidly until the financial crisis of 2008–2009. Some of the growth in consumer debt during this period was due to the increased availability of credit cards and a rapid expansion of student loans, but, as in previous periods of debt growth, the primary driver of consumer debt was the rapid growth of mortgages.

Over the past fifty years, consumer debt per household has been increasing in all developed countries. In most countries, the ratio of household debt to household wealth has lagged that of the United States. A notable exception is Canada, where the ratio of household debt to wealth surpassed that of the United States in 2014. Mortgages are by far the largest component of consumer debt in most developed countries. Table 1.1 shows the components of total household debt in the United States as of Q1 2017.

## CREDIT PRODUCTS

Some of the important characteristics that differentiate credit products are the following:

- The *payment period* is the time interval between payments. A lender will typically charge a late fee if a minimum payment is not made when due at the end of each payment period.

- The *compounding period* defines the intervals when interest is computed on the outstanding balance. At the end of a compounding period, the corresponding interest rate will be applied to the current balance (including any accrued and unpaid interest) to determine additional interest due. Typically, the compounding period is less than or equal to the payment period.

- The *amortization period* is the total "life" of the loan used to calculate payments. For a simple loan with a fixed balance, a borrower who made the periodic payment each period would exactly pay off the loan in the last period.

TABLE 1.1
*Composition of household debt in the United States in the first quarter of 2017*

| Type of debt | Total for all households ($ trillions) | Total per household carrying this debt ($) | Total household debt (%) |
|---|---|---|---|
| Mortgages | 8.95 | 168,614 | 71.1 |
| Student loans | 1.34 | 48,172 | 10.6 |
| Auto loans | 1.17 | 27,141 | 9.3 |
| Credit cards | .76 | 15,762 | 6.0 |
| Other | .37 | 4,302 | 2.9 |

SOURCE: Federal Reserve Bank of New York (2017).
NOTE: "Mortgages" refers to all debt secured with real estate, including home-equity loans and lines.

- The *term* of a loan is the length of time over which loan payments are due. If the term is less than the amortization period, then the remaining balance is typically due with the last payment. For example, in Canada, the most common mortgage has a 5-year term but a 20-year amortization period. At the end of the fifth year, the remaining principal is due as part of the final payment.

- A *line of credit* (or simply a *line*) allows a borrower to borrow up to a certain amount (the *limit*) with payments calculated on only the current balance. Thus, a $100,000 line of credit allows a borrower to borrow any amount up to $100,000. Most lines are *revolving*, which means that the limit is applied to the total amount borrowed less total balance repayments.

- A *fixed-rate loan* is one in which the interest rate does not change over the term of the loan. In contrast, the rate associated with a *variable-rate* loan can change periodically on the basis of changes in some specified market index rate. For example, the rate on a variable-rate mortgage might be adjusted every six months to the prime rate plus .5%.

- A *simple loan* is one with a fixed interest rate and equal payments throughout its term.

- *Collateral* is property pledged as security for a loan. If a borrower defaults, the lender is typically allowed to seize the collateral and sell it to recoup all or part of the unpaid balance. A *secured* loan is a loan with collateral, and an *unsecured* loan is a loan without collateral.

---

**Example 1.1: Revolving and Non-Revolving Credit Lines.** Alice is granted a $10,000 revolving credit line. She immediately withdraws $6,000, which means that she has $4,000 remaining on the line. Alice then repays $2,000 along with all outstanding interest. Since her credit line is revolving, she now has $6,000 remaining that she can draw upon. If the credit line were non-revolving, she would have only $4,000 remaining.

---

Each of these characteristics of credit products influences the expected profitability of a loan or line. For example, given the same balance and interest rate, a longer-term loan is more profitable than a short-term loan to the lender if it goes to term but is also riskier. A $10,000 line of credit is likely to be less profitable than a $10,000 loan at the same rate because there is a chance that the customer will utilize only part of the line of credit (or perhaps not utilize it at all). The risk associated with a secured loan will depend on the value of the collateral as well as the difficulty and expense that would be required for the lender to seize the collateral in the event that the borrower defaults. (How risk influences the profitability of a loan is discussed in detail in Chapter 3.)

The characteristics of a credit product not only influence risk and profitability to the lender; they also influence the price sensitivity of customers. As an example, all else being equal, customers are more sensitive to the price of a longer-term loan than they are to the price of a shorter-term loan. The sometimes subtle interactions among the characteristics of loan products with both profitability and price sensitivity generate much of the complexity of price optimization for consumer lending.

In the remainder of this section we describe some of the most common credit products and their characteristics.

## Unsecured Lines and Loans

An *unsecured loan* is the simplest credit product: a lender advances money to a borrower with no collateral. An unsecured *line* allows the customer to choose how much to borrow and to draw more if needed up to a specified limit. Borrowers use the money from unsecured loans for many different purposes, including automobile purchase, debt consolidation, home improvement, and travel. In the United Kingdom typical unsecured loan amounts range from £1,000 to £25,000, and typical terms range from 12 months to 5 years. Average rates for different types of loans in 2016 in the United States are shown in Table 1.2, which shows a typical pattern: unsecured loans carry a higher rate than a mortgage but a lower rate than a credit card.

Unsecured lines and loans are popular in Canada, the United Kingdom, and Western Europe. In contrast, unsecured loans represent less than 3% of outstanding household debt in the United States, where they are much less popular than in many other developed countries. Auto loans and home equity loans, both of which have lower rates (and, in the case of a home equity loans, tax advantages), fill much of the need met by unsecured loans in other countries. It could be argued that peer-to-peer lending in the United States is growing because it fills the niche between relatively low-cost secured debt and much higher-cost credit card debt—the same niche filled by unsecured lines and loans in other countries.

## Mortgages and Home Equity Loans and Lines

We use the term *mortgage* to refer to a loan that is used to purchase real estate and is secured by the property purchased. Virtually all banks in the developed world offer mortgages, and mortgages by far represent the largest portion of consumer debt. Specifically, debt secured by real estate represents about 70% of household debt in Canada and the United Kingdom, about 71% in the United States, and slightly more than 50% in Japan.

The most popular form of mortgage varies from country to country. In the United States, a wide variety of mortgages are on offer, but the most popular is the 30-year fixed mortgage, which has a term of 30 years at a fixed annual percentage rate (APR). 15- and 20-year fixed-rate mortgages are also common. An *adjustable-rate mortgage* (ARM) is one in which the APR is updated periodically on the basis of an index rate, such as the prime rate. A hybrid

TABLE 1.2
*Average APRs for different forms of credit in the United States
on June 1, 2016*

| Product | Description | Average APR (%) |
|---|---|---|
| Mortgage | 30-year fixed | 3.81 |
| Auto loan | 5-year, new car | 4.26 |
| Home equity | $30,000 HELOC | 4.82 |
| Unsecured | $30,000 5-year | 12.20 |
| Credit card | — | 16.03 |

SOURCE: bankcredit.com.

mortgage (also known as a *hybrid ARM*) is one in which the initial rate is fixed for some period of time—typically 1, 2, 3, or 5 years—but then converts to a variable rate for the remainder of its term. To make things even more complicated, many lenders offer optional "points," which enable borrowers to pay a fixed amount (usually incorporated into the balance) to receive a lower APR. The availability of these options in myriad combinations can make mortgage selection a difficult and complex decision for consumers.

In the United States, the market for mortgages has been shaped by government policies designed to encourage home ownership. For one thing, mortgage interest is deductible (up to a limit) from both national and state income taxes. In addition, two quasi-governmental organizations—Fannie Mae and Freddie Mac—provide a reliable secondary market for conforming mortgages, substantially reducing the default risk that lenders face.

The most common form of mortgage in Canada, the United Kingdom, and much of Western Europe has a 5-year term but a 20- or 30-year amortization period. This means that, in theory, the entire remaining balance of the mortgage is due as a lump sum after five years. In practice, the lender will typically offer to renew the mortgage for another five years. The short term has an advantage for the lender, who can decide to offer the renewal at a different rate from that of the original mortgage. Reasons for changing the rate might be changes in the underlying cost of capital, in the competitive landscape, or in the customer's credit score. In fact, if a customer's credit has been severely impaired, the lender may not offer a renewal at all. Of course, renewal is also an opportunity for the borrower to shop for other, possibly cheaper, alternatives. Determining the right prices and marketing offers for mortgage renewals is an important decision for lenders, especially since mortgage retention—the fraction of maturing mortgages that renew with the same lender—is tracked by analysts and considered an important measure of corporate performance.

A borrower with a long-term fixed-rate mortgage would appear to be bearing interest-rate risk. Specifically, if the market rate goes down substantially, she is stuck with monthly payments that are higher than the market rate. However, the borrower usually has the option to *refinance* her mortgage—that is, to take out a new mortgage at the lower market rate for the remaining balance and use that loan to pay off her previous mortgage. This is a particularly attractive option if the original mortgage has no prepayment penalty and the new mortgage is available at a much lower rate. In addition, some borrowers refinance as a way to lower monthly payments by extending the term of the loan.

---

**Example 1.2: Refinancing.** A borrower has a balance of $50,000 remaining on a simple loan with monthly payments at an annual interest rate of 6.0%, compounded monthly, with 15 years remaining. (A simple loan is one with a fixed interest rate and equal payments over its term.) Her current payments are $417.65 per month. (Equation 3.2 shows how to calculate the payment associated with a simple loan as a function of the balance, rate, and term.) If she refinances at a 5.0% annual rate with a 15-year term, her monthly payments will be reduced to $392.51 per month. However, if she refinances at a 6.5% annual rate with a 30-year term, her payments will be only $309.94 per month. A borrower who is highly sensitive to the monthly rate might be willing to refinance at the higher rate.

## Auto Loans

An auto loan is a loan secured by the vehicle it is used to purchase. Auto loans are an important source of credit in the United States and Canada: in 2013, about 79% of new vehicle sales and about 52% of used vehicle sales in the United States were financed with an auto loan. As Table 1.1 shows, auto loans represent slightly more than 9% of consumer debt in the United States—substantially less than mortgages but more than credit cards.

Auto loans are primarily originated through one of two different channels. A customer may take out a loan to purchase an automobile directly with a bank—this is called the *direct channel.* More commonly, a customer may take out an auto loan from the dealer who sells her the car—this is the *indirect channel.* In the indirect channel, the loan is originated through the finance and insurance division of a dealership. The dealer typically does not hold on to the loan—rather, the dealer seeks to sell it to one of any number of competing lenders. In the United States, this process is facilitated by two electronic systems—Dealertrack and RouteOne—that allow lenders to bid on auto loans by offering different interest rates. The dealer decides which of the competing lenders can purchase the loan. The rate at which the loan is purchased is the *buy rate,* and the rate offered to the customer is the *customer rate.* Typically the dealer gets to keep all or part of the difference in total interest between the customer rate and the buy rate. The fraction of the difference that the dealer is allowed to keep is the *participation rate.* Lending is often more profitable for a dealership than are vehicle sales.

---

**Example 1.3: Customer Rate and Buy Rate in Auto Lending.** A dealer issues a five-year auto loan of $20,000 at a customer rate of 5.5%, which the dealer then sells to a lender at a buy rate of 4.0% with interest on both loans compounded monthly. Assume that the dealer participation rate is 50%. Then, if the loan goes to term, the total interest over the term of the loan would be $2,847.27 at the customer rate and $2,061.12 at the buy rate. The difference between the two is $786.15, and the dealer participation is 50% of this, or $393.07. Thus, under this agreement, the lender would buy the loan from the dealer for $2,061.12 + $393.07 = $2,454.20.[5]

---

In the United States, many banks purchase auto loans, as do specialized lenders such as the Credit Acceptance Corporation and the finance arms of auto manufacturers, such as Toyota Motor Credit and the Ford Motor Credit Corporation. The original motivation for dealers and manufacturers to extend auto loans to customers was to sell more vehicles, and this still holds true today. Manufacturers commonly offer reduced rates as a mechanism to sell more cars. For example, in 2017, Ford advertised a "summer sales event" that included a 0% APR for 72 months for a loan on a new Ford Focus. Such reduced rates usually involve a so-called *subvention,* through which the manufacturer pays a lump sum to the lender (often the credit company associated with the manufacturer) for each loan funded at the promotional rate. The amount of the subvention is calculated to "make the lender whole" relative to the interest income that the dealer would have received if it had made the loan at the market rate.

---

**Example 1.4: Subvention.** The total interest income from a five-year $20,000 loan is $2,847.27 at an annual rate of 5.5% and $510.14 at an annual rate of 1.0%. If the market rate for the loan is 5.5% and the manufacturer wants a dealership to offer the loan at a 1.0% annual rate, the manufacturer would need to make a subvention payment to the lender for the difference, or $2,337.13.[6]

---

In the United States, dealers are the primary source of credit for automobile purchases, and the risk profile of prime auto loans is not significantly different from that of other prime portfolios. The situation is different, though, in other countries. In Canada and Great Britain, unsecured loans are more often used to finance vehicle purchases than are auto loans. In these countries, auto loans are targeted primarily at customers who have difficulty obtaining credit elsewhere. For this reason, auto-loan portfolios in these countries tend to be more risky than in the United States. Furthermore, auto loans in the United States are commonly securitized and sold to third parties, but this is rare in other countries.

### Credit Cards

While there are many variations, credit cards typically provide consumers and businesses with a revolving credit line with a specified limit. Credit card issuers determine minimum monthly payments based on the current balance at a specified interest rate and a standard amortization period (typically 20 years). If a borrower misses a monthly payment or makes less than the minimum payment, she is charged a late-payment fee. Revolving balances are charged a relatively high interest rate, typically much higher than mortgages and other secured and unsecured loans. As Table 1.2 shows, in June 2016, the average rate on a credit card in the United States was 16.03%, compared to 4.82% for a home equity loan and 3.81% for a mortgage. In addition to late fees, some credit cards charge an annual fee that is independent of the level of usage of the card.

The primary pricing decision associated with a credit card is the APR to charge for revolving debt. Secondary pricing decisions include the annual fee and the late-payment fee. Experience has shown that customers tend to be very sensitive to annual fees, and as a result, many issuers do not charge one. Customer sensitivity to APR and late-payment fees is difficult to estimate. Published estimates of the elasticity of credit card usage to APR range from .7 to 1.1 (an elasticity of .7 means that a 1.0% increase in the APR would lead to a .7% decrease in credit card usage). Most studies have suggested that customer sensitivity to late-payment fees is much lower. It has been hypothesized that low sensitivity to late fees may be either because customers are less aware of the fees—a saliency effect—or believe that they will not ever incur the fee.

Because the "price" of a credit card may include fees along with the interest rate, consumer advocates and regulators have worried that credit card issuers will bury information about fees in the fine print at the bottom of the credit card agreement resulting in unpleasant surprises for users. In the United States, regulation specifies that all the rates and fees associated with a credit card, including the APRs for purchases and cash advances, along with annual fees and late-payment fees, be listed in all promotional materials in 12-point (or larger) type. The cost summary in credit card promotional materials is sometimes called the Schumer box, after Charles "Chuck" Schumer, the New York congressman who sponsored the legislation. Similar rules are in place in the United Kingdom and elsewhere.

While a credit card is unquestionably a form of consumer credit, most credit card holders in the United States pay off their balances in full each month. This would suggest that many credit card holders use their credit cards primarily as a convenient substitute for cash rather than as a loan.

## Small-Business Loans and Lines

Small-business loans are typically priced in a fashion similar to consumer loans. Companies such as Dunn & Bradstreet provide credit ratings for many small and medium-sized businesses. For those businesses (usually very small ones) that do not have a commercial credit rating, the credit scores of the owners are typically used as a measure of credit risk. The price of a loan offered by a lender will depend on the estimated credit risk, the size and term of the loan, and the value of collateral. For small loans, the price offered by a lender may be nonnegotiable; however, for larger loans or loans to more established customers, the final rate may be set through negotiation.

## Student Loans

Student loans are a category of unsecured loans used to finance college education. In the United States, student loans have been the fastest-growing category of consumer debt since 2010. In the first quarter of 2017, the total outstanding balance on student loans was $1.34 trillion, exceeding both auto debt and credit card debt (see Table 1.1). The rapid growth of student lending in the United States can be attributed to the confluence of both increasing demand and increasing costs of college education. Student debt in the United States has raised considerable alarm not only because of its magnitude but also because of the difficulty in estimating the underlying risk (student loans had a delinquency rate of 11.6% in 2015) and the financial burden that the loan represents for many graduates (the average 2016 graduate carried more than $37,000 in student debt at the time of graduation). A variety of government programs provide subsidized student loans, merit- and need-based grants, and other forms of relief for graduates who have difficulty repaying their debt.[7]

In most other countries college education is either free or highly subsidized, so student lending is much less prevalent than it is in the United States (except for those students who choose to attend a university outside of their country). Nonetheless, a number of countries have established government agencies to provide loans to students. For example, the Student Loan Company in the United Kingdom is a government-owned not-for-profit company that provides loans for students to pay for tuition and room and board.

## Payday Lending and Pawnshops

Throughout history there have been individuals who have been willing to extend loans to people who are unable or unwilling to access credit through "mainstream" lenders.

These loans are usually at high—sometimes extremely high—rates of interest. Often these lenders operate at, or even slightly beyond, the borders of legality. Pawnbrokers had appeared in England by the eighteenth century and in the United States in the early part of the nineteenth century. Then, as now, they provided small loans at high rates of interest that were secured by items of personal property. In 2012 there were more than 11,000 pawnshops in the United States—largely concentrated in the Southwest and Southeast—doing more than $14.5 billion in business annually. While many pawnbrokers are independent, CashAmerica and EZCorp are both publicly traded chains of pawnshops.

In a typical pawnshop transaction, a customer provides a piece of property—say, a necklace—as collateral for a loan. The pawnbroker estimates the value of the property and, assuming the property is judged to be sufficiently valuable, offers a loan for a fraction of the appraised value. In the United States, a typical pawnshop loan is for 90 days, with an interest rate of 4% per month. If the borrower repays the loan plus interest within the specified period, the property will be returned to her. Alternatively, in most cases, the borrower can pay only the interest and the pawnshop will extend the loan for another 90 days. If the borrower does not return to pay the loan, the pawnshop will keep the property used as collateral, which it will typically seek to sell. In 2012, approximately 50% of the income of US pawnshops came from interest payments and 50% from merchandise sales.[8]

In the late nineteenth and early twentieth century, hundreds of small lenders—known as loan sharks—provided loans often between $10 and $50 to thousands of working-class families at interest rates that ranged from 20% to 300% annually. More recently, payday lenders are filling the role formerly played by loan sharks and pawnbrokers. Payday lenders specialize in small loans (80% of the loans they make are for less than $300) with short terms (typically 7–30 days). Payday lenders typically charge a fee of $15–$30 per $100, which corresponds to an annual percentage rate (APR) between 183% and 1,564%. The growth of the US payday lending industry has been explosive, with the number of outlets growing from a handful in 1990 to approximately 22,000 in 2014. Payday lending grew rapidly over the same period in Australia and Canada. The industry took longer to get established in the United Kingdom, but it has also experienced explosive growth there, from virtually nothing in 2000 to £3.7 billion by 2012, with balances growing between 35% and 50% annually.[9]

Pawnshops, loan sharks, and payday lenders have all been condemned for "predatory lending," or taking advantage of financially vulnerable individuals by lending at extremely high rates. Payday lenders have been accused of creating a "cycle of dependence" in which excessive interest rates lead to high payments that require additional borrowing, which then leads to higher payments, and again and again in a vicious spiral. Supporters argue that payday lenders provide much-needed access to credit to individuals who have no other legal recourse to credit. Empirical studies have reached mixed conclusions: some have provided evidence that payday lending indeed creates a cycle of dependence in some borrowers, whereas other studies have shown that access to payday loans leads to a decrease in personal bankruptcies.[10] Given the negative connotations of the term *predatory lending* and the lack of clear results from empirical studies, it is likely that the industry will be subject to increasing regulation in many countries.

## Peer-to-Peer and Marketplace Lending

*Peer-to-peer* or *marketplace* lenders operate websites that match a prospective borrower with one or more prospective lenders. The prospective borrower is usually an individual or a small business, and the prospective lender might be an individual or an institution. The motivation behind peer-to-peer lending is to reduce the cost of lending by eliminating the overhead costs borne by traditional lenders. Peer-to-peer lending enables some consumers to obtain loans at rates lower than those available from banks and other institutional lenders. As the name implies, many peer-to-peer lenders started out with the goal of providing a platform on which individuals could extend loans to other individuals. However, an increasing share of the funds provided for loans through such platforms have originated with large institutions, which makes the term *marketplace lender* more appropriate.

The first peer-to-peer lender was Zopa, which began operations in the United Kingdom in 2005. As of early 2014, there were at least 37 peer-to-peer lenders active in 20 different countries. In the United States, the two largest peer-to-peer lenders are LendingClub and Prosper. LendingClub, for example, originated $8.7 billion in loans in 2016. Peer-to-peer lending has grown rapidly since its inception: the outstanding volume of peer-to-peer loans grew from approximately $31 million at the end of 2006 to approximately $1.2 billion at the end of 2011. While this represents a growth rate of more than 200% per year, peer-to-peer lending still represents less than .2% of global debt. Peer-to-peer lending has grown particularly rapidly in China, where, as of March 2015, $67 billion in consumer and small-business loans have been originated through peer-to-peer platforms—almost four times the amount in the United States.[11]

Many marketplace lenders offer unsecured loans at rates that are lower than those offered by banks and other institutional rates. The ability of marketplace lenders to do this can be attributed in part to lower operating costs, since they do not need to maintain expensive branch networks. In addition, marketplace lenders are currently not subject to the same capital requirements as banks, which gives them an additional cost advantage. In many cases, the effective cost of capital for marketplace lenders has been lower than that experienced by other retail lenders because their investors are willing to accept a low (or negative) rate of return in the short run in return for balance growth.

Many marketplace lenders have established a risk-based pricing system in which the price of a loan depends on a customer's credit score, and in some cases, on the size of the loan. Prosper, a US-based marketplace lender, initially established an auction in which a prospective borrower would specify an amount and a maximum APR that she would accept for the loan. Prospective lenders would bid a minimum APR and the amount they wished to lend to that borrower in units of $50. If a sufficient number of prospective lenders bid below the reserve APR, the loan would be funded at the highest APR among the qualified bids. If the total amount proffered by prospective lenders at rates below the borrower's APR was less than the requested loan amount, the loan was not funded. Prosper has abandoned this pricing model in favor of fixed and published rates for different loans based on size, term, and risk. Most peer-to-peer lenders have put themselves in the business of pricing loans, which means that they face the same pricing challenges as their bricks-and-mortar competitors.

## LENDING INSTITUTIONS

Institutional lenders can be broadly grouped into banks and nonbank lenders. The difference between the two is that a bank is licensed by the government to take deposits. Under this broad definition, the term *bank* includes several different types of institutions, including credit unions in the United States and building societies in the United Kingdom. Deposits provide banks with a useful source of funding for loans; however, taking deposits means that banks are subject to more stringent regulation than nonbank lenders. The purpose of that additional regulation is to protect depositors and prevent bank runs. In most countries, banks are required to carry capital reserves—basically cash on hand—to provide a financial cushion in case loan defaults are much higher than anticipated. In addition, in the United States, banks are required to insure their deposits through the Federal Deposit Insurance Corporation (FDIC). Many other countries, including Canada and member countries of the European Union, also require banks to hold deposit insurance. In this section, we discuss the role of lending and how it contributes to profitability for both bank and nonbank lenders.[12]

### Banks

Table 1.3 shows the major income and expense items for a hypothetical but typical bank. Interest from loans is the most important source of income. The bank also receives income from various investments, here classified as "other interest income." Interest income is reduced by a provision for potential losses due to defaults. Noninterest income includes income from credit card operations, merchant fees, investment services, and various other sources. Interest expense includes interest paid to depositors as well as to other banks for funds. Noninterest expense includes all other operating expenses such as salaries and rent.

TABLE 1.3
*Example bank income statement (all entries in $US millions)*

| REVENUE | |
|---|---:|
| Loans | $10,113 |
| Other interest income | 2,115 |
| **Total interest income** | 12,228 |
| Provision for losses | (1,229) |
| **Net interest income** | 10,999 |
| Noninterest income | 9,164 |
| **Total revenue** | **20,163** |
| EXPENSES | |
| Interest expense | (1,453) |
| Noninterest expense | (10,715) |
| **Total expense** | (12,168) |
| **Income before taxes** | 7,995 |
| Taxes | (2,087) |
| **Net income** | **5,908** |

For a bank with the income statement shown in Table 1.3, a 5% increase in interest income from loans would—all else being equal—lead to an increase in net income of about 8%. This is consistent with the gains that many banks have seen from improvements in loan pricing.

Table 1.4 shows the consolidated balance sheet for all commercial banks in the United States as of May 11, 2016. Loans represent more than half of the assets of the banking system. The value of the loans on the balance sheet is adjusted to reflect estimated losses due to defaults. Cash reserves provide liquidity for withdrawals but are also required by law to hedge against possible lending losses. The "Other Assets" category includes real estate and equipment. The assets of the banking system are primarily funded by deposits but also with borrowings from the Federal Reserve, the Federal Home Loan banks, and other sources.

*Bank capital* is the difference between bank assets and real liabilities. If bank capital is negative, then the bank is technically bankrupt. In this case, the government will step in and close the bank or take other action, such as a forced sale. Table 1.4 shows that the total bank capital for large commercial banks in the United States in May 2016 was $1.7 trillion. This means that, if macroeconomic conditions suddenly deteriorated so badly that expected loan losses increased by more than $1.7 trillion, without additional action, the entire banking system would be bankrupt. Equivalently, if the banks did not hold any cash reserves and the rest of the balance sheet remained unchanged, the banking system would be bankrupt. Because the required cash reserves are an asset of the bank, they are not themselves a cost; however, the income that could reasonably be earned on them is an opportunity cost and needs to be accounted. We discuss the implications of this fact for loan profitability and pricing in Chapter 3.

TABLE 1.4

*Consolidated balance sheet for all large commercial banks in the United States as of May 11, 2016*

| ASSETS | | | LIABILITIES | | |
|---|---|---|---|---|---|
| Description | Amount ($ trillions) | Percentage | Description | Amount ($ trillions) | Percentage |
| Total loans | 8.9 | 55.7 | Deposits | 11.2 | 70.4 |
| Commercial and industrial | 2.1 | | Borrowings | 3.0 | 18.9 |
| Residential real estate | 2.1 | | Bank capital | 1.7 | 10.7 |
| Home-equity lines | .4 | | | | |
| Mortgages | 1.7 | | | | |
| Commercial real estate | 1.9 | | | | |
| Consumer loans | 1.3 | | | | |
| Credit cards | .7 | | | | |
| Automobile loans | .4 | | | | |
| Other consumer loans | .2 | | | | |
| Other loans and leases | 1.5 | | | | |
| Interbank loans | .1 | | | | |
| Securities | 3.1 | 20.0 | | | |
| Cash reserves | 2.6 | 16.6 | | | |
| Other assets | 1.3 | 7.7 | | | |
| Total | 15.9 | | Total | 15.9 | |

SOURCE: www.federalreserve.gov/releases/lbr.

## Nonbank Lenders

Nonbank lenders provide credit but do not accept deposits. Many credit card issuers, payday lenders, and lenders offering credit through peer-to-peer platforms fall into this category. The finance arms of vehicle manufacturers (e.g., Ford, Harley-Davidson, Toyota) and heavy equipment manufacturers (e.g., John Deere, Komatsu) are also nonbank lenders. The balance sheet for a nonbank lender is similar in structure to the bank balance sheet shown in Table 1.4, with the notable exception that the bulk of liabilities would be borrowings rather than deposits. Furthermore, the cash reserves carried by a nonbank lender are generally not determined by the same formula as those carried by a bank. Nonetheless, all prudent lenders—bank and nonbank—carry some level of cash reserves to hedge against the possibility of higher-than-expected losses from the lending portfolio and the consequent shrinkage of assets.

By definition, nonbank lenders do not have access to deposits to fund their loans. Nor, as a rule, do they have access to loans from the US Federal Reserve, the Bank of England, or any other central bank. Instead, they rely on the capital markets for funds. This means that the cost of funds for nonbank lenders is typically higher than for banks. Many nonbank lenders make up for this cost disadvantage by providing specialized or niche services, such as subprime lending.

## Securitization

Table 1.4 shows that in 2016, about 56% of the assets of large commercial banks in the United States were loans. However, many banks and nonbank lenders do not carry all the loans that they originate on their balance sheets. Instead, they bundle large numbers of loans together and sell them—or at least the cash flow generated by the bundle—to third parties, in a process known as *securitization*. Securitization is not a new practice—lenders securitized and sold bundles of farm mortgages in the United States in the late nineteenth century. However, securitization has become increasingly common since the 1980s, particularly in the United States. About 85% of mortgages originated in the United States in 2015 were securitized.

The popularity of securitization appears to pose a puzzle. In an ideal world, the sale of a securitized bundle of loans should be "balance sheet neutral" for both buyer and seller— the sale price would be exactly equal to the expected net present value of the income from the loan. Neither the buyer nor seller would see a change in market value. However, there are a number of potential advantages of securitization to both a seller and a buyer. For the seller, selling loans reduces overall risk since it means cash now instead of an uncertain income stream later. For a regulated lender, selling loans also reduces the total lending on the balance sheet, which reduces the need to hold capital reserves. For a purchaser, a securitized bundle of loans can represent an attractive investment if the anticipated stream of interest income minus expected losses is greater than the return available from other alternatives.

Loans are not only securitized by simply bundling them and selling them; they can also be combined to create various *mortgage-backed securities*. For example, a bundle of loans can be divided into tranches, so the income from the best-performing loans is realized by the holder of the top tranche, the next-best-performing loans by the holder of the second tranche, and so on, down to the bottom tranche, which receives the income from the poorest-performing loans. More complex securities such as collateralized debt obligations and collateralized mortgage obligations can also be created. The proliferation of increasingly complex mortgage-backed securities and other credit-based derivative products has been blamed as a major contributor to the financial crisis of 2008–2009. Critics have argued that the securities became so complex that buyers did not understand the risks involved, that rating agencies did not take account of the amount of systemic risk involved in many of the securities, and that, by selling off the loans, lenders lost interest in ensuring that the loans they issued were actually repaid. Notwithstanding these criticisms, securitization remains popular, and in the United States and other member countries of the Organization for Economic Co-operation and Development (OECD), the proportion of mortgages, auto loans, and other consumer loans that is securitized is at or above levels from before the crisis.[13]

## WHAT IS THE PRICE OF A LOAN?

Defining the "price" of a loan is not entirely straightforward. The standard definition of the unit price of a good or a service is the total expenditure divided by the amount purchased: if three loaves of bread cost $7.50, then the price of bread is $2.50 per loaf. Applying this logic to lending, the price of a loan would be the net present value of expected future payments calculated using a consumer's discount rate divided by the amount borrowed.

---

**Example 1.5: The Price of a Loan.** Consider a customer with 0% personal discount rate who is considering borrowing $5,000 and is deciding between a 10-year loan with a .5% monthly rate and a 5-year loan with a .4% monthly rate. The first loan has no fees or penalties, and the second loan has a $20 origination fee. Then, the total payments would be $1,661.23 on the first loan and $653.92 on the second loan. The ratio of discounted payments for the first loan to the amount borrowed would be $1,661.23/$5,000.00, or about $.33 per dollar borrowed, whereas the ratio for the second would be $653.92/$5,000.00, or about $.13 per dollar borrowed. Using this logic, the "price" of the first loan is more than double the price of the second loan.

---

The calculation of price in Example 1.5 is logical and straightforward; however, it does not correspond with the way most consumers choose among alternative loans. In the real world, there are plenty of customers who would choose the 10-year loan with a .5% monthly rate over the 5-year loan with a .4% monthly rate, despite the fact that the second loan is ostensibly cheaper. The 10-year loan has a monthly payment of $55.51, compared to $93.90 for the 5-year loan—a customer who was intent on minimizing monthly payment would prefer the first loan to the second. Unfortunately, there is no single useful definition of price that enables us to classify loans with different terms, rates, and conditions as "cheaper" or "more expensive." For this reason, we consider loans of different terms and conditions to be different products.

The monthly payment for a loan is an increasing function of its rate, which means that, for loans with the same terms and conditions, we consider the periodic rate to be the "price" of the loan. The situation is more complicated for lines. Here, the cost to the consumer depends both on the interest rate and on the compounding period—for a given stream of payments and withdrawals, it is impossible to calculate payments without knowing both. If the interest on a credit card is compounded monthly, a customer who pays off her bill in full at the end of the month will pay no interest. However, if the interest is compounded daily, even a customer who pays off her bill in full every month will still end up paying the interest accrued for each purchase between the date of purchase and the end of the month. For this reason, a number of different formulas have been devised to enable a consistent comparison among different lines with different compounding periods and different fees.

For lines, the *nominal annual percentage rate* (nominal APR) incorporates both the compounding period and the interest into a single number. Nominal APR was created to provide consumers with one number to use in comparing credit products. It is equal to the interest rate per compounding period times the number of compounding periods in a year. Thus, if interest is compounded monthly and $r$ is the monthly periodic rate, then the nominal APR is equal to $12 \times r$. If the compounding period is equal to the payment period, the nominal APR is the amount that a borrower who makes interest-only payments each period would have paid at the end of the year, expressed as a percentage of the balance.

A related quantity is the *annual percentage yield* (APY), which incorporates the effect of compounding over the year. The APY is the fraction of the amount borrowed that would be owed as interest at the end of a year in the absence of fees if a borrower made no payments during the year. Because it includes the effect of compounding, APY is always greater than or equal to APR.

---

**Example 1.6: APR and APY.** A credit line has a monthly rate of 1%. The nominal APR is $12 \times 1\% = 12\%$. Assume a borrower has withdrawn $1,000 on January 1 and makes no payments or further withdrawals during the year. If she makes interest-only payments each month, then she would make a payment of $10 each month and would have paid $120, or 12% of $1,000, in total at the end of the year. Now, assume that she makes no payments. In the absence of penalties and fees, she would owe $1,010 on January 31 and $1.01 \times \$1,010 = $1,020.10 on February 28. At the end of the year, she would owe $(1.01)^{12} \times \$1,000 = $1,126.83. This means that the corresponding APY is 12.68%.

---

Assume that there are $n$ periods in a year, and let $r$ denote the periodic interest rate expressed as a percentage. The relationships between $r$ and APY and APR are

$$APR = nr, \quad r = APR/n, \quad APY = (1+r)^n - 1, \quad r = (APY+1)^{1/n} - 1.$$

One shortcoming of using nominal APR as the price of a line is that it does not include fees or penalties. To address this shortcoming, the United States and some other countries require that lenders report an *effective APR*, which includes all fixed charges, such as setup fees and periodic fees (but typically not prepayment or late-payment penalties), associated with a loan or line. The calculation of effective APR is illustrated in Example 1.7.

---

**Example 1.7: Effective Annual Percentage Rate.** A $1,000 loan has a monthly rate of 1% and an annual servicing fee of $20. In the absence of fees, the total interest payments plus servicing fee due for the loan would be $120 + $20 = $140. The effective APR for this loan is 14%.

---

While the calculation in Example 1.7 is relatively simple, the devil is in the details, and the calculation of effective APR depends on exactly which fees and other charges are included. The calculation is different for loans than for lines. Furthermore, the rules for calculating effective APR differ from country to country and can even be different when applied to different loans in the same country. In the United States, effective APR is calculated differently for mortgages and auto loans, and both calculations are different from the calculation used in the European Union.[14] Like many initiatives aimed toward simplification, the attempt to find a reasonable and widely applicable single "price" that consumers can use to compare different loans and lines has instead generated considerable complexity.

For simplicity, we use the term *price* to refer to the periodic interest rate of a loan and the term *APR* to refer to the nominal APR unless otherwise specified.

## PRICE DISPERSION IN LENDING

Table 1.5 shows the APRs offered by different lenders in the United Kingdom for a 3-year unsecured personal loan of £5,000 to "good credit" customers older than 55 years of age, along with the corresponding monthly payments and total costs. (In the United Kingdom, unlike the United States, it is both legal and common practice to price loans differently depending on the age of the borrower.) It is immediately apparent that this market supports a wide range of rates—the highest APR is more than three times the lowest APR. Price variation is the rule rather than the exception in customer lending, and this has a number of important implications. First, it can be beneficial for loan customers to shop for lower prices. As we discuss in Chapter 4, differences in the propensity to shop among customers are a major source of price sensitivity. A second implication of price variation is that customer loans cannot be considered a commodity. In a commodity market there is no price variation—the price is set by the market, and the job of each supplier is to produce as much as he can at a cost as far below the market price as he can manage. In a commodity market, there is no potential to increase profit through price optimization—or indeed by any other action other than cost reduction. The fact that price variation is commonplace in lending markets suggests that lending is not a commodity and lenders have scope to improve their business results through better pricing.

TABLE 1.5

*Selected annual interest rates, monthly payments, and total interest for a 3-year unsecured personal loan of £5,000 for a 55-year-old borrower with good credit who is not a current customer, as published by various UK lenders online in May 2017*

| Provider | Annual rate (%) | Monthly payment (£) | Total interest (£) |
|---|---|---|---|
| TSB | 3.3 | 145.96 | 254.56 |
| M&S Bank | 3.6 | 146.60 | 277.60 |
| AA | 3.8 | 147.03 | 293.08 |
| Tesco | 3.9 | 147.25 | 301.00 |
| First Direct | 4.9 | 149.39 | 378.04 |
| Nationwide | 5.5 | 150.68 | 424.48 |
| HSBC | 6.1 | 151.97 | 470.92 |
| RBS | 6.9 | 153.68 | 532.48 |
| Barclays | 7.9 | 155.82 | 609.52 |
| Halifax | 8.9 | 160.11 | 763.96 |
| Admiral | 14.9 | 170.82 | 1,149.52 |

SOURCE: www.moneyfacts.co.uk.

There are likely a number of different reasons that prices vary among lenders to the extent shown in Table 1.5. The differences in price may reflect differences in cost, risk appetite, goals (market share versus profitability), and customer segmentation among lenders. It is also likely that lenders differ in the amount and quality of information they have available as well as in their levels of pricing sophistication. Price differences among lenders tend to be greater in relatively opaque markets, such as unsecured personal lending in Canada, than in more transparent markets, such as mortgages in the United States. When the cost of capital is low, there tends to be relatively little price dispersion. When the cost of capital increases, price variation tends to increase as well. Price variation is typically greater in subprime lending than in prime and superprime lending; however, some degree of price variation can be found in all consumer lending markets.

## LOAN-PRICING PROCESSES

The way that loan prices are determined and communicated to customers is different from most retail products. In most retail markets, the same price is displayed to all customers arriving through the same channel at the same time. By contrast, lenders require that each customer fill out an application providing information about her financial situation before they quote her a price. Information from the application is usually supplemented with additional information acquired from one or more credit bureaus (e.g., Experian, TransUnion) about the current debts and payment history of the customer. In addition, the lender may have an existing relationship with the customer that might provide even more information about her financial situation and payment behavior. All of this information can be used by a lender to determine whether the risk of default is too great to offer a loan. The decision of whether to offer a loan to an applicant is called the *underwriting* decision (discussed in more detail in Chapter 2). Information about applicants is not only necessary for underwriting; it is also useful in determining the price to offer if the customer's application is successful. The ability to use extensive information about customers and their desired loans in setting prices is an advantage that lenders enjoy over most retailers.

As shown in Figure 1.2, three different processes are involved in pricing a loan. The *price-segmentation process* determines which customer attributes and which loan attributes will be used in setting prices. For example, a lender may decide that 1-year loans of £1,000 to £4,999 can have a different price than 5-year loans of £5,000 to £14,999, which can have a different price than 5-year loans of £15,000 to £24,999. Each of these combinations of loan characteristics defines a pricing segment, and the job of the segmentation process is to classify all possible loan requests into discrete *pricing segments* such that the lender may charge a different price to each segment.

Given a set of pricing segments, the *price-setting process* determines the list price associated with each segment. This essentially involves creating a price list—for example, specifying that 1-year loans of £1,000 to £4,999 should have a list APR of 6.5% while 5-year loans of £5,000 to £14,999 should have a list APR of 5.4%. The *price-quotation process* includes the steps that a customer seeking a loan goes through before being quoted a final price. This process starts when a customer makes an inquiry or applies for a loan, and it ends with a successful applicant being quoted a price. For most retailers, the price-quoting process is trivial—the price of an item is predetermined and shown on a price tag or displayed online. However, in lending, the price-quoting process can involve several steps in which additional information about the customer is obtained at each step. This information can then be used to update the price offered to the customer. Finally, in some cases, the final price of a loan is the result of negotiation between the customer and the lender or his agent.

The three processes operate on different time scales. Price segments are rarely changed: for most lenders, the time between updating of pricing segmentations can be measured in months or years. List prices are typically updated weekly or monthly with ad hoc changes when market rates change or in response to competitive actions. By contrast, the price-quotation process is triggered every time an application is received, which might be hundreds or even thousands of times a day for a large lender.

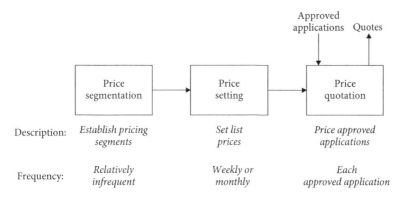

**Figure 1.2**  Processes involved in loan pricing

The following two sections describe the price-quoting and price-setting processes, how they differ in different lending markets, and the implications for how prices should be computed. Chapter 6 discusses price segmentation in more detail.

### Price-Quotation Processes

In most cases, the final price for a loan is not determined until after the customer has filled out an application and been accepted. This enables the lender to incorporate information about characteristics of the loan (e.g., size, term), characteristics of the customer (e.g., credit score, geography), and the channel through which the application was submitted into the calculation of the price of the loan. Typically, a lender will establish a number of pricing segments based on combinations of characteristics and will set a different price for each segment. When an application is accepted, the lender determines which pricing segment the transaction falls into and quotes the price associated with that segment.

This overall approach is called *customized pricing*, and it has three important properties:

1. The full price structure is not known to customers. A successful loan applicant knows only the price that she is quoted—she typically does not know the prices quoted to others.

2. The lender obtains information about the customer and her desired loan before quoting a price. This allows the lender to "customize" a price for each application.

3. The lender has information not only about the customers who accepted his offered loans but also about customers who were offered loans but did not accept them. This information can be extremely useful in understanding how price sensitivity varies among different customer segments.[15]

These properties of the price-quotation process have profound implications for loan pricing. In particular, the customized pricing approach enables lenders to differentiate prices according to customer and product information that would not be available in the absence of a loan application. Furthermore, because final prices are not advertised, prices can be differentiated without a customer learning which prices were quoted to other customers. Customized pricing enables lenders to differentiate prices at a much more granular level than the vast majority of retailers are able to do.

Credit cards would seem to be an exception—the APR and APY for a particular card is usually sent to a customer in a mailing before she fills out an application. However, credit cards are able to customize prices by determining which customers will receive which mailings and thus which customers are qualified to receive which credit card products at which prices. The information used to segment customers before determining which offers are available to which customers is similar to that available on a loan application and is used in a similar fashion. Thus, even though the details of the process are somewhat different, the overall approach and the techniques used to segment customers are the same or very similar.

A typical single-stage price-quotation process is shown in Figure 1.3. Customers enter the process by filling out an application that includes detailed personal information as well as information about the type of loan desired. The lender then determines whether to offer a loan to the customer depending on the lender's estimate of her creditworthiness. If the lender decides to offer the loan, he also determines the price to quote. After the price is quoted, the customer decides whether to take the loan at the quoted price. The fraction of offered loans that are taken up is called the *take-up rate*. The lender shown in Figure 1.3 approved 48% of the loan applications, and the take-up rate for approved loans was 78%, which means that 48% × 78% = 37% of original applicants actually took a loan.

An alternative to the single-stage price-quotation process is the *two-stage* process, illustrated in Figure 1.4. In a two-stage process, a customer inquiring about a loan is quoted an initial rate. She then decides whether to fill out an application. If she fills out an application, the process proceeds as in the single-stage process. In the case shown in Figure 1.4, 80% of inquiries submitted an application, and 55% of those applications were approved. 82% of approved applicants took up the loan. In this case, about 36% of inquiries and 45% of applications resulted in a funded loan.

A slight variation on the two-stage quote process occurs when customers are screened prior to the initial quote. In this case, an inquiring customer will be questioned about her income and outstanding debt obligations when inquiring about a loan. As a result of this

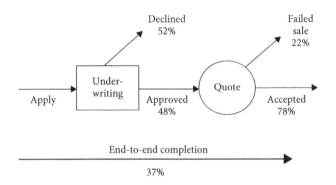

**Figure 1.3**    A single-stage loan quote process

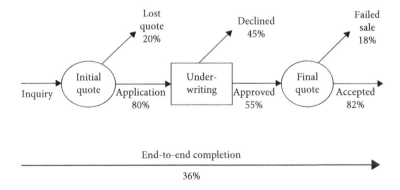

**Figure 1.4**    A two-stage loan quote process

voluntary disclosure, the customer may be informed that she will not qualify for a loan and the process ends. Only if she meets this initial test will she be quoted an initial rate and encouraged to fill out an application. This approach is used by some unsecured lenders in Australia and the United Kingdom, as well as a number of home-equity lenders in the United States. The existence of this initial step does not affect the pricing process; however, the initial screening means that a higher percentage of applicants will be approved.

Another variation on the standard price-quotation processes occurs when field staff has the authority to negotiate the final price with the customer. In this case, management typically establishes a suggested price for each deal, but field staff have the ability to agree to a different price. Typically, management limits the amount by which the final price can differ from the list price—for example, field staff may have the authority to agree to prices that are within a range of .5% above or below the list price. This type of price-quotation process is called *list pricing with discretion*. A 2010 Oliver Wyman survey found that local staff used some level of discretion in pricing more than 50% of unsecured loans and more than 70% of secured loans offered by major European banks. Another survey found that between 30% and 40% of unsecured loans and lines of credit originated or renewed at major Canadian banks in 2011 involved some level of local price discretion. Price discretion is also very common in direct auto lending in the United States—field discretion was applied to more than 70% of non-subvened loans offered by a major lender.[16]

The presence of discretion in the price-quotation process has three important implications:

1. When the field has pricing discretion, headquarters loses some control of prices. The price list becomes a list of suggested prices (or a list of price ceilings) rather than a list of final prices. In this case, price optimization requires setting both the list prices and the discretion limits within which the field staff can adjust prices.

2. The final prices in a price-quotation process with discretion can be systematically influenced by customer characteristics that are not captured in the data. This has implications for the estimation of customer price sensitivity that are discussed in detail in Chapter 5.

3. The ability of a lender to meet a specific goal, such as maximizing profitability, depends on the extent to which field staff have incentives that are aligned with corporate goals as well as the staff's negotiation skills.

Understanding what type of price-quotation process a lender is using is a critical prerequisite for effective pricing. If the price-quotation process does not include discretion, then a centralized pricing function can fully control the final prices offered to customers by specifying either list prices or list prices and loadings in the case of a two-stage process. If the price-quotation process involves discretion, then the process needs to determine both list prices and discretion limits. In this case, headquarters cannot directly determine the final prices quoted to customers, but headquarters can (and should) determine the list prices and discretion limits that will work together to best meet corporate goals.

## Price-Setting Processes

When banks initially started offering consumer loans, they generally offered a single *house rate* to all successful applicants. Typically the house rate was established by adding a provision for risk to the cost of capital and then an adding a fixed margin to cover other costs and generate a profit. The job of a loan officer was primarily to determine which customers should be extended loans and which should not. While rates might differ by category—the rate for a mortgage might be different from that for an auto loan—the rates charged to two different individuals at the same time for the same type of loan would be the same. In this world, the primary job of the loan officer was to determine which applicants should be approved and which rejected—pricing was an afterthought.

Two developments combined to make loan pricing more complex. The first development was the widespread adoption of automated credit scoring. The ready availability of individualized credit scores not only facilitated underwriting but also enabled lenders to understand the different levels of risk associated with successful applicants. The second development was the increased availability of cheap computing power. This enabled banks to manage large volumes of loans issued at different rates. The availability of credit scores combined with advanced computation led to *risk-based pricing* in which lenders divide successful applicants into different risk tiers. For each risk tier the risk-based price is the cost of capital plus a loss provision based on the average risk for that tier plus a constant margin that covers other costs and a desired rate of return.

---

**Example 1.8: Risk-Based Pricing.** A lender using risk-based pricing has a target margin of .50% and a capital cost of 4.25%. The expected average loss rates for two different risk tiers are .25% and .75%. The lender would quote a rate of 4.25% + .5% + .25% = 5.00% to the first tier and a rate of 4.25% + .5% + .75% = 5.50% to the second tier.

---

Risk-based pricing is still practiced at many banks. The adoption of risk-based pricing led to a significant extension of credit—albeit at higher prices—to customers who would have been too risky to accept under a single price policy. It also led to substantial improvements in lending profitability by enabling loan prices to better track costs. However, risk-based pricing falls short of the goal of price optimization because it adds the same margin to every risk tier and does not segment prices on the basis of any consideration other than risk.

Over time, banks began to increase the number of rates they offered by differentiating prices on additional dimensions, such as term, size of loan, loan-to-value ratio, and geography. As the number of pricing dimensions increased, so did the number of prices that needed to be managed and updated over time. Computers were necessary to keep track of the different products and prices on offer and to keep track of the changing rates on variable rate products. By the 1990s a large bank might have a computerized rate sheet with thousands or even hundreds of thousands of different rates. Simply managing this number of rates—let alone determining the "optimal" rate for each loan—became a daunting task requiring specialized software. The increased complexity of loan pricing necessitated the establishment of new processes to manage pricing.

Many lenders set prices using a pricing committee that includes representatives from product management, marketing, sales, and finance who come together and agree on prices. Because pricing affects all of these groups, it is often considered only fair to give each group a voice in pricing decisions. While incorporating different perspectives and information into pricing can be beneficial, pricing committees often lead to poor pricing. As with any committee, the decisions made by a pricing committee are often driven by the most vocal, persistent, or organizationally powerful members of the committee—not necessarily the ones with the most insight. In addition, a pricing committee can usually consider either detailed changes to a handful of prices or simple changes to all prices. This can be a limitation when considering a pricing structure that includes thousands or hundreds of thousands of prices: it means that most prices are changed (or not) without serious scrutiny or consideration of the impact on the market, customers, and expected profitability.

However, perhaps the most serious shortcoming of a committee-based process is the lack of clear responsibility: if the committee is responsible, then no one is responsible. As a result, most lenders do not apply the same rigor to pricing decisions that they apply to other critical decisions. Lenders often lack clarity about what they are trying to achieve from pricing and, as a result, cannot evaluate the outcomes of pricing decisions. Not only does this lack of rigor lead to poor decisions; it also inhibits organizational learning—if lenders don't track the effects of current pricing, how can they hope to improve pricing in the future?

The most effective pricing processes in lending, as in any business process, are closed-loop—that is, an effective process explicitly evaluates the outcomes of pricing decisions and incorporates what is learned into future pricing decisions. Such a closed-loop pricing process is illustrated in Figure 1.5 and proceeds in five steps:

1. *Analyze.* Quantify the response of different customer segments to different prices for different products through different channels.

2. *Optimize.* On the basis of the relationship between prices and performance, choose the set of prices that will best meet corporate goals.

3. *Implement.* Communicate the new prices to the marketplace.

4. *Evaluate.* Measure the performance of the new prices.

5. *Update.* On the basis of the results of the evaluation, update the parameters of the models used to relate performance to prices.

A closed-loop pricing process requires explicit measurement of what a lender is trying to achieve—a pricing metric. This metric can usually be expressed in terms of balances, risk profile, and profitability. Prices are set to maximize the metric based on the current understanding of customer price response. Regardless of the method actually used to set prices, a closed-loop process is highly recommended to enable continuous improvement.

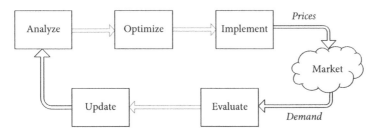

**Figure 1.5**    A closed-loop pricing process

## REGULATORY INFLUENCES ON PRICING

Regulation can play an important role in loan pricing. Financial services are among the most highly regulated sectors of developed economies, and lenders (especially banks) are among the most highly regulated financial service providers. Regulation of financial services was always stringent and it became even more stringent in most countries following the financial crisis of 2008–2009. While many aspects of lending are regulated, we concentrate on the three categories of regulation that are most relevant to pricing: minimum capital requirements, nondiscrimination, and usury laws.

### Minimum Capital Requirements

Wherever and whenever they have occurred, economic recessions and depressions have either been precipitated by or exacerbated by bank failures. In the extreme case, the failure of a single bank can lead to a bank run in which panicked depositors rush to withdraw their money from other banks. This can lead to more bank failures and ultimately to a credit crunch in which banks do not have sufficient funds to make loans. This scenario has occurred many times in many countries, notably in the United States in October 1929 at the start of the Great Depression. A related phenomenon is *contagion*—banks borrow extensively from one another, and the failure of one large bank could reduce the assets of creditor banks to the extent that they are also forced to declare bankruptcy. Concerns about contagion were a large part of the motivation of the US government to rescue AIG in 2008. Because the failure of financial institutions can have catastrophic implications for the health of the economy as a whole, governments have instituted regulations designed to ensure that financial service companies in general and banks in particular remain on a sound financial footing.

Loans are the largest asset class held by most banks, and the greatest risk to the solvency of a bank is the quality of the loans on its balance sheet. These loans are valued on the basis of their remaining balances minus expected losses from defaults. Thus, if a bank has $5 billion in outstanding loans but expects 1% of that value to be lost due to default, the value of loans on the balance sheet will be $.99 \times \$5$ billion = $4.95 billion. If the bank has $1 billion in additional assets (including reserves) and carries liabilities of $5.5 billion in deposits and borrowings, then the bank capital is the difference between the assets and the liabilities, in this case $450 million—the bank's net worth. Now, assume that, due to deteriorating economic conditions, the bank begins to see increased levels of default in its loans, leading its officers to believe that the loans on the balance sheet will actually experience a 15% loss rate. As a result, the value of the loan portfolio is only .85 × $5 billion = $4.25 billion and the bank capital is –$250 million: the bank is technically bankrupt.

To reduce the probability that a bank will go bankrupt as a result of a deterioration in the quality of its loan portfolio, governments have imposed capital requirements on both banks and, increasingly, nonbank lenders. The simplest capital requirement is that the *leverage ratio*—defined as the ratio of capital to total assets—must exceed a certain amount. For example, into the 1980s a bank was considered well capitalized if its leverage ratio was above 5%. Table 1.4 shows that the total leverage ratio of large commercial banks in the United States in May 2016 was 1.7/15.9 = 17%, indicating that, on the basis of the leverage ratio criterion, the banks were on average well capitalized.

Historically, standards for evaluating risk and setting minimum capital requirements were established on a country-by-country basis. Entering the 1980s, it became increasingly apparent that global standards were needed. The increased globalization of financial services meant that the failure of a bank (or banks) in one country could lead to failures in other countries and, potentially, global financial collapse. In response to this need, the G-20 nations, joined by some other countries with important banking industries, such as Singapore and Saudi Arabia, formed the Basel Committee on Banking and Supervision (BCBS). In 1988, the BCBS adopted the first set of Basel Accords, known as Basel I, which, among other things, set standard minimum capital requirements for banks. In 2004, Basel II was adopted and superseded Basel I. Implementation of Basel II was delayed by the global financial crisis and a stricter set of standards, Basel III, was adopted in 2011. Basel III has a variety of provisions that are to be adopted at different times from 2015 through 2019. Basel II and Basel III specify a number of different minimum capital requirements based on both risk-weighted loan value and non-risk-weighted loan value (total exposure). These minimum requirements have been adopted by all the BCBS countries and serve as the basis for minimum capital requirements adopted by many non-BCBS countries. In some cases, individual countries have adopted standards that are more stringent than those specified by the Basel Accords.[17]

Several different types of capital requirement are specified in Basel II and Basel III; however, each requirement is specified in terms of a minimum level of bank capital that must be held as a function of the different assets held by the bank. For example, one requirement of Basel III is that the ratio of bank capital to the value of risk-weighted assets must be at least 6%. Referring to Table 1.4, there are three ways that a bank could increase this ratio:

1. The bank could improve the risk-weighted value of the portfolio by issuing fewer risky loans and more less-risky loans.

2. The bank could issue fewer loans and increase the amount it holds in its cash reserve (which is riskless).

3. The bank could rely less on savings and borrowings and more on bank capital (equity) as a source of funding.

Each of these actions would make the bank less susceptible to high levels of default. However, each of them comes at a cost. To attract more less-risky loans, the bank would presumably need to offer lower prices for those loans, which would reduce their profitability. Typically, bank capital is the most expensive source of funds for a bank because equity holders require a market rate of return, which is much higher than the rate that the bank pays for deposits or for money borrowed from other banks. As a result, increasing bank capital increases the cost of lending, which must be recouped through higher prices. According to one estimate, the increased capital reserve requirements from Basel III that became effective in 2015 increased lending costs for banks by 15 basis points (.15%) and the additional reserve requirements that are to be put in place by 2019 will increase lending costs by an additional 50 basis points.[18] In Chapter 3 we show how bank capital requirements influence the pricing and profitability of loans.

## Nondiscrimination

It has been shown that lack of access to credit at reasonable terms for a group within society can impede the economic advancement of individuals in that group. Lack of access to credit can also stand in the way of other goals that are widely considered to be socially desirable, such as home ownership. With this in mind, the United States passed the Equal Credit Opportunity Act (ECOA) of 1974 to make it illegal for lenders to discriminate "with respect to any aspect of a credit transaction . . . on the basis of race, color, religion, national origin, sex or marital status, or age." Despite this legal prohibition, an influential 1988 study conducted by the Boston Federal Reserve concluded that, when controlling for all other factors, lenders were systematically discriminating against black and Hispanic mortgage applicants, and this discrimination was a significant contributor to the lower rates of home ownership among these groups.[19] In addition, some banks have been accused of the practice of redlining, denying loans en masse to people living in neighborhoods with a high proportion of minorities, without considering any other factors.

Two types of discrimination are distinguished by the ECOA: disparate treatment and disparate impact: "Disparate treatment occurs when a creditor treats an applicant differently based on a prohibited basis such as race or national origin. Disparate impact occurs when a creditor employs facially neutral policies or practices that have an adverse effect or impact on a protected class unless it meets a legitimate business need that cannot reasonably be achieved as well by means that are less disparate in their impact" (Consumer Financial Protection Bureau 2012, p. 192).

Disparate treatment of protected groups is expressly prohibited by the ECOA, whereas disparate outcomes can be justified by a "legitimate business need" that cannot be met in a more equitable fashion. Underwriting and pricing decisions based on credit scores clearly create disparate outcomes; however, they are justified by the argument that credit-based pricing and underwriting meets the legitimate business need of the bank to be compensated for funding higher-risk loans. Without this justification, credit scores could not legally be used in underwriting or pricing decisions in the United States. For example, a 2016 study showed that on average men have a higher average credit score (630) than women (621).

Older men and women tend to have higher credit scores than younger men and women. This means that a risk-based pricing approach would price the same loan higher (possibly much higher) for an average young woman than it would for an average older man. Furthermore, it means, all else being equal, that more older men than younger women would be approved for the loan.

Do such disparate outcomes indicate discrimination? In general, regulators have ruled that decisions based on credit scores that accurately predict default risk meet the "legitimate business need" criterion, provided that the score is not itself based on membership in any protected group. However, regulators have ruled that credit scoring algorithms not only cannot incorporate membership in a protected group; they cannot utilize any variable or variables that might be serving as a proxy for membership in a protected group. This was the basis of the complaint against redlining: "neighborhood" is not itself a protected category, but neighborhood was being used a proxy for race, which is a protected category. This means that in the United States, a credit-scoring approach (or any other pricing segmentation) will not ex ante be declared compliant simply because it does not include any variables that directly indicate membership in a protected group. Rather, it must be tested statistically ex post to ensure that no variables used in scoring served as proxies for membership in a protected group. The statistical issues involved in determining whether a scoring variable is or is not a proxy for membership in a protected group can be quite complex, since, as noted above, probability of default is empirically correlated with race, gender, and age, among other factors.[20]

The US government has paid more attention to the issue of discrimination in lending than any other developed country. In addition to passing legislation focused specifically on discrimination, there is a federal agency—the Consumer Financial Protection Bureau (CFPB)—that is tasked with protecting consumers from abuses by financial service companies. Since its establishment in the wake of the 2008–2009 financial crisis, the CFPB has taken action against a number of major auto lenders, claiming that the use of discretion by dealerships has resulted in higher rates for auto loans for members of protected groups. As of May 2016, the CFPB had negotiated settlements with Toyota Motor Credit Corporation, Ally Bank, American Honda Financial Corporation, and Fifth Third Bank, requiring each to pay millions of dollars in restitution to borrowers from the affected groups.[21] Avoidance of discriminatory pricing and underwriting is a key business imperative for lenders in the United States.

Nondiscrimination has three important implications for pricing:

- Lenders should make sure that their pricing segments are not based on membership in any protected groups.
- Lenders should be sure that their pricing segments are not based on any variables that could be construed as a proxy for membership in a protected group. Verifying this may require the use of sophisticated statistical tests.
- If the price-quotation process involves field discretion, a lender should be especially vigilant to ensure that field staff are not using their price discretion in a manner that could be construed to be discriminatory. This requires, at a minimum, explicit

training and ongoing monitoring of field staff. It may also include ex post statistical studies to ensure that the field is not using its discretion in a discriminatory fashion.

## Usury Laws

In some jurisdictions, usury laws specify a maximum interest rate that can be charged to consumers. In Canada, the maximum annual APR was 60% in 2017. In the United States, usury laws vary by state and the caps vary widely. Delaware caps interest on consumer loans at the Federal Reserve rate plus 5%, whereas Nevada essentially has no limits at all. In the United States, usury is governed by the state of the lender rather than the borrower, which explains why credit card companies tend to be concentrated in states such as Nevada. As of 2017, the United Kingdom had no statutory limit on interest rates.

When usury laws are in place, lenders can use fees as a way to extract more revenue from a borrower while keeping the interest rate within the usury limit. For example, a payday lender might charge a $15 up-front fee for a $200 advance for 30 days. This fee is equivalent to an interest rate of 7.5% per month, or 138% per year—an illegally usurious rate under the laws of many states. Subprime auto lenders sometimes charge a so-called placement fee to fund a highly risky loan. The placement fee is added to the initial balance of the loan and results in a higher monthly payment for the borrower. In both cases, the fees can be seen as a way to circumvent interest-rate caps.

There is evidence that usury laws reduce consumption of credit. A 2015 Federal Court ruling limited the ability of banks that securitize and sell their loans to charge interest rates in excess of the usury cap in the borrower's state. This limited the ability of peer-to-peer lenders to offer high-interest loans in those states, and as a result, in the following seven months, loan volumes to those with lowest credit scores grew by 124% in states not affected by the decision, whereas in states affected by the decision, volumes shrank by 48%. Whether or not this is a good thing depends on your view of high-priced subprime credit: is it an important source of funding to people without access to other alternatives, or does it create a cycle of dependence in the most financially vulnerable (or both)?[22]

## SUMMARY

- Institutional consumer credit is a relatively recent invention, dating from the use of installment credit in the nineteenth century to help sell big-ticket items such as harvesters and sewing machines. Since then, both the number and the types of providers and the forms of consumer credit have proliferated. Common forms of credit include unsecured loans, mortgages, home-equity loans, student loans, and credit cards. Sources of credit include both banks and nonbank lenders. Debt per household has generally been increasing in industrialized countries for the past century or more.

- Consumer credit is not only available from a wide variety of sources; it is also available in many different forms. Consumer credit is available as loans and lines, it may be secured or unsecured, and it may have a fixed or variable interest rate. Consumer credit is also available with a wide range of terms and amortization periods.

- Loans are offered by both banks and nonbank lenders. The primary distinction between banks and nonbank lenders is that banks are licensed by the government to accept deposits. This means that banks generally have a lower cost of capital than nonbank lenders; however, this cost advantage is somewhat mitigated by the fact that banks are typically subject to more stringent regulation than nonbank lenders.

- Many consumer loans have multidimensional prices; that is, the amount that a borrower will pay depends not only on the interest but also on various fees that might be assessed. Nonetheless, we generally consider the price of a loan to be its interest rate. This can be justified by observing that, for most consumer credit products, the vast majority of the lender's income will be from interest, and the most significant variation among customer payments for the same loan will be due to differences in the interest rate.

- Loan markets typically support wide variations in interest rates. This wide variation applies even across similar loans offered to similar customers. The high level of price variation in lending indicates that consumer loans are not commodities in the strict microeconomic sense, and hence there is scope for lenders to improve their performance through improved pricing methodologies.

- Loan pricing involves three related processes: the *price-segmentation process*, in which the lender decides which characteristics of a customer and a loan he will use to differentiate prices; the *price-setting process*, in which the lender determines the list prices to associate with each pricing segment; and the *price-quotation process*, which determines the price that will be actually quoted to a particular applicant. Pricing segments are infrequently updated, whereas list prices are typically updated weekly or monthly and a price is quoted each time an application is received.

- Depending on the lender and the market, the price-quotation process may either involve a single stage in which case the price is quoted only after a successful application or two stages, in which case an initial price is quoted upon inquiry and a second (possibly higher) price quoted upon successful application.

- In some markets, price quotation may involve field discretion. That is, field staff (or an intermediary) have some authority to agree on a rate with a customer that may be different from the list price. In this case, the price-setting process requires not only setting a list price for each pricing segment but also determining limits on the maximum amount by which the final price can differ from the list price—so-called *discretion limits*.

- The ideal price-setting process should explicitly incorporate market feedback. That is, prices should be set with explicit expectations on how customers will respond. Actual customer response should be compared to these expectations, and the parameters of the underlying model should be updated accordingly. This type of closed-loop process is required to ensure that prices respond to changes in the market environment.

- Lenders are typically highly regulated, and this regulation can influence pricing. Three categories of regulation have the greatest influence on pricing: capital requirements increase the cost of lending, nondiscrimination laws limit the customer attributes that can be used to differentiate pricing, and usury laws may set a ceiling on the interest rate.

## NOTES

1. For an extensive discussion by a sociologist of the broader concept of debt and credit, see Graeber's (2012) book *Debt: The First 5,000 Years*. Babylonian tablets describing the calculation of compound interest are discussed in Knuth's (1996) "Ancient Babylonian Algorithms."

2. Charles Dickens based the scenes in *Little Dorrit* on his father's time in the Marshalsea debtors' prison (Ackroyd 1991).

3. Much less has been written about the history of consumer credit than about the history of banking. Much of the history in this section was drawn from *Financing the American Dream*, by Lendol Calder (1999), which provides an excellent and readable survey of the growth of consumer credit in the United States from the middle of the nineteenth century to the present day. Chapter 5 in *Horsetrading in the Age of Cars*, by Stephen Gelber (2008), is a useful source for the early days of lending for bicycle and automobile sales.

4. The origin of the standardized system of mortgages in the United States is told in Carter (1999).

5. Example 1.3 is substantially simplified. Dealer-lender agreements are typically more complex, and participation is adjusted for the risk of the loan and probability of prepayment among other factors.

6. The subvention calculation in Example 1.4 is substantially simplified. In reality the payment would be adjusted to account for the possibility that the borrower would default or prepay the loan prior to term and for other factors.

7. Student loan statistics are from Haughwout et al. (2015).

8. For the history of pawnshops in the United States, see Woolson (2009). Statistics on the current pawnshop industry are from La Rosa (2012).

9. Statistics on US payday lending are from Stegman (2007) and the size of the UK market is from Beddows and McAteer (2014).

10. Academic research is mixed on the balance of costs and benefits of payday lending to communities. One researcher concluded: "I find no evidence that payday loans alleviate economic hardship. To the contrary (payday) loan access leads to increased difficulty paying mortgage, rent and utilities bills" (Melzer 2011, 517)—Stegman and Faris (2003) reach a similar conclusion. Other studies have found that payday lending leads to reduced check bouncing but increases personal bankruptcies (Morgan, Strain, and Seblani 2012). In the United States, it has been estimated that the typical payday lender realizes a return on capital roughly consistent with other financial service industries (Huckstep 2007), suggesting that the high interest rates charged by payday lenders are not generating excessive profits but are necessary to offset risk. For a survey of the literature on payday lending, see Caskey (2010).

11. Statistics on peer-to-peer lending in the United States and Western Europe are from Moenninghoff and Wieandt (2013). The statistics for China are from Citigroup (2016). LendingClub origination volumes can be found on their website at https://www .lendingclub.com/info/statistics.action.

12. Additional information on the differences among different types of lending and depository institutions as well as more details of bank finance can be found in any textbook on banking such as Mishkin (2010).

13. More information on the mechanics of securitization can be found in Baig and Choudry (2013). The effect of bank securitization on valuation is discussed in Dermine (2009). An extensive discussion of the role of securitization in the financial crisis of 2008 and 2009 can be found in Simkovic (2013).

14. The details of the FDIC calculations of APR for loans can be found at their websites, http://www.fdic.gov/regulations/laws/rules/6500-3500.html. and http://www.fdic.gov/regulations/laws/rules/6500-1650.html, respectively.

15. Additional information on customized pricing can be found in Phillips (2012a) and Bodea and Ferguson (2014).

16. The statistics on price discretion in lending in Europe and Canada are from Phillips (2012b), and the statistics on discretion in auto lending are from Phillips, Simsek, and van Ryzin (2015). More discussion on the relationship between incentives and the outcome of pricing discretion can be found in Phillips (2014).

17. More details on the capital requirements mandated by Basel II and Basel III can be found in documents on the BCBS website at http://www.bis.org/bcbs.

18. The estimate of the impact of the Basel III capital requirements on loan prices are from Slovik and Cournéde (2011).

19. The results of the Boston study are described in Munnell, Browne, McEneaney, and Tootell (1996).

20. An extensive discussion of statistical tests for lending discrimination can be found in Ross and Yinger (2002).

21. Information about the CFPB settlements is from a series of press releases that can be found at the CFPB website at http://www.consumerfinance.gov/about-us/newsroom/. It is illegal for dealers or lenders to record the race of loan applicants, which makes it difficult ex post to determine the race of rejected loan applicants. The CFPB employs a *Bayesian improved surname geocoding* approach, which uses a borrower's surname and neighborhood to determine the probability that she belongs to a particular ethnic group (Consumer Financial Protection Bureau 2014). The validity of this approach has been challenged by many lenders, several of whom settled without admitting wrongdoing.

22. For a study of the effects of usury laws on the consumption of credit, see Honigsberg, Jackson, and Squire (2016).

# 2 CREDIT RISK

Every loan entails risk and every lender needs to understand risk: a lender who cannot distinguish high-risk loans from low-risk loans will quickly go out of business. Understanding risk is also critical for pricing loans: not only does the risk of a loan influence the price of a loan; the price of a loan influences the risk.

Loan pricing interacts with risk in three important ways:

1. **Risk is a variable cost.** If a borrower defaults on a loan, the lender is likely to lose all or part of the outstanding balance. This means that risk needs to be considered just like any other cost in determining the price to charge for a loan. This is the primary justification for risk-based pricing: high-risk customers are more costly than low-risk customers.

2. **Risk is correlated with price sensitivity.** More risky customers tend to be less price sensitive than less risky customers. For a lender who is seeking to maximize expected return, it makes sense to segment customers on the basis of their riskiness in order to take advantage of this relationship.

3. **Price influences risk.** Everything else being equal, raising the price of loans will lead to higher losses from the loans that are funded, and by the same token, lowering the price of loans will lead to lower losses. This phenomenon is called *price-dependent risk*.

In this chapter we demonstrate how the riskiness of a loan influences its price and how the price of a loan influences its risk. We begin by defining risk and showing how risk affects loan profitability. We discuss how the riskiness of a prospective loan can be estimated and quantified. We then define price-dependent risk, discuss some of the reasons for it, and show how price-dependent risk explains the fact that credit is *rationed*—that is, credit is not available to everyone who wants it.

## ELEMENTS OF RISK

Broadly speaking, *risk* refers to the possibility of adverse business outcomes due to unanticipated events. The Basel Accords classify risk into four categories:

1. *Credit risk.* The risk of financial loss in credit assets due to the deterioration in the credit conditions of borrowers.

2. *Market risk.* The risk of financial loss where the value of assets held are affected by changes in market variables such as interest rates, security prices, and foreign exchange rates.

3. *Liquidity risk.* The risk that a poor financial position will require funding at an interest rate markedly higher than anticipated.

4. *Operational risk.* The risk of loss resulting from inadequate or failed internal processes, people, or systems, or from unanticipated external events that disrupt normal operations.

One of the fundamental principles of banking regulations such as the Basel Accords is that risk should be quantified and banks should hold sufficient capital to hedge against losses that might arise from any or all risks. In this chapter we focus entirely on credit risk—namely, the risk that a borrower will *default*—in which case the lender may need to write off all or part of the remaining balance. Credit risk is far more important than the other three categories in setting the price of loans.[1]

The Basel Accords (sec. III.F, para. 146) defines *default* as follows:

A default is considered to have occurred with regard to a particular obligor when *one or more* of the following events has taken place.

1. It is determined that the obligor is unlikely to pay its debt obligations (principal, interest, or fees) in full;

2. A credit loss event associated with any obligation of the obligor, such as charge-off, specific provision, or distressed restructuring involving the forgiveness or postponement of principal, interest, or fees;

3. The obligor is past due more than 90 days on any credit obligation; or

4. The obligor has filed for bankruptcy or similar protection from creditors.

Once a borrower is deemed to be in default, most lenders will initiate a collection process. In many cases, collection is automatically initiated when a borrower is 90 days overdue on a payment. A collection process involves a sequence of actions that typically begins with a series of increasingly urgent telephone calls and mailings. These may induce the borrower to pay in full, or the borrower may reach an agreement with the lender to settle for some portion of the remaining balance. If the loan is secured, the lender may seize the collateral and sell it to recoup all or part of the remaining balance. Alternatively, the lender may institute legal action or sell the defaulted loan at a discount to a third party. Unless the collateral is more valuable than the outstanding balance at the time of default, default will typically result in a loss to the lender, particularly when the variable costs of collection and recovery are considered.[2]

Three quantities are critical in any discussion of lending risk:

- *Exposure at default* (EAD) is the total balance remaining on a loan or line at the time of default.

- *Loss given default* (LGD) is the fraction of the remaining balance that a lender loses in the event of a default. LGD is equal to 1 if the entire balance is lost, and it is less than 1 if the borrower is able to recover all or part of the remaining balance through collection and recovery. If a loan defaults, the amount lost is equal to $LGD \times EAD$.
- *Probability of default* (PD) is the probability that a borrower will default at some point before the loan is repaid in full.

Of course, when a loan is funded, the lender does not know whether or not the borrower will default. For this reason, both EAD and LGD are random variables. The exposure at default is much higher for a borrower who defaults early than for one who defaults near the end of term. Loss given default depends on the value of the collateral (if any) associated with a loan and the effectiveness of the lender's collection activities.

In evaluating a prospective loan, a risk-neutral lender is concerned only with the expected values of EAD and LGD; that is, he would only care about expected exposure at default (EEAD) and expected loss given default (ELGD). Assume that a risk-neutral lender is considering a loan with term $T$ that has probability of default, loss given default, and exposure at default in each period of $p_d(t)$, $LGD_t$, and $EAD_t$, respectively, for $t = 1, 2, \ldots, T$. We assume that $p_d(t) > 0$ for at least one value of $t$ so that $PD > 0$. In this case:

$$PD = \sum_{t=1}^{T} p_d(t), \tag{2.1}$$

$$EEAD = \frac{\sum_{t=1}^{T} p_d(t) \times EAD_t}{PD} \tag{2.2}$$

$$ELGD = \frac{\sum_{t=1}^{T} p_d(t) \times LGD_t \times EAD_t}{\sum_{t=1}^{T} p_d(t) \times EAD_t} \tag{2.3}$$

and the *expected loss* (EL) for the loan is given by

$$EL = \sum_{t=1}^{T} p_d(t) \times LGD_t \times EAD_t.$$

Simple algebra can be used to show that

$$EL = PD \times ELGD \times EEAD. \tag{2.4}$$

Estimating the expected loss from an individual loan or a portfolio of loans is important for many reasons. For one thing, the value of a portfolio of loans depends on the total expected losses from loans in the portfolio. Second, the risk associated with a prospective loan is an important determinant of whether a lender will be willing to make that loan: most lenders establish a "risk threshold" such that they will not accept loans with estimated risk greater than the threshold. Finally, and most important for our purposes, the expected loss from a loan is a major determinant of the expected profitability of a loan and thereby influences the price that a lender should charge for the loan.[3]

Consider a loan of $1 that a customer agrees to pay back after one period at an interest rate of $p$. The lender believes that the customer has a probability of defaulting of $PD$, and if the customer defaults, he will lose the entire balance (i.e., $LGD \times EAD = 1$). To fund the loan, the lender borrows $1 at a one-period rate of $p_c$ from another entity—for example, the Federal Reserve.[4] If the customer pays back the loan, the lender will receive a net profit of $p - p_c$. If the customer defaults, the lender will lose an amount equal to $1 + p_c$. Thus, the expected profit from the loan is given by

$$E[\pi] = (1 - PD)(p - p_c) - PD \times (1 + p_c). \qquad (2.5)$$

A risk-neutral profit-maximizing lender would offer the loan if and only if $E[\pi] > 0$.

Assume that the lender cannot influence the price of the loan—that is, he is a *price taker*. In this case a risk-neutral lender would offer the loan only if

$$\frac{p - p_c}{p + 1} > PD. \qquad (2.6)$$

Equation 2.6 defines the risk cutoff that a risk-neutral profit-maximizing lender would use in underwriting decisions.

---

**Example 2.1: Risk Cutoff.** A lender has a cost of capital of 2% and is offering one-period loans at 4%. Using the formula in Equation 2.6, he would offer loans only to customers whose estimated probability of default satisfied $PD < (.04 - .02)/1.04$ or $PD < 1.92\%$.

---

The risk cutoff in Equation 2.6 is appropriate for a lender who is a price taker. However, more relevant to the problem of price optimization is the case in which the lender *can* set the price to charge for a loan. In this case, the profit-maximizing lender would set a price for each loan such that $E[\pi] > 0$. That is, given cost of funds $p_c$ and probability of default $PD$, he would set a price $p$ such that

$$p > \frac{PD(1 + p_c)}{1 - PD} + p_c. \qquad (2.7)$$

According to Equation 2.7, a lender should charge a rate for each loan that is greater than the cost of capital plus a risk premium. The minimum risk premium is an increasing function of $PD$, which suggests that riskier customers should be charged higher rates.

---

**Example 2.2: Price Cutoff.** A lender with cost of capital of 2% is considering offering a loan to a customer who has a probability of default of 5%. Following Equation 2.7, a positive expected profit from the loan requires the lender to offer a rate higher than $.05 \times (1 + .02)/(1 - .05) + .02 = 7.37\%$. This corresponds to a minimum risk premium of 5.37%.

---

Equation 2.7 only establishes a lower bound—it does not specify the price that the lender *should* offer. The price that the lender should offer will depend both on what the lender is trying to achieve—whether he is looking to maximize profitability or maximize bookings subject to profitability constraint—and on the price sensitivity of customers. We describe how customer price sensitivity can be estimated in Chapter 5 and how price sensitivity can be used along with loan profitability to determine price in Chapter 7.

The expected profit calculation in Equation 2.5 is extremely simplistic. It ignores the dynamics of payment and default in a multiperiod loan. It also ignores the fact the probability of default is not independent of the price at which the loan has been offered. We address those issues in detail in Chapter 3. However, even the simplistic calculation in Equation 2.5 should be sufficient to show that risk is an important consideration in loan pricing.

## ESTIMATING RISK

Equations 2.6 and 2.7 show that pricing and underwriting decisions both depend on estimates of the expected loss from a prospective loan. The more accurate the estimate of expected loss, the better the pricing and underwriting decisions the lender can make. One approach to estimating the expected loss from a loan is to use the average behavior of similar loans in the past. Assume that a lender has full history for a large number $i = 1, 2, \ldots w,$ $N$ of similar loans. (Here, "full history" means that all of the loans have either gone to term or defaulted.) Let $D_i = 1$ if loan $i$ defaulted and $D_i = 0$ if the loan went to term without defaulting. One way to estimate the probability of default is to use the fraction of loans that historically defaulted; that is:

$$\widehat{PD} = \frac{\sum_{i=1}^{N} D_i}{N}.$$

The use of the caret over $PD$ distinguishes statistical estimates of random variables from the random variables themselves, thus $\widehat{PD}$ is a statistical estimate of the random variable $PD$.

Let $EAD_i$ be the exposure at default for loan $i$ and let $LGD_i$ be the loss given default for loan $i$, with $EAD_i = 0$ and $LGD_i = 0$ if the loan went to term without defaulting. The average historical exposure at default, loss given default, and loss are given by

$$\widehat{EEAD} = \frac{\sum_{i=1}^{N} EAD_i}{\sum_{i=1}^{N} D_i},$$

$$\widehat{ELGD} = \frac{\sum_{i=1}^{N} LGD_i \times EAD_i}{\sum_{i=1}^{N} EAD_i},$$

$$\widehat{EL} = \frac{\sum_{i=1}^{N} LGD_i \times EAD_i}{N}.$$

These equations are the statistical versions of the relationships in Equation 2.3. From simple algebra, $\widehat{EL} = \widehat{PD} \times \widehat{ELGD} \times \widehat{EEAD}$, which is the statistical equivalent of Equation 2.4.

**Example 2.3: Risk Estimates.** A lender has records on the full history of 100,000 loans issued in the past. Of these loans, 1,300 defaulted and the remainder were repaid in full. The total balances due on the loans that defaulted equaled $10,000,000, of which, through collection efforts, the lender was able to recover $6,000,000. In this case:

$$\widehat{PD} = 1,300 / 100,000 = .013,$$

$$\widehat{EEAD} = \$10,000,000 / 1,300 = \$7,692,$$

$$\widehat{ELGD} = \$4,000,000 / \$10,000,000 = .40$$

$$\widehat{EL} = \$4,000,000 / 100,000 = \$40.$$

The lender can use these values as estimates of future PD, EEAD, ELGD, and EL for similar loans.

The basic assumption underlying the estimates in Example 2.3 is that the performance of future loans can be estimated based on the performance of past loans. This assumption is problematic—future changes in macroeconomic conditions or other factors can lead to future losses that differ from the past. The problem is exacerbated because the estimates used in Example 2.3 require a database of loans that have had an opportunity to go to term. If the loan in question is a 35-year mortgage, the database must include loans that were originated at least 35 years ago. It is a stretch to believe that the performance of loans issued today will be similar to those issued 35 years earlier. The risk estimates in Example 2.3 are also based on the aggregate performance of a large number of disparate loans. For purposes of underwriting and pricing, it would be useful to have an estimate of loan risk that incorporated information about the characteristics of the borrower and the loan itself, as well as the underlying macroeconomic conditions.

## Individual Credit Risk

Broadly speaking, there are three reasons a borrower might default on a loan. It might be that the loan was fraudulent, meaning that the borrower took out the loan under false pretenses (e.g., a stolen identity) and had no intention of repaying. Another possibility is that the borrower was the victim of an unpredictable financial shock, such as a medical emergency or being laid off from her job. Finally, it could be that financial mismanagement or bad decisions by the borrower put her into a position such that she cannot repay her debts.

Lenders expend considerable time and resources developing algorithms to determine whether a particular loan application or transaction—such as a credit card charge—is fraudulent.[5] In addition, random shocks clearly play a role in many non-fraudulent defaults. Job losses, divorce, and accidents can all lead to default. In the United States, it has been estimated that more than 46% of personal bankruptcies result from medical expenses.[6] Notwithstanding the importance of fraud and random shocks, most modern risk estimation approaches are based on the premise that poor individual decisions are the dominant contributor to default and that a history of poor decisions predicts that an individual is likely to make poor decisions in the future. Simply put, certain people are more creditworthy than others. Furthermore, cases of default that might be attributed to random shocks may in part be the consequence of poor personal decisions: unanticipated medical expenses are much more likely to lead to default for a household that is underinsured than one that is properly insured. Modern risk estimation focuses primarily on using the past financial behavior of a borrower to predict her probability of default.

For most of history, evaluating loan applicants was expensive and time consuming. In the United States, through the 1970s, a credit manager would interview a prospective borrower to determine "loan purpose, amount of loan, how secured, antecedents of the applicant, profession, employment, income, assets and liabilities," in order to "evaluate character, capacity, and creditworthiness." Ascertaining the facts required some skill:

> The applicant through convenience or short memory frequently fails to provide the interviewer with a complete listing of all fixed and open accounts or revolving credit obligations. The experienced interviewer will, in many instances, detect a hesitancy on the part of the applicant to be forthright in identifying creditors along with the amount of obligation and terms. (Baughn and Walker 1978)

The interview would usually be followed by a series of phone calls to verify the applicant's information and to obtain additional information. The final evaluation of the applicant's creditworthiness would be based on "character of the applicant, evidence of stability of residence, employment, prospects of future advancement and increased earnings, extent of obligations, performance on fixed and open account obligations, and the relations of applicant's obligations to uncommitted disposable income."

Undoubtedly, experienced credit managers at most banks did a good job of weeding out risky applicants and identifying good prospects. Indeed, in the decades following the Great Depression, banks were highly conservative in lending, and default rates were extremely low. However, the "interview and investigate" process of credit evaluation suffered from two major drawbacks. First of all, it was expensive and time consuming: "Direct lending is expensive for the lender. The components that must be taken into account in analyzing the cost of providing this credit includes: facilities to accommodate the person-to-person interview; credit investigation and loan closing . . . and the time element required for the disclosure and the credit investigation," as Baughn and Walker (138) noted in 1978.

In addition to the time and expense involved, the process was subject to biases—conscious or unconscious—on the part of the lender. Elements considered in evaluating creditworthiness such as the character of the applicant and prospects of future advancement were highly subjective. As a result, credit was extended more readily to local "insiders"—members of the Rotary Club and owners of established businesses—than to "outsiders" such as members of minority groups or new arrivals to the community.[7] In addition to being discriminatory, the need to interview and investigate limited both the size of consumer lending operations and their geographical scope—local knowledge and access was critical to evaluate the creditworthiness of a loan applicant. In the years following World War II, a number of retailers and consumer lenders began to institute more systematic approaches to making credit decisions. Specifically, they began to score loan applicants.

### Credit Scoring

The statistician David Durand (1941) is generally credited with developing the first numerical credit score based on historical loan performance. He analyzed the outcomes of about 7,200 installment loans issued by 37 firms and used statistical techniques to estimate an efficiency index to predict which customers were more likely to default. His key finding was that a statistically reliable predictor of default could be calculated using observable customer characteristics. While Durand's report was academically influential, it is not clear if his approach was ever directly adopted. However, as computational power became increasingly available in the early 1950s, more retailers and lenders began to implement credit scoring systems. During this period, Spiegel's—a giant mail-order company based in Chicago whose business required extending credit to millions of customers—implemented a credit scoring system that required a team of women working with punch cards and Friden calculators.[8]

Several companies began to develop analytic credit scoring approaches in the 1950s and early 1960s. With the assistance of professors at the University of California, Los Angeles, and the University of Southern California, the Universal Financial Company (or UFC, which purchased mobile-home loan contracts) developed a credit scoring system based on analysis of historical default data. They considered explanatory variables such as age of the principal applicant, whether or not the applicant had a phone, time at present job, percentage down payment, and other factors. They used linear regression to determine the weights for the variables that best estimated the probability of default. For example, an applicant with no bank account received a weight of 0, one with a single bank account (checking or savings alone) received a weight of 2, and one with both a checking and a savings account received a weight of 4. The sum of the weights (or score) for a particular application could be used to predict the probability of default: a higher sum of weights corresponded to a lower chance of default. The lender could use the predictions to set a cutoff score such that UFC rejected applicants with scores below the cutoff and accepted those with scores above it.

The results of the Universal Financial Company scoring system are summarized in Table 2.1, which shows the impact of different cutoff scores on the fraction of loans predicted to be *good* (i.e., go to full term) versus *bad* (i.e. default). The first column shows the fraction of bad applications that will be rejected with each cutoff score, and the second column shows the fraction of good applications that will be rejected. As the cutoff score is increased, an increasing number of both bads and goods are rejected; however, the percentage of bads rejected initially increases faster than the percentage of goods rejected. This means that by setting a cutoff score and rejecting all applications below that score, a lender can ensure that his population of accepted loans is less risky than the total population. Perhaps more important, the lender can determine a cutoff score that maximizes profit. The fourth column in Table 2.1 shows the expected profit that UFC would achieve using each cutoff score,

TABLE 2.1
*Scoring system results applied to holdout sample for the Universal Financial Company*

| Cutoff score | Bads rejected (%) | Goods rejected (%) | Profit ($) |
|---|---|---|---|
| 19 | 13 | 0.5 | 144,400 |
| 20 | 19 | 1 | 154,800 |
| 21 | 23 | 2 | 159,600 |
| 22 | 26 | 3 | 162,400 |
| 23 | 34 | 6 | 168,800 |
| 24 | 40 | 7 | 177,600 |
| 25 | 42 | 10 | 172,000 |
| 30 | 71 | 43 | 124,400 |
| 35 | 91 | 74 | 65,200 |
| 40 | 99 | 97 | 7,600 |
| 45 | 100 | 100 | 0 |

SOURCE: Myers and Forgy (1963).
NOTE: Columns 2 and 3 show the fraction of bad and good applications rejected for the corresponding cutoff score in Column 1. Column 4 shows the corresponding expected profit per application assuming that the profit per good loan is $4,000 and the loss per bad loan is $10,000.

assuming that profit from a good loan for the Universal Financial Company is $4,000 and loss per bad loan is $10,000. In this case, the company would maximize its expected profit by setting a cutoff score of 24.

The Universal Financial Company scoring system illustrates the most important features of modern credit-scoring mechanisms: applicants are assigned a score based on analysis of historical data, a higher score indicates lower risk, and the score can be used as an acceptance threshold for underwriting decisions. Credit scoring was originally used to supplement the judgment of credit analysts, but over time, credit scores proved better than analyst judgment, and lenders began to rely increasingly on credit scores as the primary criterion in underwriting decisions. While some lenders developed their own proprietary scoring methodologies, a number of firms—most notably Fair, Isaac and Company—began to specialize in developing credit-scoring algorithms that lenders could apply to their historical performance data to calculate scores. During this period, credit-scoring methodologies were *customized*—that is, both the variables used in scoring and the weights applied to each variable were different from lender to lender.

These early scores would be classified as *application scores*, because they were based entirely on information submitted with a loan application. However, from the early 1960s many banks used information from *credit bureaus* to supplement their interview-and-investigate processes of credit decision making. Credit bureaus began by collecting information about loan applicants such as bankruptcies and court judgments, which they would supply to banks for a fee. The credit bureau business gradually consolidated until, by the end of the 1980s, there were three large credit bureaus in the United States: TransUnion, Equifax, and Experian. Through agreements with banks and other agencies, credit bureaus gather and store information about the status of all commercial debt held in the United States and, more recently, other countries. This information includes outstanding balances, outstanding delinquencies, and utilization for all loans and lines held with commercial lenders.

In the 1980s, Fair, Isaac developed a credit scoring system in the United States based entirely on bureau information.[9] Under this system, every potential borrower in the United States with a credit history received a numerical score—her *FICO score*—that measured creditworthiness. The FICO score differed from previous scores in two important ways:

1.  It was a universal score rather than a custom score. This means that there was a single score for each person based on his or her credit history obtained from the bureaus rather than a custom score based only on the information available to a single lender.

2.  The score was based entirely on bureau information regarding an applicant's current balances, delinquencies, defaults, and other behavior. It did not use many of the factors that had previously been incorporated into many of the custom scores, such as age and gender.

While the score has changed through the years, the original FICO score ranged from 300 to 850, with a higher score representing lower risk. The division between prime and subprime is often considered to be a FICO score of 640.

The FICO score was rapidly adopted in the United States following its introduction in the early 1980s. Its adoption accelerated following the 1995 recommendation of Freddie Mac and Fannie Mae that banks use the FICO score to evaluate mortgage risk. The success of the FICO score encouraged others—notably, credit bureaus—to create their own, competing scores. Each of the credit bureaus now sells its own score in addition to the Vantage score, which was developed through cooperation among the bureaus. Credit scoring has spread to many other countries: either through the entry of one or more American credit bureaus or through development by a local company, such as Veda Advantage in Australia and New Zealand.

The rapid growth in the use of credit scores was driven partly by the need to streamline and automate underwriting decisions to support large-volume consumer lending—it would be impossible for a credit card company to perform an interview-and-investigate procedure for millions of applicants. The adoption of credit scoring was also boosted by regulatory and institutional needs: basing underwriting decisions on credit scores has generally been allowed by regulators even though the results may have a disparate impact on protected groups such as women and the elderly. Credit scores have also provided a convenient numerical metric for the risk associated with a loan portfolio—average and quartile credit scores for a portfolio of loans are used as measures of the riskiness of a security based on that portfolio.

At the end of the day, however, the primary driver behind the widespread adoption of credit scoring was the fact that using credit scores results in better risk estimates than unaided human judgment. For example, one subprime auto lender saw profitability increase by about $1,000 per loan when he converted from reliance on local dealer judgment to using credit scores to evaluate creditworthiness. Given that the average initial balance of the loans was $9,000, this was highly significant and corresponded to an increase on return on capital of 16%. The use of credit scores increases profit in two ways: it enables lenders to set down payment requirements and prices based on risk, leading to lower default rates; and it enables lenders to offer larger loans to lower-risk customers.

## Defining a Credit Score

As of 2015, a typical credit file in the United States included from 120 to more than 200 variables summarizing all the credit held by an individual. Typical entries in a credit file include total number of revolving accounts, total balances on revolving accounts, total balances on revolving accounts more than 30 days delinquent, and time on file (i.e., time elapsed since first entry). Credit files contain only information about an individual's credit history—they do not include information about income, employment history, wealth, or investments.

A credit score converts credit file information into a numeric score that is correlated with the probability that an individual will default. Denote the credit file information associated with an individual by the vector $\mathbf{x}$, and define the probability that an individual characterized by information $\mathbf{x}$ will not default by $Pr\{G|\mathbf{x}\}$, where $G$ denotes that a customer is "good." We wish to derive a numerical score $s(\mathbf{x})$, such that $Pr\{G|\mathbf{x}\}$ is an increasing function of $s(\mathbf{x})$. That is, we want a higher credit score to correspond to a higher probability that a customer is good. There are many different ways this can be done, but the most popular approach—pioneered by Fair, Isaac—is the *log odds score*. A log odds score is based on the logarithm of the odds that a customer will not default:

$$s(x)= ln\left( \frac{Pr\{G|x\}}{Pr\{B|x\}} \right),\tag{2.8}$$

where $Pr\{B|\mathbf{x}\} = 1 - Pr\{G|\mathbf{x}\}$ is the probability that a customer with information $\mathbf{x}$ will be "bad," that is, will default. The *odds* corresponding to a customer with associated information $\mathbf{x}$ are defined by $o(x) \equiv \dfrac{Pr\{G|x\}}{Pr\{B|x\}}$. This definition matches the common use of the term *odds* in betting—odds of "10 to 1" mean that it is 10 times more likely that a customer will be good than bad or, equivalently, that a customer's probability of being good is 10/11 or 91%.

The quantities $Pr\{G|\mathbf{x}\}$ and $Pr\{B|\mathbf{x}\}$ are the probabilities that an applicant will be good or bad, respectively, given information $\mathbf{x}$. Let $p_G$ and $p_B$ be the fractions of the underlying population that are good and bad. We may be interested in the probability of observing the information $\mathbf{x}$ given that a customer is either good or bad. By applying Bayes' theorem, we obtain

$$Pr\{G|x\} = \frac{p_G Pr\{x|G\}}{Pr\{x\}} \quad \text{and} \quad Pr\{B|x\} = \frac{p_B Pr\{x|B\}}{Pr\{x\}},\tag{2.9}$$

where $Pr\{\mathbf{x}|G\}$ and $Pr\{\mathbf{x}|B\}$ are the probability of observing the information $\mathbf{x}$ given that a customer is good or bad, respectively, and $Pr\{\mathbf{x}\}$ is the probability of observing the information $\mathbf{x}$. We can substitute these quantities into Equation 2.8 to obtain

$$s(x)= ln\left( \frac{p_G Pr\{x|G\}}{p_B Pr\{x|B\}} \right)$$

$$= ln\left( \frac{p_G}{p_B} \right) + ln\left( \frac{Pr\{x|G\}}{Pr\{x|B\}} \right).\tag{2.10}$$

The ratio of goods to bads in the underlying population, $p_G/p_B$, is the *population odds*. It is a characteristic of the population as a whole and does not depend on the information associated with any particular customer. The first term on the right-hand side of

Equation 2.10 is the logarithm of the population odds. The second term on the right side of Equation 2.10 is the logarithm of the ratio of the probability of observing **x** given that a customer is good divided by the probability of observing **x** given that she is bad. This ratio is called the *weights of evidence*. From Equation 2.10 it is evident that the *relative* scores of two different customers depends only on their corresponding weights of evidence. Changing the number of goods and bads in the population changes the population odds, which moves everyone's score up or down by the same amount but does not change the relative scores of any two customers.

From the relationships in 2.9, we can see that

$$ln\left(\frac{Pr\{x \mid G\}}{Pr\{x \mid B\}}\right) = ln\left(\frac{Pr\{G \mid x\} / Pr\{B / x\}}{p_G / p_B}\right);$$

that is, the weight of evidence is equal to the logarithm of the ratio of the odds for the group with information **x** divided by the population odds. If customers with information **x** have a higher chance of being good than the overall population, then this ratio will be greater than 1 and the logarithm of the ratio will be greater than 0. This means that customers with lower-than-average risk will have scores higher than the population odds, whereas customers with higher-than-average risk will have scores lower than the population odds. Thus, the population odds "center" the score while the weights of evidence determine how far above or below the population odds a particular customer will be ranked.

Denote the probability of being bad for a customer who is assigned score $s$ by $Pr\{B|s\}$. Using Equation 2.8, we can write

$$e^s = \frac{1 - Pr\{B \mid s\}}{Pr\{B \mid s\}},$$

which implies

$$Pr\{B \mid s\} = \frac{1}{1 + e^s}, \quad Pr\{G \mid s\} = \frac{e^s}{1 + e^s} \quad \text{and} \quad o(s) \equiv \frac{Pr\{G \mid s\}}{Pr\{B \mid s\}} = e^s,$$

where $o(s)$ denotes the odds at score $s$.

Consider two customers, one with score $s$ and one with score $s + h$, where $h > 0$. Then from the formula above for $o(s)$, we have

$$o(s + h) = e^{s+h} = e^h e^s = e^h o(s).$$

This means that any constant difference in scores corresponds to the same multiplier on the odds, independent of the scores themselves. As a consequence, scores can always be scaled by choosing the reference odds and a corresponding reference score and reference interval. For example, the FICO score was originally calibrated so that an increase of 20 in FICO score corresponded to a doubling of the odds.

## Calculating the Credit Score

Once we have defined a credit score, we have the problem of how to estimate the score given historical data. Assume that we have a database that specifies the outcome of $i = 1, 2, 3, \ldots,$

$N$ funded loans, such that $D_i = 1$ indicates that the loan defaulted and $D_i = 0$ indicates that it went to full term. Assume further that we have a vector of $m$ characteristics associated with each borrower. These characteristics would typically be the items found in the borrower's credit file. Let $\mathbf{x}_i$ be the vector of characteristics associated with borrower $i$. We want to find some function $f(\mathbf{x})$ such that $f(\mathbf{x}_i)$ is a good predictor of $D_i$. This is called a *classification problem* in statistics and a *supervised learning problem* in machine learning. Specifically, we want to find a function $f$ such that, for a new applicant with characteristics given by $\mathbf{y}$, $f(\mathbf{y})$ is a good estimator of $Pr\{B|\mathbf{y}\}$.

Mathematically, the default prediction problem has a relatively simple structure—on the basis of an input vector $\mathbf{x}$ we want to predict the probability that the output variable $D$ will be either 0 or 1. Historically, the most common approach to calculating credit scores has been to use *logistic regression* to calculate the coefficients of a *logit function*, which is then used as the function $f(\mathbf{x})$. We discuss logistic regression and its use in the context of estimating a price-response function in Chapter 5. More recently, newly developed machine learning and artificial intelligence approaches—such as neural nets, support vector machines, and random forests—have been applied to the default prediction problem. The goal of using such techniques is, of course, to achieve more accurate prediction of the likelihood of default to support better underwriting and pricing decisions. However, some of these approaches have the drawback that it can be difficult to determine how the different credit features are combined to create a score. This can make it difficult to justify an approach either to a regulator or to a consumer who wants to understand why her score is bad and what she can do to improve it. Notwithstanding these difficulties, given the high stakes, default prediction will continue to be a fruitful area for the application of increasingly advanced artificial intelligence algorithms.

The output of each of these approaches to default prediction is a function that predicts the probability that a prospective loan will be bad based on a value of $\mathbf{x}$; that is, this approach fits a function $f$ so that $f(\mathbf{x}) \approx Pr\{B|\mathbf{x}\}$. This estimated probability can be substituted into Equation 2.8 to calculate the corresponding log odds score.

The functions underlying different credit scores along with the methods used to estimate the coefficients vary from score provider to score provider and are generally confidential. However, certain categories of credit file variables tend to have a similar influence on credit score across providers. Table 2.2 shows the relative influence of different elements in the calculation of the FICO score.

TABLE 2.2
*Categories of credit file elements and their relative influences on FICO score*

| Weight | Category | Influence |
|---|---|---|
| 35% | Payment history | Frequency, amount, and duration of delinquent accounts are all detrimental. |
| 30% | Amounts owed and percentage of credit used | More money owed in total and higher percentage of available credit used are detrimental. |
| 15% | Length of credit history | Less history is detrimental. |
| 10% | New credit | Multiple new accounts and/or hard inquiries are detrimental. |
| 10% | Types of credit in use | A variety of accounts is favorable, however too many accounts may be detrimental. |

SOURCE: Adapted from http://www.myfico.com/crediteducation/whatsinyourscore.aspx, accessed July 2015.

## Using Credit Scores

Most lenders in the United States, Canada, and the United Kingdom use credit scores as an important input to their underwriting processes. Most lenders use one or more of the commercially available scores. Some larger or more analytically inclined lenders develop their own internal scores, either scoring directly from credit files obtained from one or more of the bureaus or starting from a commercially available score and modifying it. In most cases, lenders will adjust the credit score of an existing customer on the basis of their history with that customer.

Once applications have been scored, lenders often apply triage to determine which applications to accept. A lender using triage establishes a reject cutoff and a higher accept cutoff. An application whose score falls below the reject cutoff is automatically rejected, whereas one with a score above the accept cutoff is automatically accepted. An application whose score falls between the reject cutoff and the accept cutoff is forwarded to a credit manager who will do more research. Depending on such factors as previous experience with the applicant, quality of collateral, and the lender's risk appetite, the applicant will either be accepted or rejected. A particular issue is so-called *thin-file applicants*, who have little or no credit history—college students or recent immigrants, for example—and therefore have no credit score. Some lenders reject thin-file applicants outright; others perform some research—typically of the old-fashioned interview-and-investigate type—to determine whether or not to approve a particular applicant.

Credit score providers emphasize that their scores provide only *relative* measures of risk—that is, they provide consistent rankings of applicants and a consistent measure of the *relative* risks posed by applicants. The *absolute risk*—that is, the actual probability of default and loss rate—associated with a particular applicant depends not only on the applicant's credit score but also on other factors such as current economic environment, type and size of loan being applied for, and quality of collateral associated with the loan. Furthermore, credit scores are typically estimated on the basis of historical default rates. To the extent that default rates are influenced by macroeconomic conditions, future default rates may be systematically higher or lower than those experienced in the past. The danger of assuming that the future will be like the past was painfully illustrated by the performance of mortgages in the United States during the recession of 2008–2011. From 1995 through 2006, residential mortgage default rates $(\widehat{PD})$ ranged from 1.4% to 2.4%. Most lenders did not expect that default rates would go above 4% or 5% even in the event of a recession. Delinquency rates began to creep up in 2007, reaching 3.1% by the end of that year. During 2008 and 2009 the default rate continued to increase, reaching a peak of 11.2% in the first quarter of 2010. It is fair to say that no lender had anticipated a situation in which more than one out of ten mortgages would be in default.[10]

At the end of the day, the truth is that no backward-looking approach such as credit scoring will ever be able to accurately predict default rates (or any other aspect of risk) in unprecedented future situations. Regulations such as the Basel Accords seek to ensure that large lenders maintain adequate reserves to cover the risk of future outcomes in which defaults are significantly higher than those experienced in the past.

## Product-Based Influences on Risk

The risk of a loan not only depends on the borrower; it also varies in predictable ways with characteristics of the loan. All else being equal, larger loans and longer-term loans tend to be riskier than smaller and shorter-term loans. These effects need to be combined with the applicant-specific risk in the underwriting and pricing processes. A particular applicant might qualify for a $10,000 unsecured loan but might be considered too risky for a $25,000 loan.

Larger loans are riskier in part because the monthly payment is higher—the higher monthly payment from a large loan could make a financially stressed household more susceptible to financial shocks. Another explanation for the higher risk associated with larger loans is *moral hazard*. In the words of the economist Paul Krugman, moral hazard occurs when "one person makes the decision about how much risk to take, while someone else bears the cost if things go badly" (Krugman 2009, 54). An example of moral hazard is a driver who drives more recklessly because she has purchased the collision damage waiver on her rental car and knows that the insurance company will bear all the cost of a minor collision.[11]

Moral hazard can influence loan risk because, in general, the cost to an individual for defaulting is not proportional to the size of the default—the penalty for defaulting on a large loan can be about the same as the penalty for defaulting on a smaller loan, which means that a customer with a larger loan might be willing to take greater risks.

---

**Example 2.4: Moral Hazard in Lending.** An individual who defaults on an auto loan will face impaired credit for a number of years, and the severity and duration of the credit impairment is typically not related to the size of the default: the penalty for defaulting on a $60,000 car loan is the same as that for defaulting on a $30,000 loan. In this case, an individual who is contemplating a $30,000 car loan knowing that there is a good chance that she will default in 6 months might opt for a $60,000 loan that allows her to drive a nicer car for the 6 months before she defaults. This effect has been confirmed in subprime auto lending—subprime borrowers who are more likely to default tend to take out larger auto loans than those who are less likely to default.

---

A similar effect has been found with loan-to-value ratios: all things being equal, customers who are borrowing a larger fraction of the price of their purchase (i.e., making a lower down payment) are more likely to default than those who are borrowing a smaller fraction of the price of their purchase. Longer-term loans tend to be riskier than shorter-term loans. Some of the additional risk of longer-term loans can be explained by the *random shock effect*—the likelihood of a random event such as a medical emergency increases with the length of a loan. However, there is probably also a selection effect in play—customers with more risk prefer longer terms as a way to borrow more money for the same monthly payment.

**Example 2.5: Loan Size and Selection Effect.** The e-Car data described in Chapter 6 contains information on the prices, loan and customer characteristics, and take-up for all loans offered by an online lender over a 2-year period. The e-Car data shows clear evidence of a selection effect: the average FICO score of customers requesting a 36-month loan is 736.4; of those requesting a 60-month loan it is 722.9; and of those requesting a 72-month loan it is 709.73. Given that a 20-point change in FICO score is associated with a doubling of the odds, this would imply that the odds of a 36-month loan being good are about three times as high as those for a 72-month loan, all else being equal.

## Other Approaches to Estimating Risk

Credit scoring and other analytic approaches to estimating risk have become the norm in most developed countries. These analytic approaches enable rapid, efficient, and objective evaluation of the creditworthiness of large numbers of potential borrowers. In essence, they make it possible for strangers to lend to strangers without an extensive and time-consuming process of vetting. Credit scoring has spread from its origins in the United States to many other countries, including Canada and the United Kingdom, as well as to Europe and much of East Asia. Creditinfo, an Icelandic company, has established credit bureaus in locations such as Guyana and Iraq. Whenever a credit bureau is first established in a country, credit scoring is likely to be close behind.

Despite the spread of credit bureaus and credit scoring, a substantial number of people—particularly those in developing or underdeveloped countries—do not have access to commercial sources of credit. Many of these people lack physical or electronic access to banks or other institutional lenders. Others find that the loans offered by institutional lenders do not meet their needs—for example, the minimum loan offered by commercial lenders may be more than they need to borrow. Microfinance lenders such as Kiva were established to serve this market. Microfinance lenders often use a variation of the time-tested interview-and-investigate approach to assess risk. For example, according to the Kiva website: "Each borrower is screened by a local Kiva Field Partner before being posted on Kiva's website. The Field Partner looks at a variety of factors (past loan history, village or group reputation, loan purpose, etc.) before deeming a borrower as creditworthy."

Microfinance lenders specialize in making small loans to relatively impoverished borrowers. However, there are hundreds of millions of people whose access to credit is impaired not by poverty but by the fact that lenders do not have information such as bureau files or credit scores with which to evaluate them. Their situation is similar to thin-file customers: they may be excellent credit risks, but with little or no information on past behavior, many lenders will not lend to them. Several companies have begun to supplement (or replace) the typical elements in a credit file with other indicators of credit. This can include payment history on nonfinancial accounts such as telephone or gas bills. Kredittech, an online lender, uses up to 8,000 data points that they receive from different sources such as Facebook, eBay, and Amazon in evaluating a loan application. Lenddo determines whether an applicant has Facebook friends who have borrowed from Lenddo. If they do, Lenddo uses the repayment behavior of these friends as a factor in the underwriting decision: Lenddo is more likely to approve a loan if an applicant's Facebook friends are current in their payment than if they are delinquent.

Because credit scores measure an underlying individual propensity for certain types of behavior, their use has expanded into areas well removed from consumer lending. Insurance companies commonly use credit scores in granting policies and setting rates for automobile and homeowner policies. Not only are customers with higher credit scores more likely to pay their insurance bills on time; on average, they also submit fewer claims. Studies have shown that credit scores can predict aspects of job performance; thus, not surprisingly, a 2010 poll conducted by the Society for Human Resource Management revealed that about 60% of employers used credit scores in hiring decisions. Credit scores are correlated with the risk of cardiovascular disease: people who take care of their finances are more likely to take care of their health, and vice versa. This effect persists when variables such as income and education are controlled for. These studies support the belief that creditworthiness is a function of deep-rooted behavioral tendencies.[12] Some of the implications of this fact for lenders and policy makers are discussed in Chapter 8.

## PRICE-DEPENDENT RISK

Our discussion so far has treated the risk of a loan as determined primarily by characteristics of the borrower and size and term of the loan. In reality, the riskiness of a loan is also a function of its price. Broadly speaking, as the price of a particular loan is raised, both the default rate and the loss given default of those who take up the loan will also rise. We call this phenomenon *price-dependent risk*.[13] Most lenders are familiar with price-dependent risk and take it into account in underwriting and pricing. Price-dependent risk provides the rationale behind the otherwise puzzling phenomenon of *credit rationing*—the fact that some high-risk customers cannot obtain a loan at any price.[14]

We explore the phenomenon of price-dependent risk in much greater depth in Chapter 4, but the basic idea can be seen from modifying the formula for the profit from a simple two-period loan in Equation 2.5 to incorporate a dependence of risk on price:

$$E[\pi] = (1 - PD(p))(p - p_c) - PD(p)(p+1).$$

(2.11)

When price-dependent risk is present, the probability of default increases with price; that is, $PD'(p) > 0$. Referring to Equation 2.6, if the probability of default increases with price in a way such that $PD(p) > (p - p_c)/(p+1)$, for all values of $p \geq c$, then there is no price at which the loan is profitable. In this extreme case, the expected loss rises faster than margin as the price is increased. If this property holds for an entire population of customers—say, those with credit scores below a certain value—then it is not profitable for a lender to offer loans to that population at any price. Even if it is profitable to lend to a particular population, it is important for a lender to incorporate price-dependent risk when setting the price.

**Example 2.6: Price-Dependent Risk and Underwriting.** Consider the simple two-period loan with profitability given by Equation 2.11 with $PD(p) = p/(1+p)$ for $p \geq 0$. In this case, the probability of default is 0 when $p = 0$ and approaches 1 as $p$ approaches infinity. In this case, $E[\pi] = (p - p_c)/(1+p) - p$, which is less than 0 for every value of $p$. In this case, it is unprofitable for the lender to offer the loan at any price.

Price-dependent risk is generally acknowledged as an important phenomenon in most consumer and commercial credit markets. It has been empirically detected in a wide variety of markets, including credit cards, US mortgages, US auto lending, and unsecured lending in Canada.[15] Five factors that contribute to price-dependent risk are the following:

1. *Fraud.* Because fraudulent applicants do not plan on repaying, they are insensitive to rate. As the price of a loan is raised, price-sensitive legitimate customers tend to drop away faster than price-insensitive fraudsters.

2. *Adverse private information.* Borrowers have information about likelihood of repayment that is not available to credit agencies or lenders—so-called *private information.* A borrower who has adverse private information is likely to be less price sensitive than the group average. Consider the example of Jane and Alice, both of whom have applied for an identical mortgage from the same bank and have identical credit scores. However, Jane knows that her company is planning layoffs and that she just received a bad job review. Given the higher chance that she may be without a job shortly and thus unlikely to be able to obtain a mortgage, she is more likely to accept a high rate than is Alice, who believes her job is secure and is willing to take the time to shop for a better rate. Individuals with adverse private information will tend to be both less price sensitive and riskier than the population as a whole.

3. *Competitive alternatives.* A customer who is a better credit risk is likely to have more alternatives than one who is riskier. As a result, as a lender raises his rates, less risky customers will find it easier to find cheaper alternatives than more risky customers. Consider two competing banks that classify applicants into risk tiers based on credit scores. The lowest risk tier for Bank A is 640–660, while the lowest tier for Bank B is 620–660. If Bank B unilaterally raises its rates, customers with credit scores between 640 and 660 will begin to favor Bank A. From Bank B's point of view, these low-score customers will seem to demonstrate much higher price sensitivity than customers with credit scores between 620 and 640, who do not have the option of borrowing from Bank A. Thus, if Bank B raises its prices, it will experience declining credit quality among the borrowers who accept its loans.

   A similar phenomenon will occur if lenders use different scoring methodologies or have access to different information. As a result of such differences, a customer may be considered creditworthy by one lender but not by another, even if the lenders are using the same risk cutoff. Consider two competing banks—Bank A and Bank B—who use different methodologies and/or information to evaluate default

## TABLE 2.3
*Risk categories for two competing lenders*

| | BANK B DECISION | |
| BANK A DECISION | Accept | Reject |
| --- | --- | --- |
| *Accept* | I: Low risk | II: High risk |
| *Reject* | III: High risk | IV: Highest risk |

risk. As shown in Table 2.3, there are four categories of customers: (1) *low-risk customers* whom both banks would accept (Type I); (2) *high-risk customers* whom Bank A would accept but not Bank B (Type II); (3) *high-risk customers* whom Bank B would accept but not Bank A (Type III); and (4) *highest-risk customers* whom neither bank would accept (Type IV). If Bank A unilaterally decides to raise its rates, some of the low-risk customers of Type I will begin to migrate to Bank B. However, Type II customers are not able to obtain a loan from Bank B, so they will continue to accept the loan from Bank A, even at a higher rate. For this reason, if Bank A unilaterally raises its rate, it will attract a higher proportion of high-risk customers and experience a higher default rate.

4. *Behavioral factors.* Studies have shown that individuals vary greatly in how they make financial decisions. Customers vary in terms of their attitudes toward risk, how they evaluate future outcomes relative to the present (future-mindedness), and their mathematical abilities. These variations mean that customers who are willing to accept higher prices for a loan are likely to be riskier. As an example, a customer who values current consumption very highly relative to future consumption is more likely to accept a high price for a loan. However, studies have shown that such customers will also tend to be riskier. We explore the relationship between behavioral factors, pricing, and risk more fully in Chapter 8.

5. *Affordability.* The *affordability* of a loan refers to a borrower's ability to make the monthly payments given her after-tax income and existing financial obligations, such as rent, utilities, and other debt payments. The estimated maximum monthly amount that a customer can afford given her income and other obligations is her *payment capacity*, or just *capacity*. The risk of default on a loan is high if the monthly payment would consume most or all of a customer's payment capacity. Many subprime lenders estimate the capacity of a prospective borrower relative to the monthly payment as part of the underwriting decision. Following the 2008–2009 financial crisis, capacity is being increasingly used by lenders as an underwriting criterion.

**Example 2.7: Affordability.** A 5-year unsecured personal loan of $10,000 with a 5% APR has a monthly payment of $188.71. With an 18% APR (which might be the lowest rate available to a subprime borrower), the monthly payment is $253.93, representing a difference of $782.64 per year. For a household that is already financially stressed, the cumulative effect of these additional payments could be the straw that breaks the camel's back, leading to bankruptcy or default. In addition, with an 18% APR, the household will have $65 less per month to absorb financial shocks such as unanticipated reduction in income or unplanned additional expenses.[16]

The contributions of each these factors to price-dependent risk is not fully understood and is the subject of ongoing research. Whatever the cause or combination of causes, the phenomenon of price-dependent risk is very real and is an important consideration in underwriting and loan pricing. We show how price-dependent risk can arise as a result of differential price sensitivity between good and bad customers in Chapter 4 and show how price-dependent risk should be incorporated in determining optimal loan prices in Chapter 7.

## SUMMARY

- The primary risk associated with a loan is default. Default occurs when the borrower is judged to be incapable of paying off the remaining balance of the loan. Many lenders will declare a borrower in default when no payment has been made in 90 days.
- If a borrower defaults, the remaining balance at the time of the default is the exposure at default (EAD). In case of default, the lender will lose some or all of the EAD: the fraction of the EAD that the lender loses is called the loss given default (LGD). The loss from a defaulted loan is equal to EAD times LGD, with the convention that EAD and LGD are 0 for loans that do not default. The expected loss (EL) from a loan is equal to the probability of default times the expected EAD times the expected LGD.
- The expected loss from a prospective loan is a cost to the lender and should influence the price accordingly. All else being equal, it is optimal for lenders to charge more for higher-risk loans. A price-taking profit-maximizing lender will have a cutoff risk such that he will not accept loans whose risk is greater than the cutoff. A lender who can set price should calculate a risk premium that is the expected cost on top of his cost of capital for accepting a risky loan. This risk premium can be treated as a cost in the calculation of price.
- Credit scoring forms the basis of modern risk evaluation. A customer's credit score is a formula that takes in information on her current obligations and past financial behavior and calculates a score that is proportional to her probability to default. The coefficients in the credit-scoring formula are determined through analysis of past default behavior on the part of many customers.
- The probability of default on a loan is dependent on the size and term of a loan: all else being equal, larger loans and loans with longer terms are riskier.
- Any population will contain good customers who will not default and bad customers who will default. In general, good customers will be more price sensitive than bad customers. Reasons for this difference in price sensitivity include fraud, adverse private information, competitive alternatives, affordability, and behavioral factors.
- An implication of the differential price sensitivity between good and bad customers is that loans demonstrate *price-dependent risk*: if the price offered for a loan is

increased, the default rate will increase. Similarly, if the price is decreased, the default rate will decrease. Price-dependent risk needs to be incorporated in both underwriting and pricing.

## NOTES

1. It is also possible that a borrower repays all or part of the remaining balance of a loan prior to it coming to term. This is sometimes considered a risk (*prepayment risk*), because it means that the lender will not receive the total interest income that he anticipated. We describe how the probabilities of both default and prepayment can be incorporated in the calculation of loan profitability in Chapter 3.

2. The term *collections and recovery* is often used to refer to the sequences of activities triggered by a default. *Collections* are activities focused on persuading the borrower to pay all or part of her remaining debt. *Recovery* refers to the seizure and sale of collateral as payment toward the outstanding debt.

3. The definitions of expected exposure at default and expected loss given default in Equations 2.2 and 2.3 both assume implicitly that the probability of default is greater than 0. This is a reasonable assumption for all real-world loans; however, for completeness, we assume that, if $PD = 0$, then $EEAD = 0$ and $ELGD = 0$ as well.

4. The rate $r_d$ can be interpreted as the cost of capital or as a risk-free rate available to the lender such that, instead of extending the loan, he could invest in a risk-free bond and receive a return of $1 + r_c$ with certainty. This is the approach taken by Thomas (2009).

5. Lenders sometimes distinguish between third-party fraud, which typically involves a stolen identity utilized to obtain credit, and first-party fraud, in which an applicant obtains credit that she has no intention to repay. Whether first- or third-party fraud was involved in a particular case can be difficult to determine. Often, failure to make any payment on a loan within 90 days of funding is considered the definition of fraud.

6. The statistic on default due to medical bills is from Himmelstein, Throne, and Woolhandler (2009).

7. As an example of the characteristics used to determine creditworthiness, Samuel Terry's *Retailer's Manual* (1869) recommended that store owners (the major source of consumer credit at the time) not extend credit to "people of extravagant habits, those who are intemperate or are the victims of other personal vices, people in ill health, minors and married women who are not legally responsible for their obligations, men without families."

8. Much of the history of credit scoring on this and the following pages is from Poon (2007).

9. Fair, Isaac changed its name to the Fair Isaac Corporation in 2003 and to FICO in 2009. For consistency, we refer to the company as Fair, Isaac.

10. Statistics on default can be found on the Federal Reserve Board website, at https://www.federalreserve.gov/releases/chargeoff. Part of the increased default rate can be ascribed to increased lending to subprime customers, but in 2009, prime customers were also defaulting in record numbers. This led many lenders to criticize the FICO score. Fair, Isaac responded that its credit-scoring methodology provided a relative measure of risk

among customers but that absolute risk would vary over time and among lending products at any given time.

11. For an analysis of moral hazard in subprime auto lending, see Adams, Einav, and Levin (2009), who also discuss the distinction between the roles of adverse selection and moral hazard in default.

12. The use of credit scores in insurance is discussed in Hartwig and Wilkinson (2003). For the relationship between credit scores and job performance, see Bernerth et al. (2012), and for the relationship between credit scores and cardiovascular disease, see Israel et al. (2014).

13. We use the term *price-dependent risk* to refer to the phenomenon that the loss rate experienced for a portfolio of loans is a function of the price at which the loans are funded—higher prices will lead to higher losses, and lower prices will lead to lower losses, all else being equal. The term *adverse selection* is sometimes used either as a synonym for this phenomenon or as an explanation for it. Technically, *adverse selection* refers to the situation in which the customer has adverse private information. We consider adverse selection to be one of the causes of price-dependent risk, but it is not necessarily the only cause.

14. Stiglitz and Weiss (1981) were the first to recognize that price-dependent risk explained the fact that credit was commonly rationed.

15. For the existence of price-dependent risk in credit cards, see Ausubel (1999) and Agarwal, Chomsisengphet, and Liu (2010); in US mortgages, see Edelberg (2004); in auto lending, see Adams, Einav, and Levin (2009); and in unsecured lending, see Phillips and Raffard (2011).

16. For the calculation of capacity in order to determine affordability, see Wilkinson and Tingay (2004).

# 3   INCREMENTAL LOAN PROFITABILITY

Calculating the optimal price for a loan requires answering two questions:

1. How will the profitability of a funded loan change as we change the price?
2. How will demand for the loan change as we change the price?

In this chapter, we address the first question. We do so by showing how to estimate the incremental profitability of a loan based on its price and on other characteristics such as term, amount, and risk that are known at the time the price is quoted.

In most industries, estimating the incremental profitability from a sale is a rather straightforward exercise in adding up revenue and subtracting incremental costs. At the highest level, loans are no different; the incremental profitability from a loan is equal to revenue minus cost. However, estimating the profitability of a loan is more difficult than for most products and services for three important reasons:

1. *Time value of money.* All the revenue from a loan and most of its costs will be realized at different times in the future. Calculating the profitability of a loan at the time the price is quoted requires calculating a discounted value for these future costs and revenues.

2. *Uncertainty.* At the time that a loan is extended, the future income from the loan is uncertain because it depends on the future behavior of the borrower and, possibly, on the future behavior of the market. A lender faces four sources of uncertainty:

   - *Default.* If the borrower does not pay back the loan in full, the lender is likely to lose some or all of the unpaid balance.

   - *Prepayment.* If borrower pays back the loan prior to its term, the lender will recover the full balance of the loan but will receive less interest income than if the loan were to have gone to term.

   - *Utilization.* If the credit product is a line, the lender's profit will depend on the extent to which the borrower utilizes it.

- *Interest rate.* For a variable-rate loan, the monthly payment will change if the market interest rate changes—if the market interest rate goes down, so will the monthly payment. For a fixed-rate loan, the monthly payment is constant, but the cost of capital (or the return on an alternative risk-free investment) may change over time. Most lenders reduce or eliminate interest-rate risk by hedging.

3. *Capital reserve requirements.* As described in Chapter 1, governments require banks and some other lenders to carry capital reserves as a hedge against higher-than-expected loan losses. The cost associated with this reserve is the foregone return from a risk-free alternative investment.

Because the incremental profitability of a loan is uncertain at the time it is funded, the profitability of the loan needs to be calculated as an *expected value.* Calculating the various risks associated with a loan and estimating their probabilities and impacts on expected profitability can be quite complex. This complexity is compounded by the intertemporal nature of loan payments—a borrower who defaults soon after receiving a loan will result in a much greater loss for a lender than for a borrower who defaults closer to the term of the loan. Furthermore, the expected profitability of a loan will be influenced by the characteristics of the borrower. High-risk borrowers carry much higher default risk, but they may also generate more fee income. Low-risk borrowers have low default risk but may have high prepayment risk and are much less likely to heavily utilize a line. Understanding how customer and product characteristics interact to determine expected profitability is key for lenders to segment their customer base and to design and price products appropriately for different segments.

In the remainder of this chapter, we show how the elements of loan profitability can be calculated for any price and combined into a single measure of the expected profitability of a loan. We begin by introducing the concept of incremental profit.

## THE CONCEPT OF INCREMENTAL PROFIT

For purposes of pricing, the appropriate measure of loan profitability is *expected incremental profit. Incremental* means that the costs used to evaluate the profitability of the loan do not include any fixed or semivariable costs that would be incurred independent of whether the loan is funded. Only costs that would change if the loan is made should be included in the cost. Many overhead costs—such as facilities costs and employee salaries and benefits—are sunk by the time that a price is quoted for a loan and should not be included in the calculation of incremental profit.

Which costs are variable and need to be included in incremental profit depends on the pricing process in use and the point in that process at which prices are quoted. Any costs that are incurred as the result of a pricing action should be included in the calculation of incremental profit. For example, an advertised promotional price for a credit card may drive a surge of applications. In this case, the costs of processing these additional applications should be included in calculating the profitability of the promotion. In contrast, for many loans, a final rate is quoted only after an application is approved. In this case, the costs of processing the application and the costs of underwriting are already sunk and should not be included in the calculation of incremental profit.

This approach to calculating incremental profit is based on the principle of activity-based costing which attributes costs to the activities that generate them. Because fixed costs are not generated by any specific loan, they are not incorporated into the incremental profit calculation. For this reason, the sum of the incremental profits of all loans on the book will not equal the profit of the lending activity as a whole.

In summary, only variable costs—those that would change if the loan were funded—should be used in calculating the incremental profit of a loan. Using fully allocated costs in pricing leads to systematic overpricing. A useful rule of thumb is this: if changing a price will not change a cost, then that cost should not influence the price.

## CALCULATING THE INCREMENTAL PROFIT OF A SIMPLE LOAN

Calculating the incremental profit of a loan requires determining how each of the components of expected incremental revenue and cost will vary over the life of the loan and then discounting these back to the present at the corporate discount rate. To illustrate the calculations of these components and how they are combined to calculate incremental profit, we use as an example a simple 5-year loan of $20,000 at an APR of 5% with the characteristics shown in Table 3.1. The components of incremental profit for this example loan are shown in Table 3.2. The primary source of revenue from the loan is *lending interest*, which the lender will receive from the borrower. Set against the lending interest is the amount of interest the lender pays to a third party (or the loss of return from a risk-free asset) for

TABLE 3.1
*Characteristics of the example loan*

| | | |
|---|---|---|
| **Loan characteristics** | Amount | $20,000 |
| | Term (mos.) | 60 |
| | APR | 5.00% |
| **Risk** | Probability of default (annual) | 1.00% |
| | Loss given default | 50% |
| | Collection cost | $200 |
| | Prepayment rate (annual) | 5.00% |
| **Other costs and revenue** | Origination costs | $45 |
| | Commission | $0 |
| | Servicing cost (monthly) | $2 |
| | Expected fees (monthly) | $5 |
| | Ancillary profit | $0 |
| | Capital reserve rate | 2% |
| | Tax rate | 35% |
| **Annual rates** | Cost of funds | 3% |
| | Corporate discount rate | 8% |
| | Return on equity | 10% |

TABLE 3.2

*Calculation of incremental profit for the example loan*

| | |
|---|---:|
| Lending interest | $2,110.37 |
| Equity benefit | 24.28 |
| Cost of funds | (1,259.03) |
| **Net interest income** | **875.62** |
| Fees | 216.46 |
| Ancillary profit | 0.00 |
| **Total income** | **1,092.08** |
| Origination cost | (45.00) |
| Commission | 0.00 |
| Servicing costs | (86.58) |
| Loss | (204.17) |
| Collection and recovery costs | (7.18) |
| **Net income before tax** | **749.14** |
| Tax | (262.20) |
| **Net income after tax** | **486.94** |
| Equity capital charge | (78.51) |
| **Incremental profit** | **408.44** |

the funds. The difference between these two is adjusted by the amount of interest that the lender does not have to pay for the cash reserve he will hold against the loan—the so-called *equity benefit*. Additional sources of revenue from the loan are fees and *ancillary profit* from other products and services such as insurance that might be sold along with the loan. Adding these elements to the net interest income gives the *total income* for the loan.

Among the costs associated with the loan are *origination costs* and third-party *commissions*. In addition to these onetime costs, there are likely to be periodic *servicing costs* for the loan, such as preparing and mailing statements. Finally, as discussed in detail in Chapter 2, there is the possibility that the borrower will default before repaying the loan. In this case, the lender will lose some or all of the remaining balance on the loan—the expected value of the lost balance is the *loss*. In the case of default, the lender may also pay *collection and recovery costs* arising from attempts to get the borrower to repay and/or to recover some of the remaining balance. Subtracting these costs from total income gives net income before tax. Taxes are subtracted from this amount to give the net income after tax. Finally, a capital charge is assessed reflecting income lost from the capital reserve. The resulting *incremental profit* from the loan is the amount that the loan contributes to the total value of the lender and is the amount that a lender seeking to maximize shareholder value should maximize.

The elements of incremental profit shown in Table 3.2 are based on a 5-year simple loan of $20,000 with an APR of 5%. A *simple* loan is one that has a fixed interest rate and equal periodic payments over its term. In this case, we have assumed that the amortization period of the loan is equal to the term—this is characteristic of auto loans and mortgages in the United States and unsecured consumer loans in Canada and the United Kingdom. The various inputs used to calculate incremental profitability of the loan in Table 3.2 are shown in Table 3.1. In the remainder of this section, we show how the components of incremental profitability can be calculated from these inputs. We start by showing how the periodic rates required in the calculation are calculated from the annual rates and how the probability of the loan surviving (and thus still making payments) in any period can be calculated from the annual prepayment and default probabilities. We then show how each component of incremental profitability is calculated.

## Rate Conversion

The first step in estimating the expected profitability of a loan is to convert all the discount rates and interest rates into the same period as the loan payments. For a loan with monthly payments, this means that the interest rate, discount rate, and cost of capital need to be expressed as monthly rates. The formula to convert an annual rate to a monthly rate is $r = (1 + r_A)^{1/12} - 1$, where $r_A$ is the annual rate and $r$ is the corresponding monthly rate. This conversion formula is derived in Appendix A and applies to the default rate and the prepayment rate as well as the cost of funds, return on equity, and corporate discount rate.

In contrast to the other rates, by convention, the APR for a loan is 12 times the monthly rate, which means that the monthly rate for a loan with an APR of $r$ is $r/12$.

The monthly rates corresponding to the annual rates in Table 3.1 are shown in Table 3.3.

## Survival

In most cases, the most profitable outcome for the lender would be for a loan to survive for its full term—that is, for the borrower to make every payment. (An exception can occur if the loan has a substantial prepayment penalty, in which case it can be more profitable if the borrower prepays the loan at a point when the penalty is greater than the sum of the remaining interest payments.) However, there are two reasons a loan may not survive for its full term. The first reason is that the borrower may *default*—in which case, the lender loses the remaining principal as well as future interest payments. The other reason is *early repayment*, which occurs when the borrower repays the remaining principal in full at some point prior to the full term. In this case, the lender recovers all the principal but loses all future interest payments. In either event, the loan "dies"—its value goes to 0 and it is no longer carried on the books. *Survival analysis* is used to estimate the probability that a loan will

TABLE 3.3
*Annual and monthly rates for the example loan*

| Item | Annual rate (%) | Monthly rate (%) | Symbol |
|---|---|---|---|
| APR | 5.0 | .42 | $r$ |
| Cost of funds | 3.0 | .25 | $r_f$ |
| Corporate discount rate | 8.0 | .64 | $r_c$ |
| Return on equity | 10.0 | .80 | $r_e$ |
| Default rate | 1.0 | .08 | $p_d$ |
| Prepayment rate | 10.0 | .80 | $p_p$ |

survive—that is, not have a prior default or prepayment—into periods 1, 2, ..., $T$, where $T$ is the term of the loan. In any period, a lender receives revenue and incurs costs only from loans that have survived until that period.

In each period $t$ we specify two probabilities:

1. $p_d(t)$ = the probability that a loan will default at time $t$ given that it has survived to that point, and

2. $p_p(t)$ = the probability that a loan will prepay at time $t$ given that it has survived to that point.

Both $p_d(t)$ and $p_p(t)$ are *conditional probabilities*—that is, they measure the probability that a loan will default or prepay given that it has survived until the previous period. This is different from the *unconditional probability* that a loan will default or prepay in period $t$. Example 3.1 illustrates the difference between the two.

---

**Example 3.1: Conditional and Unconditional Survival.** Consider a portfolio of 100 60-month loans issued in the same month, and assume that 80 of those loans have survived until month 30. If we expect 2 of those remaining loans to default in the next month, then $p_d(31) = 2/80 = .025$. However, the unconditional probability of an individual loan defaulting in period 31 is $2/100 = .02$.

---

If we have values of $p_d(t)$ and $p_p(t)$ for every value of $t$, we can calculate the probability that a loan will survive to any future time. The probability that a loan that has survived up to time $t$ will either default or prepay in time $t$ is equal to $p_d(t) + p_p(t)$ and the probability that it survives to period $t + 1$ is $1 - p_d(t) - p_p(t)$. Let $S(t)$ denote the probability that a loan survives until period $t$. Then $S(t) = S(t-1) \times \left[1 - p_d(t) - p_p(t)\right]$, which means that

$$S(t) = \left[1 - p_d(1) - p_p(1)\right] \times \left[1 - p_d(2) - p_p(2)\right] \times \ldots \left[1 - p_d(t) - p_p(t)\right].$$

In general, the probabilities of default and early repayment vary over the life of a loan. Default probabilities are often highest in the periods just after the loan was issued. This reflects the fact that some of the borrowers realized quickly that they couldn't make payments or, in some cases, may not have intended to pay back the loan at all. Over time, default and prepayment rates both tend to approach constant rates. For purposes of analysis, it is often convenient to assume that default and prepayment probabilities are constant over time, in which case $p_d(t) = p_d$ and $p_p(t) = p_p$ for some $p_d$ and $p_p$ for all values of $t$. In the case of constant prepayment and default rates, the probability that the loan survives to period $t$ is given by

$$S(t) = [1 - p_d - p_p]^t. \tag{3.1}$$

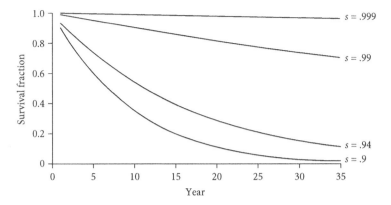

**Figure 3.1**   35-year survival curves at different values of the annual survival rate *s*

---

**Example 3.2: Survival.** Assume that a 10-year loan has a constant monthly probability of default of 1% and a monthly prepayment probability of 2%. The probability that the loan will survive for 2 years is $S(24) = [1 - .01 - .02]^{24} = .481$, or 48.1%.

---

Survival can be illustrated with a *survival curve*, which shows the fraction of loans that have survived until each period. Figure 3.1 shows the survival curves for a 35-year loan with different annual survival rates. Note that a seemingly small difference in annual survival rates can lead to a big difference over time. If the annual survival rate is 99%, then more than 70% of 35-year loans will go to term. However, if the annual survival rate is 94% (as in the example loan with characteristics in Table 3.1), then fewer than 12% of loans will survive their entire 35-year term.

## Net Interest Income

Recall that a simple loan has constant payments over its term. A simple loan with an initial balance of $B$ and a periodic interest rate of $r > 0$ for a term of $T$ has monthly payments given by

$$P(r, T, B) = rB\left[\frac{(1+r)^T}{(1+r)^T - 1}\right]. \tag{3.2}$$

This formula is derived in Appendix B.

---

**Example 3.3: Periodic Interest for a Simple Loan.** The loan in Table 3.1 has an initial balance of $20,000, a term of 60 months, and an APR of 5%. The corresponding monthly rate is .004167, and the monthly payment is

$$P(.004167, 60, 20000) = .004167 \times \$20{,}000(1+.004167)^{60}/[(1+.004167)^{60} - 1]$$

$$= \$377.42$$

We note that this is the same result as the Excel function calculation PMT(.004167, 60, 20000).

---

While the monthly payment for a simple loan is constant, the unpaid balance steadily decreases over the term. Let $B(t)$ be the balance remaining just prior to payment $t$. Then:

$$B(t) = B\left[\frac{(1+r)^T - (1+r)^{t-1}}{(1+r)^T - 1}\right]. \tag{3.3}$$

At payment $t$, an amount equal to $rB(t)$ goes toward interest, and the remainder goes toward paying down the balance. This means that the interest paid in period $t \geq 1$ is

$$I(t) = rB\left[\frac{(1+r)^T - (1+r)^{t-1}}{(1+r)^T - 1}\right], \tag{3.4}$$

and the amount that goes toward reducing the balance is

$$\Delta B(t) = P(r, T, B) - I(t) = rB\left[\frac{(1+r)^{t-1}}{(1+r)^T - 1}\right].$$

Over the term of the loan, the remaining balance decreases from $B(1) = B$ to $B(T + 1) = 0$. As the balance decreases, the fraction of the periodic payment that is used to pay down the remaining balance increases. The fraction of payment $t$ that is applied to balance reduction is $\Delta B(t) / P(r, T, B) = (1+r)^{t-T-1}$.

---

**Example 3.4: Interest and Principal Payment Split.** A 20-year mortgage has a monthly rate of 0.50%, and 42 payments have already been made. The fraction of the next payment that will be devoted to principal reduction is $(1 + .005)^{43-240-1} = .37$, which means that 63% of the payment will be interest and 37% will go to repaying the outstanding balance.

---

The speed at which the balance of a loan is paid down depends on both the interest rate and the term. Figure 3.2 shows how the split between balance reduction and interest payment changes over the life of a 5-year and a 35-year loan, both with annual interest rate of 6%. For the shorter-term loan, the majority of each payment goes toward balance reduction, with a relatively small and declining fraction of the payment going toward interest. For the 35-year loan, almost all of the early payments go toward interest, with a relatively small amount devoted to balance reduction. It is only in the 25th year of the loan that half of the monthly payment goes toward balance reduction. This helps explain why long-term mortgages are much more popular in the United States than the rest of the world—mortgage interest is deductible from income tax in the United States and a long-term mortgage front loads this tax-deductible interest to a far greater extent than a short-term mortgage does. For consumers in a higher tax bracket, this means that the after-tax payment on a long-term mortgage can be substantially lower than the pretax payment in the early years.

If a loan does not survive as a result of prepayment or default, the lender no longer receives interest (or any other income) from that loan. The expected interest in period $t$ is the probability that the loan has survived until $t$ times the interest payment in period $t$. The

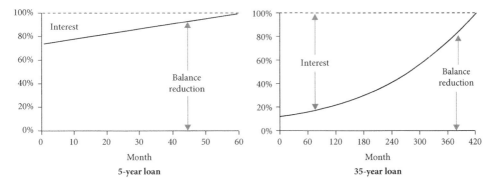

**Figure 3.2**    The fraction of each payment that is devoted to interest and to balance reduction for a 5-year simple loan (*left*) and a 35-year simple loan (*right*), both with an APR of 6%

lending interest is the net present value of the expected interest in every period over the term of the loan discounted back to the current period. That is,

$$LI = \sum_{t=1}^{T} S(t) I(t) / (1 + r_c)^t, \qquad (3.5)$$

where $S(t)$ is the probability that the loan has survived to period $t$, $I(t)$ is the interest component of the payment in period $t$ (given by Equation 3.4), and $1/(1 + r_c)^t$ is the discount factor in period $t$ evaluated at the corporate discount rate $r_c$.

The lender receives interest from the borrower. However, the lender also pays interest for the money that he used to finance the loan—this is the lender's *cost of funds*. For a bank this interest is typically paid to a government finance agency such as the Federal Reserve or the Bank of England. For other lenders, the cost of funds is the rate they paid for borrowing the funds from another lender. For a lender that is debt-free and funds the loan from cash on hand, the cost of funds can be interpreted as the interest foregone on a risk-free investment such as US Treasury bills.

The total payments that the lender needs to make depend on the fate of the loan. If the loan goes to term, he will make payments every period throughout the term. If the loan prepays, he will pay back the remaining balance and his payments will end. However, if the loan defaults, he can pay back only the amount recovered from the borrower, or $(1 - LGD) \times B(t)$, where $LGD$ is the fraction of the remaining balance that is lost in case of default. The lender will need to keep making interest payments on the amount defaulted, which is $LGD \times B(t)$. The expression for the survival rate for the expected balance for the cost-of-funds calculation is $S_c(t) = (1 - p_p - (1 - LGD) p_d)^t$.

We assume (realistically) that the lender has hedged his funding position so that his cost-of-funds rate is constant over the life of the loan. Let $r_f$ represent the lender's monthly cost of funds. Then, in each period, the lender needs to make an interest payment equal to the remaining balance of the loan times the cost-of-funds rate, or

$$C(t) = r_f B \left[ \frac{(1 + r_f)^T - (1 + r_f)^{t-1}}{(1 + r_f)^T - 1} \right]. \qquad (3.6)$$

The cost of funds that the lender needs to subtract from the lending interest is equal to the net present value of $C(t)$:

$$COF = \sum_{t=1}^{T} S_c(t) C(t) / (1+r_c)^t. \tag{3.7}$$

Because $S_c(t) \geq S(t)$, in the case of default, it is likely that the lender will still be making payments after he stopped receiving income from the loan. For a loan to be profitable, there needs to be sufficient spread between the customer rate and the cost of funds to compensate the lender for default risk.

We note that the formula for expected net present value of capital in Equation 3.7 is somewhat simplified. In particular, it has assumed that capital repayments are based on the remaining balance of the loan to the borrower. In actuality, the payments would be based on the remaining balance of the loan to the lender. Because the cost of capital is less than the rate that the borrower pays, the balance owed by the lender at the time of default will be less than the balance owed by the borrower. The impact on incremental profit of this effect is small, and we have ignored it in the calculation.

The final element of the net interest calculation is the *equity benefit*. This "benefit" arises from the fact that, by regulation, the lender cannot borrow the full amount that he lends. Instead, he must retain a reserve in each period equal to a specified fraction of the remaining balance of the loan. Because he must hold this reserve in cash, he cannot invest it. Thus, it does not contribute to the cost of funds and must be subtracted from the cost (or added to the revenue).

Assume that in each period $t$, the capital reserve requirement, is a fraction, $\alpha$, of the remaining balance. Then the equity benefit in each period is equal to $\alpha C(t)$ while the loan survives, and the expected net present value of the equity benefit is

$$EB = \sum_{t=1}^{T} \alpha S(t) C(t) / (1+r_c)^t.$$

The net interest income for the loan is equal to the lending interest minus the cost of funds plus the equity benefit; that is, $NII = LI - COF + EB$.

## Additional Revenue

For many lenders, fees are an additional source of revenues. Most lines and loans charge a fee for a late payment, and some loans and lines—particularly credit cards—charge an annual fee. Let $f$ be the expected fees paid per period. The net present value of expected fees at the time of origination is

$$F = \sum_{t=1}^{T} f S(t) / (1+r_c)^t \tag{3.8}$$

For the example loan, we have assumed $f = \$5.00$. This would be consistent with a 10% chance of incurring a late fee of $50 each period.

Many lenders impose a *prepayment penalty* if a borrower pays off a loan before it goes to term. In this case, the expected prepayment penalty in each period is $S(t) p_p(t) v$, where $p_p(t)$

is the probability of repayment in period $t$ and $v$ is the prepayment penalty. The net present value of this stream over the life of the loan evaluated at the corporate discount rate should be included in the incremental profitability of the loan. We have assumed that there is no prepayment penalty associated with the example loan.

Another potential source of income from a loan is *ancillary profit*—the profit on products or services that are sold along with the loan. The most common source of ancillary profit in lending is insurance. In the United States, mortgage lenders offer mortgage insurance, which, for a monthly fee, will pay off the mortgage if the borrower defaults as a result of injury or unemployment. Similar insurance policies are offered by banks for unsecured loans and mortgages in the United Kingdom and elsewhere. Auto lenders in the United States offer gap insurance, which pays off the remaining principal on an auto loan if the car is totaled in an accident before the loan is paid off.

Ancillary products can be quite profitable to the lender—sometimes more so than the loan itself. Thus, the incremental profitability of a loan transaction can be quite different depending on whether a customer takes an ancillary product. For this reason, it would be profitable for a lender to offer a lower price for a loan to a borrower who purchases a profitable ancillary product along with the loan than to a borrower who does not. However, in most cases, lenders do not know whether or not a customer will purchase an ancillary product at the time they quote the final price. (There are exceptions to this rule: some higher-risk borrowers might be required to take mortgage insurance as a condition of being approved for a loan.) This precludes the possibility of adjusting prices to a customer on the basis of whether she purchases an ancillary product. However, if a lender knows that certain customer segments are more likely to purchase an ancillary product than others, he can use this information to set more profitable prices. For example, in the United Kingdom, younger borrowers are more likely to take mortgage insurance than older borrowers. This would suggest that, everything else being equal, it would be profitable to price the same loan lower to a younger customer than an older customer.

In most cases, profit from ancillary products is realized in the first period, and expected ancillary profit can be simply added into total income. We assume that there is no expected ancillary profit associated with the example loan.

## Additional Costs

In some cases, a lender may pay a commission to a third party such as a broker. Typically this payment is made at the time the loan is issued. In addition, there are typically *origination costs* associated with setting up a new loan. We have assumed that the example loan has no commission and an origination cost of $45.00.

Once a loan has been funded, there are ongoing costs associated with servicing it, such as the costs of mailing statements and of processing payments. We have assumed servicing costs of $2.00 per month, which is broadly realistic for mortgages and auto loans in the United States. Let $\sigma$ be the monthly servicing cost, then the expected service cost at each period is $S(t)\sigma$, and the expected net present value of this expected cost is included in the calculation of net income before tax.

## Loss from Default

Aside from the cost of funds, the largest cost for most loans arises from the risk that the borrower will default. As described in Chapter 2, if a borrower defaults, the lender loses some portion of the remaining balance along with any future interest and fees. The loss of future interest and fees in the case of default is incorporated using the survival rate factors in Equations 3.5 and 3.8. To account for the lost balance in case of default, let $p_d(t)$ be the probability of default and $LGD(t)$ be the fraction of the remaining balance in period $t$ that is lost as a result of default. Then, the expected loss from default in each period is given by $LD(t) = LGD(t)p_d(t)S(t)B(t)$, where $B(t)$ is the remaining balance in period $t$. Expected loss at origination is the net present value of $LD(t)$.

When a loan defaults, a lender also incurs the costs of collection activities, such as mailings and telephone calls and fees paid for the recovery of collateral. Let $c$ be a fixed collection cost. Then the expected collection cost in each period is $c(t) = p_d(t)S(t)c$, and the collection cost for the loan at the time of origination is the net present value of this stream. For the example loan, we have assumed a collection cost of \$200 incurred by the lender if the borrower defaults.

## Taxes

Taxes can be calculated as $T = \tau \times NIBT$, where $T$ is the amount of tax collected, $\tau$ is the tax rate, and $NIBT$ is net income before tax. For the example loan, we have assumed that $\tau = .35$, which is consistent with the corporate tax rate in the United States. The appropriate rate to use will, of course, vary from country to country, and potentially from jurisdiction to jurisdiction within a country.

## Equity Capital Charge

The equity capital charge is a cost to the lender resulting from the capital reserve requirement. The amount of cash that is held by the bank in reserve for a loan adds to the equity of the bank. Investors require a return on the equity $r_e$ that is typically higher than the cost of capital. This required return is a post-tax capital charge to the bank. The expected equity capital charge in each period is $r_e \alpha S(t)B(t)$, and the equity capital charge is the net present value of this stream of payments evaluated using the corporate discount rate.

### CLOSED FORM APPROXIMATION OF NET INCOME BEFORE TAX

The calculation of the components of net income before tax is summarized in Table 3.4. In this table, the notation $NPV[x(t), r_d, T]$ indicates the net present value of the stream of cash flows $x(1), x(2), \ldots, x(T)$ at the interest rate $r_d$. $S(t)$ indicates that the loan has survived to time $t$, and $B(t)$ is the balance remaining at time $t$. Other variables are the following:

| | | |
|---|---|---|
| $r$ | = | Periodic interest rate on the loan |
| $T$ | = | Term of the loan |
| $\alpha$ | = | Capital reserve fraction |

$f$ = Expected fees per period

$A$ = Expected ancillary profit

$OC$ = Origination cost

$COM$ = Commission

$\sigma$ = Monthly servicing cost

In general, default and prepayment rates vary across the life of a loan. This means that an accurate calculation of net income after tax (NIAT) requires explicit calculation of the net present values of its various constituents. However, for purposes of analysis, it can be convenient to have a closed-form approximation of NIAT. It turns out that such an approximation can be derived if we make the simplifying assumption that the default and prepayment rates are the same in each period. In this case, we can replace the time-dependent default rate $p_d(t)$ and the time-dependent prepayment rate $p_p(t)$ with constants $p_d$ and $p_p$, respectively, that are independent of time. In this case, the survival function has the simplified form shown in Equation 3.1. Under this simplifying assumption, the components of net income before tax fall into three categories:

1. Revenues and costs that are independent of the size of the loan and are incurred at time of origination. Ancillary profit, origination cost, and commission fall into this category.

2. Revenues and costs that are an equal amount in each period over the life of the loan. Servicing costs, fees, and collection costs fall into this category.

TABLE 3.4
*Calculation of incremental profit*

| Element | Notation | Calculation |
|---------|----------|-------------|
| Lending interest | $LI$ | $NPV\,(rS(t)B(t),\, r_d,\, T)$ |
| Cost of funds | $COF$ | $NPV\,(r_c B^*(t),\, r_d,\, T)$ |
| Equity benefit | $EB$ | $NPV\,(\alpha r_c S(t)B(t),\, r_d,\, T)$ |
| Fees | $F$ | $NPV\,(fS(t),\, r_d,\, T)$ |
| Ancillary profit | $A$ | — |
| Origination cost | $OC$ | — |
| Commission | $COM$ | — |
| Servicing | $SC$ | $NPV\,(S(t)\sigma,\, r_d,\, T)$ |
| Losses | $LD$ | $NPV\,(S(t)p_d(t)B(t) \times LGD,\, r_d,\, T)$ |
| Collection costs | $C$ | $NPV\,(p_d(t)S(t)c,\, r_d,\, T)$ |
| Equity charge | $EC$ | $NPV\,(r_e \alpha S(t)B(t),\, r_d,\, T)$ |
| Net interest income | $NII$ | $LI + EB - COF$ |
| Total income | $TI$ | $NII + A + F$ |
| Net income before tax | $NIBT$ | $TI - OC - COM - SC - LD - C$ |
| Net income after tax | $NIAT$ | $(1 - \tau) \times NIBT$ |
| Incremental profit | $IP$ | $NIAT - EC$ |

NOTE: $B^*(t)$ indicates the balance at time $t$ computed using the cost-of-funds rate $r_c$ instead of the customer rate $r$.

3. Revenues and costs that are a constant fraction of the remaining balance in each period. Lending interest, equity benefit, cost of funds, and loss from default fall into this category.

Consider a component of the second type, say, fees. Under the assumption of constant prepayment and default rates, the expected net present value of fees, $F$, can be written as follows:

$$F = f \sum_{t=1}^{T} [(1 - p_p - p_d)/(1+r_d)]^t$$
$$= f \left[ \frac{(1 - p_p - p_d)}{(1+r_d)^T} \right] \left[ \frac{(1+r_d)^T - (1 - p_p - p_d)^T}{r_d + p_p + p_d} \right]$$
$$= f \times \phi_1 \left( p_d, p_p, r_d, T \right),$$

where we define

$$\phi_1 \left( p_d, p_p, r_d, T \right) = \left[ \frac{(1 - p_p - p_d)}{(1+r_d)^T} \right] \left[ \frac{(1+r_d)^T - (1 - p_p - p_d)^T}{r_d + p_p + p_d} \right]. \tag{3.9}$$

The first equation shows how $F$ can be expressed as the net present value of the survival-weighted value of $f$. The second equation reduces the sum using the formula for a series in Equation A.7. While the mathematical expression for $\phi_1(p_d, p_p, r_d, T)$ in Equation 3.9 may seem a bit complicated, it is actually straightforward to calculate and, after being calculated once, can be applied to each of the periodic components of the second category.

We can find a similar closed-form representation for the components of incremental profit that are proportional to the remaining balance—components in the third category. Consider lending interest, and let $R$ denote the net present value of expected lending interest. Then, we can write:

$$R = \sum_{t=1}^{T} rB(t)S(t)/(1+r_d)^t$$
$$= rB \sum_{t=1}^{T} \left[ \frac{(1+r)^T - (1+r)^{t-1}}{(1+r)^T - 1} \right] \left[ \frac{(1 - p_d - p_p)^t}{(1+r_d)^t} \right]$$
$$= \frac{rB\beta}{(1+r)^T - 1} \left[ (1+r)^T \left( \frac{\beta^T - 1}{\beta - 1} \right) - (1+r) \left( \frac{\beta^T (1+r)^T - 1}{\beta(1+r) - 1} \right) \right]$$
$$= rB\phi_2 \left( p_d, p_p, r_d, r, T \right),$$

where we define $\beta = (1 - p_p - p_d)/(1 + r_d)$, and

$$\phi_2 \left( p_d, p_p, r_d, r, T \right) = \frac{\beta}{(1+r)^T - 1} \left[ (1+r)^T \left( \frac{\beta^T - 1}{\beta - 1} \right) - (1+r) \left( \frac{\beta^T (1+r)^T - 1}{\beta(1+r) - 1} \right) \right] \tag{3.10}$$

The second equation in the calculation of $R$ is the net present value of the balance in each period from Equation 3.3 weighted by the survival probability. The third equation is derived from Equation A.7.

**Example 3.5: Closed-Form Estimation.** Consider the loan with the characteristics shown in Table 3.1 and periodic rates shown in Table 3.3. For these parameters, we can use Equations 3.9 and 3.10 to calculate $\phi_1(.0008,.0041,.0064,60)=43.2925$ and $\phi_2(.0008,.0041,.0064,.0041,60)=25.345$. Then, given the periodic expected fee of $5.00, the expected NPV of fees is $43.2925 \times \$5.00 = \$216.46$, and given the monthly consumer rate of .42% and the initial balance of $20,000, the expected NPV of interest is $.0042 \times \$20,000 \times 25.3245 = \$2,100.37$.

This implies that for a loan with constant periodic prepayment and loss rates, we can calculate net income before tax as

$$NIBT = A - OC - COM + \left(f - \sigma - p_d c\right)\phi_1\left(p_d, p_p, r_d, T\right)$$
$$+ \left(r - r_c + \alpha r_c - p_d \times LGD\right)\phi_2\left(p_d, p_p, r_d, r, T\right)$$

and incremental profit as $IP = (1 - \tau)NIBT - EC$. The closed-form solutions for net income before tax and incremental profit exactly hold only when the probabilities of default and prepayment are constant in each period for the life of the loan. As previously noted, this is not generally the case; however, the closed-form solution provides a very good approximation when the default and prepayment probabilities do not vary much over time or when they are both close to 0.

## SENSITIVITY ANALYSIS

We have gone through in rather painful detail how the characteristics of a simple loan can be combined to calculate an estimate of the loan's incremental profitability. However, it may not be immediately clear from these equations exactly how each characteristic of the loan influences profitability. In this section, we provide some sensitivity analyses to illustrate the relative influences of the term, rate, and risk associated with a loan on its incremental profitability. These sensitivity analyses can be valuable in developing an intuitive feeling for loan profitability and for understanding how and why loan prices should vary with term and risk.

Table 3.5 shows the monthly payments and net interest income at different APRs and terms for the $20,000 loan with characteristics given in Table 3.1. The relationships in Table 3.5 are shown graphically in Figure 3.3. Several patterns are evident. First of all, net interest income rises with term. The increase is more pronounced at higher interest rates. Second, monthly payment decreases with term, and it decreases much more quickly for short-term loans than for longer-term loans. Thus, for a $20,000 loan with a 10% annual rate, increasing the term from 12 months to 13 months decreases the monthly payment by $128.62 while increasing the term from 60 months to 61 months decreases the monthly payment by only $5.38. This is one of the reasons few consumer loans are for periods shorter than 5 years—short-term loans get much cheaper (in terms of monthly payment) when the term is extended even slightly. Also, as can be seen from Figure 3.3, the monthly payment for a loan approaches a minimum as the term is increased. This minimum is the payment for an *interest-only* loan in which each payment covers only the interest, with no balance reduction. The monthly payment for an interest-only loan is equal to *rB*.

The relationships among interest rate, monthly payment, and net interest income have important implications for the way that loans are positioned in the marketplace. Table 1.5 shows the advertised interest rates, monthly payments and total interest for a 3-year unsecured personal loan of £5,000 as advertised by 11 different lenders in the United Kingdom in May 2017. As in many consumer-lending markets, there is great variation in annual rate—from 3.30% to 14.90%. By this measure, the rate offered by Admiral (the most expensive lender) is 352% higher than the rate offered by TSB (the cheapest lender). However, it is likely that many prospective borrowers are more interested in the monthly payment. By this measure, Admiral's loan is only 17% more expensive than TSB's. Clearly, lenders charging rates at the lower end of the spectrum would do well to feature interest rates in their advertisements, while those offering rates at the higher end of the spectrum should highlight monthly payment rather than annual rate.

Consumers who are more concerned with the size of the monthly payment than they are with the interest rate often have in mind a maximum monthly payment that they can afford

TABLE 3.5

*Monthly payments and total interest income (TII) for a simple loan of $20,000
at different rates and terms*

| | ANNUAL INTEREST RATE | | | | | |
|---|---|---|---|---|---|---|
| | 5% | | 10% | | 25% | |
| Term (years) | Monthly payment ($) | TII ($) | Monthly payment ($) | TII ($) | Monthly payment ($) | TII ($) |
| 1 | 1,712.15 | 545.80 | 1,758.32 | 1,099.81 | 1,900.88 | 2,810.61 |
| 5 | 377.42 | 2,645.48 | 424.94 | 5,496.45 | 587.03 | 15,221.59 |
| 10 | 212.13 | 5,455.72 | 264.30 | 11,716.18 | 454.99 | 34,598.31 |
| 20 | 131.99 | 11,677.88 | 193.00 | 26,321.04 | 419.64 | 80,714.38 |
| 35 | 100.94 | 22,393.76 | 171.93 | 52,212.48 | 416.74 | 155,030.34 |

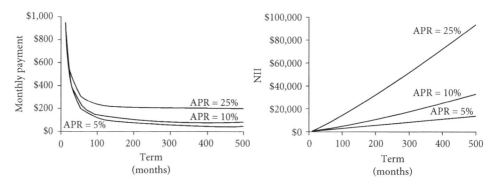

**Figure 3.3**   Monthly payment (*left*) and net interest income (*right*) from the simple loan in Table 3.1 at three different APRs

and will consider only loans with a monthly payment less than their maximum. A customer seeking to borrow $10,000 may prefer a 5-year loan at 6% with a monthly payment of $193.33 to a 3-year loan at 5% with a monthly payment of $299.71, even though she would end up paying considerably less interest with the second loan. Evidence of this can be found from the US mortgage market, where the 30-year fixed mortgage is the most popular product even though 15-year fixed mortgages are typically available at significantly lower rates. Further evidence that some customers focus on monthly payment rather than rate can be found in data from an online auto lender that offered refinancing of existing auto loans. Of the customers who refinanced their auto loans, 10% did so at a higher interest rate than their existing loan. This seemingly odd behavior can be explained by noting that, in each case, the borrower reduced her monthly payment by extending the term of the loan.

In theory, lenders should also prefer longer-term loans because they are more profitable. Table 3.5 shows that a loan of $20,000 with an APR of 10% generates more than ten times as much total interest if the term is 35 years than if the term is 5 years. The 35-year loan has a monthly payment that is less than half the monthly payment for the 5-year loan, which means that a borrower who is sensitive to monthly payment would prefer the longer-term loan. Thus, there is a strong motivation for both borrowers and lenders to seek longer terms. In the US auto-lending industry, 5 years was long the standard term for an auto loan. However, beginning around 2000, lenders began issuing greater numbers of 6- and 7-year loans. This trend was reversed during the 2008–2009 financial crisis, but has resumed following the crisis: the average term of a new car loan in Q2 2017 was 66.53 months compared to 60.27 months in Q3 2009. (St. Louis Federal Reserve Board, 2017). Counteracting the natural drift toward longer-term loans is the fact that longer-term loans have higher risk of default.

Risk strongly influences loan profitability. Table 3.6 shows the incremental profit for the example loan with the characteristics listed in Table 3.1 for three different APRs and five different annual loss rates. The same information is shown graphically in Figure 3.4. Not surprisingly, incremental profit decreases with increasing default risk. For any APR, there is a cutoff default rate such that the loan is unprofitable for default rates higher than the cutoff—this is the equivalent of the risk cutoff described in Chapter 2. One implication of the relationship between risk and profit is that the profit-maximizing price is increasing in risk. Another implication is that underwriting and pricing decisions should be linked—

TABLE 3.6
*Incremental profit for the example loan at different annual default rates and APRs*

| Annual Default Rate (%) | APR | | |
|---|---|---|---|
| | 3% | 5% | 7% |
| 0 | $5.46 | $562.10 | $1,134.31 |
| 0.5 | (66.72) | 484.49 | 1,051.08 |
| 1.0 | (137.45) | 408.44 | 969.51 |
| 1.5 | (206.75) | 333.89 | 889.55 |
| 2.0 | (274.68) | 260.83 | 811.17 |

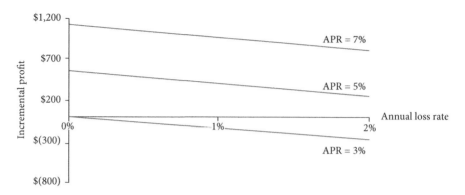

**Figure 3.4**    Incremental profit as a function of annual loss rate for the example loan in Table 3.1 at three different APRs

loans with different level of risk should be priced differently, and loans with different prices should have different cutoff default rates.

### ALTERNATIVE LOAN STRUCTURES

We have described in detail how to calculate the expected incremental profit of a simple loan—one with a fixed interest rate and constant periodic payments. But loans come in many different forms and the calculation of incremental profit depends on the form of the loan. In this section we discuss three of the most important alternative loan structures and their implications for the calculation of incremental profit.

#### Variable-Rate Loans

For a simple loan, the interest rate does not change over the term of the loan. In a variable-rate loan, the interest rate is periodically changed on the basis of some specified market rate such as the prime rate or the London Interbank Offered Rate, or LIBOR. Thus, "prime plus 2%" means that the APR is periodically adjusted—say, every six months—to be equal to the prime rate plus 2% (200 basis points). The idea behind a variable-rate loan is to shift some or all of the interest-rate risk from the lender to the borrower.

It may seem that the computation of expected net interest income for a variable-rate loan should be significantly more complex than for a simple loan. In reality, this is not the case. The primary reason is that the net interest income from a loan in any period is, with minor adjustments, a function of the difference between the periodic rate and the cost-of-funds rate. In general, the cost-of-funds rate tracks the market rate—thus, the difference between the variable rate and the market rate is likely to be more-or-less constant. This is the same assumption that we used to calculate net interest income in the case of the simple loan.

#### Renewable Loans

In Canada, the United Kingdom, and parts of Western Europe, the most common mortgage is a *renewable mortgage*, in which the term of the mortgage is less than the amortization period. For example, the term of a mortgage may be 5 years, while the amortization period might be 20 years. In theory, the borrower owes the lender the remaining balance of the loan at the end of the 5-year term in a large balloon payment. In practice, the lender is likely to renew the mortgage for another 5 years, possibly at a different interest rate.

---

**Example 3.6: Renewable Loan.** A borrower takes out a $100,000 mortgage at an APR of 6.0%. The term of the mortgage is 5 years and the amortization period is 20 years. The monthly payment on the loan can be computed using Equation 3.2 with $r = .005$, $T = 240$, and $B = \$100,000$, namely, $716.43. From Equation 3.3, the remaining balance at the end of 5 years is $85,190.08. The borrower owes this full amount in her last payment.

---

A 5-year renewable loan is similar to a variable-rate loan with a 5-year adjustment period. However, unlike a variable-rate loan, the lender can also change the rate on the basis of the borrower's payment history or changes in the borrower's credit rating. If, for example, a borrower's credit rating has declined over the 5 years since the mortgage was issued, or if the borrower has been consistently late with payments, the lender may choose to increase the interest rate upon renewal. Alternatively, the lender may offer renewal at a lower rate if the lender perceives the borrower's creditworthiness to have improved.

The ability to adjust the interest rate at renewal on the basis of new information is a clear benefit for the lender. However the renewable loan has the drawback that the renewal notice may encourage a borrower to shop for a new lender. One approach to incorporating this risk into pricing is to associate a high probability of prepayment with the renewal points. For example, a bank might offer a 5-year renewable mortgage with simple monthly payments and a 20-year amortization. Retention at each of the 5-year renewal points is expected to be 90%, and the prepayment rate otherwise is .1% per month. This situation can be modeled by specifying that $p_p(t) = .10$ for $t = 60, 120, 180$, and $p_p(t) = .001$ for all other values of $t = 1, 2, \ldots, 239$.

## Mortgage Points

In the United States, some mortgage lenders offer *discount points* as an option for borrowers. Discount points (or simply *points*) enable the borrower to obtain a lower interest rate by prepaying some interest at origination of the loan. Typically each point costs 1% of the balance and results in a 25-basis-point (.25%) reduction in the annual interest rate, although there are many variations. Lenders often offer the option of buying 0, 1, 2, or 3 points for a 30-year fixed-rate mortgage.

---

**Example 3.7: Mortgage Points.** A 30-year $150,000 mortgage with an annual interest rate of 6% would incur monthly payments of $899.33. The borrower could purchase 2 points for $3,000, and in return the annual interest rate of the loan would be reduced to 5.50%, with an associated monthly payment of $868.72. The $3,000 additional payment up front results in a $30.61 reduction in monthly payment. If the loan goes to term, purchasing the points would result in a total of $11,019 in reduced payments.

---

Evaluating the effect of points on incremental profitability is not difficult. As a first order approximation, the profitability of the standard loan without points can be compared to the profitability with points at the lower rate. For the example loan, the expected incremental profitability at 5.00% with no points is $115.98. If the lender offered a .25% reduction for a single point, the lender would receive an additional $200 up-front payment in return for reducing the annual interest rate to 4.75%. The expected incremental profitability for this loan including the points paid is $186.34, so, everything else being equal, the lender would be happy for borrowers to take the point in return for the reduced interest rate for this loan.

The trade-off of a .25% reduction in annual interest rate for 1 point is not a very good deal for the borrower when the term of the loan is only 5 years. However, for 30-year mortgages it may be a different story—the choice of the number of points for such a mortgage that minimizes the expected value of a borrower's future payments is quite complex and depends on the borrower's expectations of future economic conditions and her own future income-tax rate, as well as her expectation of how long she will own the home before selling it.

In analyzing whether to offer points—and if so, on what terms—a lender would also need to incorporate the selection effect: borrowers who take the option of points will tend to be those who benefit most from them. The most common way to evaluate whether a borrower should accept points is to calculate a breakeven point such that the points save the borrower money if they do not prepay before the breakeven point. Thus, borrowers who do not take points will tend to prepay more quickly than those who do take points.

### Credit Lines

Assuming that the borrower makes her payments, the balance outstanding on a loan decreases over time in a predictable fashion. However, the situation is different for a line in which the borrower can choose how much she wishes to draw from the line at any time. Specifically, given a credit limit of $L$, at any time the borrower can choose how much she wishes to borrow up to $L$. Her decision at any time $t$ can be represented by a utilization level $u(t)$ between 0 and 1 so that, at any time, her remaining balance is given by $u(t)L$.

Typically, the payments on a line are calculated in the same fashion as a simple loan; that is, the periodic payment, interest charge, and balance reduction are calculated as for a simple loan with balance $u(t)L$. Thus, the interest income in any period from a line is simply $ru(t)L$. If the lender knew the future pattern of utilization on the part of the borrower, he could calculate the expected profitability of the line using the formulas in Table 3.4 by setting $B(t) = u(t)L$. Complexity arises from the fact that the pattern of utilization for a particular borrower is unknown at the time the loan is offered. Unless the lender charges a periodic fee, a customer who does not utilize a line will generate no profit. For credit cards, this is called the *activation problem*—a certain number of customers who take out credit cards will never use them, resulting in no profit for the lender—or even a loss when servicing costs are considered.

This means that estimating the expected incremental profit from a line requires forecasting the extent to which the customer will utilize the line. One approach is to classify borrowers into three categories: nonutilizers, partial utilizers, and full utilizers based on line utilization 6 months after activation. Typically, a nonutilizer is a borrower who utilizes less than 5% of the limit after 6 months, a full utilizer is one who utilizes more than 95%, and a partial utilizer falls between 5% and 95% utilization. Statistical classification approaches applied to characteristics of the borrower—such as size and type of business, credit score, and other variables—can be used to predict the probability that a customer will be a nonutilizer, partial utilizer, or full utilizer. These probabilities can be used to estimate the expected incremental profitability of the customer.

## RISK AND PROFITABILITY

A risk-neutral lender would evaluate the profitability of an individual loan on the basis of its incremental profit: loans with positive expected incremental profit make a positive contribution to shareholder value. In theory, funding a loan with positive expected incremental profit would increase the market value of a lender, whereas funding a loan with negative incremental profit would decrease the lender's market value.[1] However, a loan (or a portfolio of loans) is a risky asset—its future return is uncertain at the time it is acquired. It would seem that a risk-averse lender should consider the risk of a loan along with its expected profit in making pricing and underwriting decisions. In this section, we show that this is not necessarily the case for a lender who holds a large portfolio of loans, each of which is small relative to the total size of the portfolio.

The most likely return for most loans is the incremental profit assuming that the loan goes to term, possibly with some additional fee income. The potential downside for the loan comes from the risks of prepayment and default. As we have seen, this downside can be considerable, especially if a borrower defaults early in the term. The only upside for a loan comes from the possibility that the borrower will end up paying more fees or ancillary revenue than anticipated. In the vast majority of cases, this potential upside is extremely small compared to the downside risk due to default. As a result, the returns from a typical loan follow a distribution similar to that on the left in Figure 3.5. The peak corresponds to the most likely return. The distribution to the right of the peak corresponds to outcomes in which the borrower does not default but pays more fees or ancillary revenue than the average. The distribution to the left of the peak corresponds to the cases in which the borrower prepays or defaults. Intuitively, the potential loss due to default is much greater than the potential gain from additional fees.

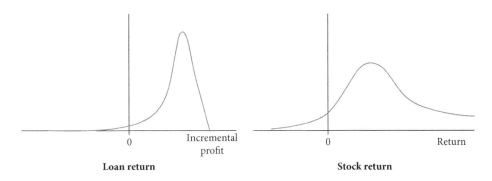

**Loan return**                                        **Stock return**

**Figure 3.5**    Sample return distributions for a simple loan (*left*) and a stock (*right*)

The distribution of returns from a loan can be contrasted with the distribution of re-turns from a typical stock, as shown on the right in Figure 3.5. The stock certainly has a downside: the total investment can be lost if the firm goes bankrupt. However, stocks typically have a much greater upside than a loan, as shown by the "fatter" right tail of the distribution. Does this mean that loans are intrinsically riskier than stocks? If so, why would investors choose to lend money rather than invest in equities? And how should the risk be incorporated into loan pricing?

Several approaches can be used to measure the risk associated with a distribution of returns. Some of the most common are the following:

1. *Standard deviation,* which measures the spread of a distribution—larger standard deviations mean a larger spread. The standard deviation of a distribution is typically denoted by $\sigma$.

2. *Variance,* which also measures the spread of a distribution. It is equal to the square of the standard deviation and is typically denoted by $\sigma^2$.

3. *Value at risk* (VaR), which is a measure of downside risk. For a given probability $p$, the corresponding value at risk is the level of incremental profit such that there is a probability $p$ that incremental profit will be below that value. For example, saying that a loan has a 5% VaR of –$212 means that there is a 5% chance that the actual incremental profit realized from the loan will be less than or equal to –$212 or, equivalently, a 95% chance that the incremental profit will be greater than –$212.

4. *Conditional value at risk* (CVaR, sometimes called *expected shortfall*), which meas-ures the expected loss if the loan performs poorly. For example, saying that a loan has a 5% CVaR of –$1,212 means that, in a large portfolio of identical, independent loans, the worst-performing 5% of loans would have an average loss of –$1,212.

5. *Probability of loss,* which is the probability that the loan will lose money; that is, *IP* < 0. A threshold other than 0 could also be specified; for example, the lender could be interested in the probability of a loss greater than $100, in which case he could measure the probability that *IP* < –$100.

No single number can capture all the information in a full distribution of returns: every risk measure has its shortcomings. Standard deviation and variance are both based on the full spread of the distribution—both above and below the mean. But risk-adverse investors are more worried about the risk of loss—the left tail of the distribution—than they are about the possibility of exceptional gains. Value at risk establishes only the probability that incre-mental profit might fall below a certain level—it does not say anything about how bad it is likely to be *if* that happens. For example, if every loan in a portfolio has a 5% VaR of –$212, it means that we would expect about 1 in every 20 loans to lose more that $212. However, VaR says nothing about how big the loss is likely to be when it occurs. Most investors would consider the risk to be quite different if the average loss for the bottom 5% of loans were $213 versus $5,000. CVaR does give an idea of the potential magnitude of loss but is sensi-tive to the level specified: 1% CVaR may be very different from 5% CVaR.

Table 3.7 shows several risk metrics, along with mean incremental profit, for the exam-ple loan with characteristics given in Table 3.1 at three different combinations of interest

TABLE 3.7
*Risk metrics for the example loan estimated for different
combinations of annual interest rate and annual default rate*

|  | Loan 1 | Loan 2 | Loan 3 |
|---|---|---|---|
| APR | 5% | 6% | 7% |
| Annual default rate | 1% | 2% | 3% |
| **Mean incremental profit** | **$333.99** | **$442.11** | **$583.71** |
| Standard deviation | $954.61 | $1,359.32 | $1,593.98 |
| Variance | 911,281 | 1,847,749 | 2,540,774 |
| 5% VaR | ($743.29) | ($2,194.94) | ($3,422.68) |
| 1% VaR | ($5,450.45) | ($6,472.30) | ($6,633.59) |
| Prob. of loss | 11.99% | 14.00% | 15.97% |

N O T E : All metrics were estimated using Latin hypercube simulation and 20,000 trials.

rate and annual default rate. A loan at a 6% annual interest rate and a 2% annual default rate has significantly higher expected incremental profit than a loan with a 5% annual interest rate and a 1% annual default rate; however, it is also significantly more risky according to all four risk measures. Default rate has a particularly strong effect on VaR and CVaR, since both measures are highly sensitive to the risk of high losses from early default. This can be seen by comparing the loan with the 6% annual interest rate and 1% annual default rate to the one with a 6% annual interest rate and a 2% annual default rate. The 1% increase in the annual default rate increases the 5% VaR by $1,680.92, whereas the standard deviation goes up by only $304.41. Increasing the default rate has a much stronger effect on the left tail of the distribution than it does on the overall spread. For this reason, VaR is often a better measure of downside risk than either standard deviation or variance.

A *risk-neutral* lender cares nothing about risk and will always choose the loan with highest expected incremental profit. Given the choice among the loans in Table 3.7, a risk-neutral lender would prefer to fund Loan 3. However, most lenders—like most investors—are *risk averse* in the sense that they would be willing to give up some expected incremental profit in return for avoiding some downside risk. A risk-averse lender might prefer funding the less-risky Loan 2 or Loan 1 rather than Loan 3, even though Loans 1 and 2 both have lower returns.

---

**Example 3.8: Risk Aversion.** One way to incorporate risk-aversion in decision making is to quantify the trade-off between risk and expected return. Let us assume that a lender has a risk preference that weights return four times as high as 5% VaR in making investing decisions. This lender would calculate the utility of a loan as $.8 \times IP + .2 \times (5\% \ VaR)$, which equals $118.46 for Loan 1, –$85.30 for Loan 2 and –$217.57 for Loan 3. This lender would choose to fund Loan 1, but not Loan 2 or Loan 3, even though Loans 2 and 3 have higher expected returns.

---

Example 3.8 would seem to imply that a lender's pricing decision should depend on his risk preference. A risk-neutral lender would be indifferent between two loans with the same expected incremental profit and would be willing to fund both if they both had expected incremental profit greater than 0. A risk-averse lender would prefer the loan with the lower risk and may not be willing to accept a loan with a positive incremental profit if it is too risky. Alternatively, the risk-averse lender would want to charge higher rates offered for more risky loans relative to a risk-neutral lender since, for the loan to be acceptable the risk-adverse lender would require a higher return to offset the risk.

Risk aversion can be important to a lender who is issuing only a very large single loan or a relatively small number of loans. However, a lender with a large number of loans can use his portfolio to hedge against the risk of any individual loan. As a lender's portfolio grows, he should act more and more risk neutral with respect to underwriting and pricing new loans. To illustrate this idea, assume that a lender has an existing portfolio of $N$ loans such that each loan has a return (expected incremental profit) of $\mu$ and a standard deviation of $\sigma$. Furthermore, assume that the loan returns are independent and that the lender is risk averse: in particular, his utility on a portfolio of loans is given by $\mu_p - \alpha\sigma_p$ for some $\alpha > 0$. The lender's expected portfolio profitability is $N\mu$, and his portfolio standard deviation is $\sqrt{N}\sigma$. The condition for his portfolio to have positive utility is $N\mu - \alpha\sqrt{N}\sigma \geq 0$, or

$$\mu \geq \alpha\sigma / \sqrt{N}. \tag{3.11}$$

As $N$ gets larger, the right side of Inequality 3.11 becomes smaller, which implies that, as his portfolio grows, the lender should act increasingly risk neutral in underwriting and pricing decisions. A lender with a sufficiently large portfolio—or who is acting as an agent on behalf of someone else who has a large portfolio—should act as if he were risk neutral. In fact, Inequality 3.11 can be rearranged to read $N \geq \alpha^2(\sigma/\mu)^2$. This specifies the minimum size for a portfolio of independent loans with mean return $\mu$ and standard deviation $\sigma$ to have a positive utility for a lender with risk preference parameter $\alpha$.

---

**Example 3.9: Individual Loan and Portfolio Risk.** As shown in the left-hand column of Table 3.7, the example loan has an expected incremental profit of $333.99 and a standard deviation of $954.61. Assume that a lender has a risk-weighted utility of $\mu - 10\sigma$. If the lender planned to make only a single loan, he would not be interested in the example loan because $\mu - 10\sigma = -\$9,212.11$. However, a portfolio of $10^2 \times (954.61/333.99)^2 = 817$ or more independent loans with the same return and standard deviation would meet his risk criterion.

---

It is not necessary for this general argument to be valid for all of the loans to be identical—it just makes the math easier. The basic idea is that—because of the law of large numbers—the risk of a portfolio of loans, each of which has expected incremental profitability greater than 0 relative to its mean return, will shrink relative to the expected return as the portfolio grows. With a sufficiently large portfolio, a lender should price and fund new loans as if he were risk neutral; that is, he should evaluate loans strictly on the basis of their expected incremental profitability. For this reason, we consider lenders to be risk neutral when optimizing prices.

The argument that a lender should act as if he were risk neutral in evaluating new loan opportunities requires two important caveats: it is not a good assumption for a company that does not have a portfolio to use as a hedge. Second, the risk reduction implied by Inequality 3.11 assumes that the default and prepayment risks of all the loans in the portfolio are independent. If the risks are positively correlated, the relative reduction in risk from adding loans will be less—possibly much less—than that implied by 3.11.

## Securitization and Incremental Profit

Expected incremental profit is the right measure for a lender to use to evaluate the contribution of a loan, assuming that the lender is planning to keep the loan on his balance sheet for its duration. However, in the United States the majority of auto loans and mortgages are securitized—meaning that the lender will bundle a large number of loans together and sell them on the secondary market. In the case that a loan is going to be sold, its value should be equal to its expected incremental profit (adjusted for tax considerations)—no one should be willing to purchase it for more, and the lender should not be willing to sell it for less. This presumes a perfect world in which all buyers and sellers have common information and risk preferences—an assumption that seems unlikely given the size of the secondary market in mortgages and other asset-based securities. However, it is not clear if or how the possibility of securitization should influence the pricing of individual loans. In particular, a loan with a higher incremental profitability should be a more valuable asset than a loan with a lower incremental profitability whether it is held on the lender's balance sheet or securitized and sold (and therefore held on someone else's balance sheet). For this reason, maximizing expected profitability is a reasonable goal for any lender whether he plans to retain the loans on the balance sheet or sell them to a third party.

## SUMMARY

- For pricing purposes, the profitability of a loan should be measured on an *incremental* basis. That is, only costs that would change depending on whether or not a loan is funded should be included in evaluating its profitability.

- Loans differ from most other products and services in that both the costs and revenues from a loan will be realized over time and that the magnitudes of both costs and revenues realized is uncertain at the time the loan is issued. The incremental profitability of a loan includes the expected net present value of all of the incremental cash flows associated with the loan including interest income, capital costs, loss from default, servicing costs, fees, taxes, and capital charge. The elements of the incremental profitability for an example loan are shown in Table 3.2.

- Net interest income is the largest source of income from most loans. Net interest income is the net present value of the future interest payments from a loan plus the equity benefit minus the cost of funds. Additional sources of income include fees and the potential of ancillary profit from other products sold with the loan.

- Other costs associated with a loan include origination costs, commissions, and servicing costs. In addition, if the loan defaults, the lender will lose some or all of the remaining balance and will also incur some collection and recovery costs. The probability-weighted net present value of these costs is incorporated in the net income before tax of a loan.

- The incremental profit from a loan is equal to the after-tax net income plus the equity capital charge.

- Survival curves illustrate the probability that a loan will still be active at each period up to its term in the face of possible prepayment or default. If default and prepayment rates are constant over the life of the loan, the expected discounted present value of various cost and revenue elements associated with a loan can be calculated using closed-form discount and amortization factors ($\phi_1$ and $\phi_2$ in the text). If default and/or prepayment rates vary significantly over the life of the loan, then there is no closed-form solution for expected incremental income. In this case, expected incremental income can be estimated using the assumption of constant prepayment and default rates. Alternatively, the expected income and costs for each period during the term of the loan can be calculated and discounted back to the first period using the corporate discount rate.

- The lending interest that a lender will receive from a simple loan is a function of the size of the loan, the interest rate, and the term. In particular, lending interest increases with all three factors. The monthly payment for a simple loan is also a function of the balance, interest rate, and term. The monthly payment increases with the balance and interest rate but decreases with the term. Because many borrowers are more sensitive to monthly payment than interest rate, and longer-term loans are more profitable, lenders are potentially motivated to favor longer-term loans.

- All else being equal, increased probability of default reduces the expected incremental profit from a loan. To some extent, this reduced profitability can be outweighed by higher rates—this is a justification for the practice of risk-based pricing.

- A loan is a risky asset to the lender. Various metrics such as standard deviation, value at risk, and conditional value at risk can be used to measure the risk associated with a single loan or a portfolio of loans. A risk-averse lender considering a single loan in isolation—or a lender considering a loan that is very large relative to his existing portfolio—would need to understand the risk of the loan and incorporate the appropriate risk measure both in evaluating the loan and in determining which price to quote. However, a lender with a sufficiently large portfolio of loans should act risk neutral with respect to evaluating and pricing new loans because his existing portfolio can hedge against the risk of the individual loans. This is true, however, only if the risk of the new loan is not highly correlated with the portfolio risk.

## NOTE

1. The idea that profitable loans increase a lender's market value while unprofitable loans decrease its market value is highly idealized. For example, the market value of a lender might also be influenced by the total value of loans on the books or by market share, among other factors. In this case, taking on unprofitable loans might actually increase the lender's market value.

# 4 THE FUNDAMENTALS OF PRICE RESPONSE

*Price response* refers to the relationship between the price of a product and its demand. For consumer lenders, all else being equal, raising the price of a loan will result in lower demand, and lowering the price will result in higher demand: this is consistent with the so-called *law of demand*. We are interested in the price response that will be experienced by an individual lender—that is, we want to understand how the demand for loans offered by a particular lender will change as that lender changes his prices. The focus on an individual lender distinguishes the *price-response function*, which we consider in detail, from the *market-demand function*, which specifies how the total market for a product changes as a function of the average market price. In price optimization, a lender estimates how different customer segments respond to changes in the prices of the different product that he is offering through different channels. Price optimization uses this information along with specifications of how the incremental profitability of different loans varies with price (discussed in detail in Chapter 3) to determine the price that maximizes expected total profitability.

Classical economic theory posits that, for each product offered by each seller, a rational consumer has a maximum willingness to pay such that she would achieve a positive surplus from purchasing the product from a particular seller if and only if her willingness to pay is less than the price offered by that seller. If a number of sellers are offering competing products, she will purchase the product from the seller that provides the highest positive surplus, defined as the price minus her willingness to pay. If the price offered by every seller is less than her willingness to pay, she will not purchase. Note that a rational consumer can have preferences among sellers—she does not necessarily purchase from the seller offering the lowest price even if the products on offer by each seller are otherwise identical.

The idea that each consumer has a willingness to pay for each product offered by each seller can be derived from the axioms of consumer behavior that form one of the foundations of classical economics. Appendix C provides a brief overview of these axioms and discusses how the existence of a maximum willingness to pay for each customer can be derived from the axioms. Differential willingness to pay among customers gives rise to a price-response function for a product. The link between the axioms and the price-response function is important in part because it provides the intellectual grounding for the price-response function that is a key element in price optimization. The link is also important because consumer behavior can deviate from the predictions of the axioms, and these deviations from "rationality" have implications for pricing, which we discuss in detail in Chapter 8.

In this chapter, we introduce the price-response function and show how it arises from the variation in customer willingness to pay across a population. We introduce some common price-response functions and describe the most widely used measures of price sensitivity and some of their properties. This material is standard and can be skipped or skimmed by a reader familiar with pricing theory. In the last section of the chapter we show how a systematic relationship among price sensitivity and risk will lead to the situation in which increasing the price for a loan will also increase the default rate, or *price-dependent risk*.

## THE PRICE-RESPONSE FUNCTION

The classical theory of consumer behavior implies that, at any time, every consumer has a maximum willingness to pay (henceforward called simply *willingness to pay* or *WTP*) for every loan offered by every lender. A consumer's WTP may be different for the same loan offered by different lenders for a number of reasons. For one thing, a consumer may not be aware of all of the options available to her—we treat her willingness to pay for options that she is not aware of as 0. A consequence of this is that the WTP of a particular consumer is determined in part by how much time and energy she is willing to expend in comparing alternatives (i.e., loan shopping), which is, in turn, influenced by her value of time. Thus, variation in value of time among consumers induces variation in willingness to pay. In addition to different shopping behavior among consumers, as discussed in Chapter 2, not all lenders are willing to lend to all consumers. A consumer who has fewer alternatives is likely to have a higher willingness to pay for a loan from a lender who is willing to extend her credit. Finally, a consumer may have preferences among lenders; for example, a consumer may prefer her current bank over the competition. If she values service and convenience, she may accept a higher price from a lender that meets her service standards than one who does not.

An important consequence of differential preferences among consumers is that different lenders will face different price-response curves for the same loan. Each price-response curve specifies the demand that the lender would experience at each price, which will depend on five factors:

1. The total number of consumers who are interested in that particular loan.
2. The number of those consumers who apply for the loan with the lender in question.
3. The number of those applicants whom the lender deems creditworthy and quotes a price.
4. The number of accepted applicants who would achieve a positive surplus from taking the loan from the lender at the offered price.
5. The number of accepted applicants who take up the offered loan. These applicants must not only have a positive surplus for taking up this loan from this lender at the offered price; this surplus must be greater than the surplus for any other loans that they were offered by other lenders.

The upshot is that the willingness to pay of a consumer for a loan from a particular lender depends on the price offered by that lender, the prices for similar loans by other lenders, which lenders she applies to, which lenders accept her application, and, finally, her preference among lenders who accepted her application. All these factors play a role in determining which lender a borrower will choose.

---

**Example 4.1: Lender-Specific Willingness to Pay.** Three competing lenders—Bank A, Bank B, and Bank C—offer a 5-year $15,000 loan at APRs of 7.5%, 8.0%, and 8.5%, respectively. Customer 1 is indifferent among these three lenders, has a willingness to pay for the loan of 8.25%, and applies to all three. Customer 2 has a willingness to pay for the loan of 9.0% from Bank C, which is the only bank she applies to. Customer 3 has a willingness to pay for the loan of 9.0% from Banks A and B. She has a strong preference for the service offered by Bank C and is willing to pay a .75% premium so that her WTP from Bank C is 9.75%. She applies to Banks B and C. All three customers are accepted by the banks they applied to. In this case, Customer 1 will borrow from Bank A, and Customers 2 and 3 will borrow from Bank C.

---

Example 4.1 illustrates why consumer-lending markets can support price variations of the magnitude shown in Table 1.5. Price variation reflects not only differences in preferences among consumers but also the fact that not all consumers apply to all (or even most) lenders. In Example 4.1, Bank C enjoys the most demand of the three competitors even though it charges the highest rate.

It is evident that the demand for a loan is equal to the number of successful applicants for the loan times the fraction of the successful applicants who take up the loan at the offered price. As noted in Chapter 1, in most lending markets, the final price is unknown to a customer at the time she applies for the loan. This means that we can generally assume that the number of customers who apply for a loan is not strongly influenced by the price. In this case, we can express the price-response function for a loan as:

$$d(p) = D\bar{F}(p), \tag{4.1}$$

where $d(p)$ is the total number of the loans offered by a lender that would be taken up at the price $p$, $D$ is the number of successful applicants for the loan, and $\bar{F}(p)$ is the *take-up rate*, which is defined as the fraction of successful applicants who will take up the loan at price $p$.[1] Because demand is a decreasing function of price, $\bar{F}'(p) \leq 0$ for all $p \geq 0$.

An example price-response function is shown in Figure 4.1. For the loan in Figure 4.1, the number of funded loans would be close to 1,000 at an APR of 0%, dropping to around 500 at 5% and close to 0 at 8%. Figure 4.1 is similar to the demand curve familiar to anyone who has taken a microeconomics course; however, there are two important differences. First of all, the price-response function in Figure 4.1 has price on the horizontal axis and quantity on the vertical axis, but demand curves are typically shown with quantity on the horizontal axis and price on the vertical axis. This reflects the fact that we view price as the lender's decision variable, and we are interested in how demand responds as the lender changes his price.

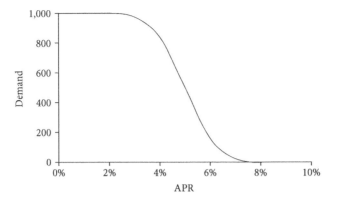

**Figure 4.1**   Example price-response function

Second, a demand curve typically reflects industry-level demand for a good assuming that all competitors are offering an identical good at a single market price. The price-response function represents demand for the output of a single firm. It reflects the fact that competitors may well be offering the same (or similar) loans at the same (or different) prices.

Equation 4.1 is based on the assumption that each consumer has a willingness to pay, $W$, specific to this lender such that she will take the loan if $p \leq W$ and will not take the loan if $p > W$. For any price $p$, $\overline{F}(p)$ is the fraction of prospective consumers who have a willingness to pay that is greater than or equal to $p$. As $p$ increases, demand decreases as the price exceeds the willingness to pay of more and more customers. Again, we stress that the price-response function is lender specific: a different lender offering the same loan would face a different price-response function. The price-response function arises from the distribution of willingness to pay across a population: as the price changes, the number of successful applicants stays the same, but the number of them who take the loan changes. If the willingness to pay is distributed across the population with probability density function $f(w)$, then:

$$\overline{F}(p) = \int_{p}^{\infty} f(w)\,dw. \tag{4.2}$$

**Example 4.2: Probit Price-Response Function.** A lender believes that willingness to pay for a loan that he offers is normally distributed with mean 5% and standard deviation 1% and that the potential market for this loan is 1,000 approved applicants in the next quarter. The corresponding density function and price-response function are shown in Figure 4.2. At any price $p$, Equation 4.2 specifies that the fraction of accepted applications that will take the loan is equal to the probability that a normal random variable with mean 5% and standard deviation 1% will be greater than $p$. This quantity is commonly written as $1 - \Phi[(p - .05)/.01)]$, where $\Phi(x)$ denotes the cumulative distribution function for the standard normal variable—that is, one with mean of 0 and standard deviation of 1. For this loan, at a price of 4%, the lender would expect to fund 841 loans; at a price of 5%, he would fund 500 loans; and he would fund 159 loans at a price of 6% (Figure 4.2).

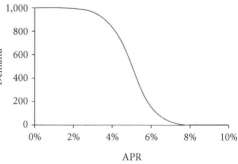

**Figure 4.2**   Willingness-to-pay distribution (*left*) and associated price-response function (*right*) for the willingness-to-pay distribution described in Example 4.2

TABLE 4.1
*Common price-response functions and their corresponding probability distributions*

| Price-response function | Formula $d(p) = D\bar{F}(p)$ | Parameter conditions | Probability distribution | Density function $f(p) = -\bar{F}'(p)$ |
|---|---|---|---|---|
| Linear | $D(1 - p/b)^+$ | $b > 0$ | Uniform | $1/b$ for $0 \le p \le b$ |
| Probit | $D[1 - \Phi((p - \mu)/\sigma)]$ | $\sigma > 0$ | Normal | $\varphi((p - \mu)/\sigma)$ |
| Logit | $De^{a+bp}/(1 + e^{a+bp})$ | $b < 0$ | Logistic | $\dfrac{-be^{a+bp}}{(1 + e^{a+bp})^2}$ |

NOTE: The notation $(x)^+$ denotes the maximum of $x$ and 0.

Every price-response function corresponds to a willingness-to-pay distribution and vice versa. Given a probability density function on willingness to pay $f(w)$, the corresponding price-response function $\bar{F}(p)$ can be computed using Equation 4.2. For a given price-response function $\bar{F}(p)$ the corresponding density function for willingness to pay at $p$ can be calculated as $f(p) = -\bar{F}'(p)$ This means that common willingness-to-pay distributions can be derived from well-known probability distributions and that any probability distribution can be converted into a price-response function. Table 4.1 shows three common price-response functions and their corresponding willingness-to-pay distributions.[2]

## MEASURING PRICE SENSITIVITY

Price sensitivity refers to the change in demand that a lender would experience from a small change in price. There are three common measures for price sensitivity: absolute slope, hazard rate, and elasticity. In each case, a higher value of the measure indicates a higher degree of price sensitivity:

1. *Absolute slope.* The absolute slope of the price-response function measures the rate at which demand changes as a function of price. The price-response function $d(p) = D\bar{F}(p)$ has an absolute slope $|d'(p)| = -D\bar{F}'(p) = Df(p)$. In some cases, we are interested in the absolute slope of the take-up rate $\bar{F}$, in which case $\bar{F}'(p) = |d'(p)|/D = f(p)$.

2. *Hazard rate.* The hazard rate (sometimes called the *failure rate*) of a price-response function at price $p$ is equal to its absolute slope divided by the demand. That is,

$$h(p)=\frac{|d'(p)|}{d(p)}=f(p)/\overline{F}(p). \qquad (4.3)$$

Unlike absolute slope, hazard rate is independent of the total market size $D$.

3. *Elasticity.* Elasticity is the percentage change in demand that would result from a 1% change in price; for example, an elasticity of 1.2 means that a 1% increase in price would result in a 1.2% reduction in demand. Elasticity is equal to the hazard rate times the price:

$$\varepsilon(p)=ph(p)=-pd'(p)/d(p)=pf(p)/\overline{F}(p). \qquad (4.4)$$

Elasticity is a unitless measure that does not depend on the size of the potential market $D$, but only on the function $\overline{F}(p)$.

In general, the slope, hazard rate, and elasticity associated with a price-response function will not be constant but will change as the price changes. Figure 4.3 shows the absolute slope, hazard rate, and elasticity for the probit price-response function described in Example 4.2 and shown in Figure 4.1. In this case, the absolute slope is close to 0 at low prices, increases to a maximum at $p = .05$, and then begins to decrease. For this price-response function, both the hazard rate and the elasticity increase with price. In fact, increasing hazard rate and elasticity are a characteristic of most common price-response functions.[3] This property is useful in establishing the existence of a unique profit-maximizing price, as we will see in Chapter 7.

Any of the three measures can be calculated from any of the others if we know the price and corresponding demand. Thus, the elasticity is equal to the absolute slope times the price divided by the quantity. Furthermore, each of the three measures can be used to estimate the effect of small change in price. Let us assume that the current price is $p$ with expected demand $d(p)$ and that we want to estimate the demand that we would see if we charged a price of $p + \Delta p$. Here, $\Delta p$ can be either less than or greater than 0. If we know any one of the price-sensitivity measures, we can estimate $d(p + \Delta p)$ using the appropriate formula:

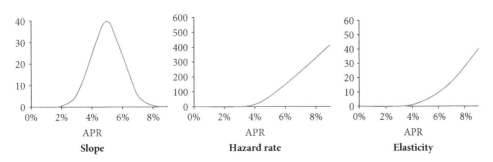

**Figure 4.3** Slope, hazard rate, and elasticity as a function of APR for the price-response function described in Example 4.2 and shown in Figure 4.2

$$
\begin{aligned}
d(p+\Delta p) &= d(p)-|d'(p)|\Delta p \\
&= d(p)\big[1-h(p)\Delta p\big] \\
&= d(p)\big[1-\varepsilon(p)\Delta p/p\big]
\end{aligned}
\tag{4.5}
$$

**Example 4.3: Approximating the Effect of a Price Change.** Assume that a lender has been charging a rate of 5.75% for his loans and that, of the last 1,000 accepted applications, 620 took up the loan. He believes that the absolute slope of his price-response curve is 4,000 and wants to estimate how take-up would change if he increased the price of the loan to 6.00%. Applying Equation 4.5, we can estimate that, for 1,000 applications accepted at the higher rate, $620 - 4{,}000 \times (.06 - .0575) = 610$ would convert. Note that at the current rate of 5.75%, the hazard rate is $4{,}000/620 = 6.45$ and the elasticity is $.0575 \times 6.45 = .37$.

Table 4.2 gives the formulas for the slopes, elasticities, and hazard rates for the three price-response functions listed in Table 4.1.

Hazard rate and elasticity are more commonly used measures of price sensitivity than absolute slope. In part this is because they are independent of total demand $D$ and depend only on $\overline{F}$. Elasticity and hazard rate are consistent in the sense that if $h_1(p)$ and $h_2(p)$ are the hazard rates associated with two different populations at price $p$ and $\varepsilon_1(p)$ and $\varepsilon_2(p)$ are the corresponding elasticities, then $h_1(p) \geq h_2(p)$ implies that $\varepsilon_1(p) \geq \varepsilon_2(p)$ and vice versa.

The price-response function associated with a loan is something of a hypothetical construct since it cannot be directly observed. To construct the "real" price-response function would require observing demand at prices that were not offered, which is impossible. However, given a functional form, it is possible to estimate the underlying parameters of a price-response function using historical data. We describe how this can be done in Chapter 5.

### Local Estimation

The ideal situation for price optimization is to have a fully parameterized price-response function. However, estimating the parameters of a price-response function requires observations of take-up at many different prices and, in many cases, lenders only have observations of loan take-up at a few different prices. This may not be enough information to estimate the parameters of a price-response function. However, even with observations at only a few different prices, we can estimate local price sensitivity, which, as we describe in Chapter 7,

TABLE 4.2

*Formulas for the slopes, hazard rates, and elasticities of the price-response functions listed in Table 4.1*

| Price-response function | Slope | Hazard rate | Elasticity |
|---|---|---|---|
| Linear | $D/b$ | $1/(b-p)$ | $p/(b-p)$ |
| Probit | $D\phi((p-\mu)/\sigma)$ | $\phi((p-\mu)/\sigma)/[1-\Phi((p-\mu)/\sigma)]$ | $p\phi((p-\mu)/\sigma)/[1-\Phi((p-\mu)/\sigma)]$ |
| Logit | $-Dbe^{a+bp}/(1+e^{a+bp})^2$ | $-b/(1+e^{a+bp})$ | $-bp/(1+e^{a+bp})$ |

TABLE 4.3
*Two-point estimates of local price response*

| Measure | Formula |
|---------|---------|
| Absolute slope | $\lvert \hat{F}' \rvert = (\hat{F}(p_1) - \hat{F}(p_2))/(p_2 - p_1)$ |
| Hazard rate | $\hat{h} = 2(\hat{F}(p_1) - \hat{F}(p_2))/(p_2 - p_1)(\hat{F}(p_1) + \hat{F}(p_2))$ |
| Elasticity | $\hat{\varepsilon} = (p_1 + p_2)(\hat{F}(p_1) - \hat{F}(p_2))/(p_2 - p_1)(\hat{F}(p_1) + \hat{F}(p_2))$ |

can be useful for updating prices. Assume that we have observed take-up rates for a pricing segment at two different prices $p_1$ and $p_2$. These take-up rates may have been observed as the result of an A-B test, a randomized test, a natural experiment or a regression discontinuity design. Let the take-up rates be denoted by $\hat{F}(p_1) = d_1(p_1)/D_1$ and $\hat{F}(p_2) = d_2(p_2)/D_2$, where $d_i(p_i)$ is the number of funded loans and $D_i$ is the number of approved applications when price $p_i$ was offered. Table 4.3 gives the formulas for the point estimators of each of the three measures of price sensitivity.

Recall that the three measures of price sensitivity in Table 4.3 are not constant but change with price: in general, hazard rate and elasticity will tend to increase with price, whereas absolute slope may either increase or decrease. This means that, in general, the formulas for the estimates will be valid only for some price intermediate between $p_1$ and $p_2$. However, if $p_1$ and $p_2$ are not too far apart, then it is likely that the measure does not change too much across the interval.

---

**Example 4.4: Two-Point Estimators.** In a price test, the control APR was 6.0% and the test APR was 6.5%; 75% of accepted applicants in the control group and 66% of applicants in the test group took up the loan. The corresponding measures of price sensitivity are as follows:

- *Absolute slope:* $\lvert \hat{F}' \rvert = (.75 - .66)/(.065 - .06) = 18$.
- *Hazard rate:* $\hat{h} = 2(.75 - .66)/[(.065 - .06)(.75 + .66)] = 25.5$.
- *Elasticity:* $\hat{\varepsilon} = (.065 + .06)(.75 - .66)/[(.065 - .06)(.75 + .66)] = 1.60$.

---

## PRICE SENSITIVITY AND PRICE-DEPENDENT RISK

In Chapter 2 we noted that increasing the price at which a loan is offered will result in a higher default rate for consumers who take the loan. We also observed that highly risky customers are less price sensitive than less risky customers. Thus, the price elasticity of consumers with a FICO score of 750 will be higher than those with a FICO score of 600 for the same loan offered at the same price. We show in this section that the two phenomena are, in fact, the same: if price sensitivity decreases with risk in a population, then that population will demonstrate price-dependent risk. Similarly, price-dependent risk can be shown to be a logical consequence of the fact that riskier consumers are less price sensitive than less risky consumers.

## A Model of Price-Dependent Risk

Assume that a pricing segment includes a mix of bad customers, all of whom will default, and good customers, all of whom will repay the loan in full. We will call these customers *bads* and *goods*, respectively.[4] For a particular pricing segment, a lender has two decisions: whether to offer a loan product to that segment and, if so, at what price. Let $D_g$ denote the number of good consumers and $D_b$ the number of bad consumers in the segment. Denote the total size of the segment by $D = D_g + D_b$. The probability that a consumer randomly chosen from this segment will default is $D_b/D$. We can write the price-response functions for the two types of consumer as follows:

$$d_g(p) = D_g \overline{F}_g(p); \quad d_b(p) = D_b \overline{F}_b(p), \tag{4.6}$$

where $\overline{F}_g(p)$ and $\overline{F}_b(p)$ are the fractions of good and bad consumers respectively who have a willingness to pay greater than or equal to $p$. We denote the hazard rate for consumer type $i$ at price $p$ by $h_i(p)$ for $i = g$ or $i = b$; thus, $h_g(p) = -\overline{F}'(p)/\overline{F}_g(p) = f_g(p)/\overline{F}_g(p)$ is the hazard rate for goods and $h_b(p) = f_b(p)/\overline{F}_b(p)$ is the hazard rate for bads.

The default rate is the fraction of consumers who will default on the loan. If everyone in the population accepted the loan, the default rate would $D_b/(D_b + D_g)$. However, the default rate at a given price depends on the number of goods and bads who accept the loan at that price, namely,

$$DR(p) = \frac{D_b \overline{F}_b(p)}{D_b \overline{F}_b(p) + D_g \overline{F}_g(p)}, \tag{4.7}$$

where $DR(p)$ is the default rate that the lender will experience if he prices his loan at $p$.

We can differentiate Equation 4.7 with respect to $p$ and perform some algebra to obtain the following:

$$DR'(p) = (h_g(p) - h_b(p))DR(p)(1 - DR(p)). \tag{4.8}$$

We call $DR'(p)$ the *price-dependent risk rate* (or *PDR rate*). The PDR rate is a measure of the sensitivity of risk to price—a high PDR rate means that risk rises rapidly with price. If $h_g(p) = h_b(p)$—that is, the price-response functions are identical for goods and bads—then the PDR rate is 0, meaning that the default rate $DR(p)$ does not change with the price. If $h_g(p) > h_b(p)$, then $DR'(p) > 0$, which means that the default rate increases with price. Thus, price-dependent risk is a direct consequence of differential price sensitivity between good and bad consumers.

Let $z(p) = h_g(p) - h_b(p)$ denote the difference in hazard rates between good and bad consumers at price $p$. Then we can write $DR'(p) = z(p)DR(p)(1 - DR(p))$. Because good consumers are more price sensitive than bad consumers, $z(p) > 0$. If $z(p)$ does not change very much with rate—that is, if the hazard rate difference is nearly constant—the relationship between the price-dependent risk rate and the default rate will resemble the curve in Figure 4.4. The PDR rate will be 0 when the population default rate is either 0 or 1. The PDR rate increases from $DR(p) = 0$ until $DR(p) = .5$, after which it decreases. Because retail

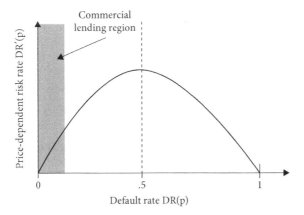

**Figure 4.4**    Relationship between price-dependent risk rate and default rate when the hazard rate difference between goods and bads does not vary with price

N O T E : The shaded area is the typical region in which consumer and commercial lenders offer loans.

and commercial lending is generally extended to populations with expected default rates much less than 50% (the shaded area in Figure 4.4), we would expect price-dependent risk to be much more salient in higher-risk populations than in lower-risk populations. This is indeed what is found in practice—the effect of price on risk is much stronger in subprime lending than in prime lending, and price has very little impact on the default rates of very low-risk superprime loans.

What does the existence of price-dependent risk imply for pricing and underwriting? Consider the case of a risk-neutral lender who seeks to maximize expected total profit. The lender knows the number of goods and bads in the population, $D_g$ and $D_b$, and their corresponding price-response functions $\overline{F}_g(p)$ and $\overline{F}_b(p)$. For simplicity we assume that every loan is of size 1 and that there is a common loss-given-default rate of $0 < \ell \leq 1$. If the lender offers the loan to the entire population at price $p$, then his total net interest income will be

$$\Pi(p) = (p-c)d_g(p) - \ell d_b(p).$$

There is a positive number $k_0$ such that if $z(p) > k_0$ for all $p \geq c$ then the lender cannot achieve a positive profit at any price. In this case, his best decision is not to offer the loan to this population. If, however, $z(p) \leq k_0$, then it is profitable for the lender to offer the loan. This means that whether or not it is profitable to offer a loan to a population is dependent not only on the overall number of bads in the population but also on the difference in price sensitivity between goods and bads. If goods and bads are similar in terms of price sensitivity, then it can be profitable to offer the loan however, if goods are much more price-sensitive than bads, then it may not be profitable to offer the loan at any price.

The situation is illustrated in Figure 4.5, which shows total profit $\Pi(p)$ as a function of price when $\ell = .9$, $c = 1$, and $D_b = .25D$. Three cases are shown, each with a different value of the hazard rate differential $k = h_b(p) - h_g(p)$. When $k = 0$, goods and bads have identical price-response functions. In this case, the default rate does not change as a function of $p$,

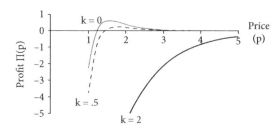

**Figure 4.5**   Dependence of profit on price for three values of the hazard-rate differential $k = h_b(p) - h_g(p)$

the price-dependent risk rate is 0, and the loan is profitable for all prices above some threshold. When $k = .5$, the population exhibits price-dependent risk, but there is still a range of prices at which the loan is profitable. In this case, the lender needs to choose his price carefully—if he chooses a price that is too high, he will lose money because of increased risk. Finally, when $k = 2$ the effect of price-dependent risk is so strong that there is no price at which the lender can make a positive profit. In this case, the lender's best decision would be not to offer the loan at all to this segment. This corresponds to the common practice of setting an underwriting threshold.

### Immediate and Latent Price-Dependent Risk

An implication of differential price sensitivity between goods and bads is that lenders will experience both *immediate* and *latent* price-dependent risk. Immediate price-dependent risk refers to the change in observable risk measures (e.g., FICO score) that occurs as a lender changes prices. Latent price-dependent risk is the additional change in default rate that is not captured by observable risk measures.

The difference between immediate and latent price-dependent risk is best introduced by an example. Table 4.4 shows the effects of a rate increase from 7.5% to 9.5% for a loan offered to consumers with credit scores between 630 and 650 inclusive. We assume that goods have a constant hazard rate of 6 and bads have a constant hazard rate of 1. The fraction of consumers in the population who are bad and the total number of approvals for each credit score are shown in columns 2 and 3. Columns 4–6 show the number of bads and goods who accept the loan and the corresponding loss rates for each credit score at a 7.5% APR. At this APR, the lender books 2,067.8 total loans, of which 189.6 would be bad and 1,878.2 good, with a corresponding default rate of 9.17%. If the lender increased the APR to 9.5%, he would book 1,851.7 loans—a reduction of 216.1. Of the booked loans, 185.9 would be bad and 1,665.8 good, for a default rate of 10.04%. Raising APR reduces the number of loans booked and increases the default rate of booked loans—this is a manifestation of price-dependent risk.

A notable aspect of the higher default rate resulting from increasing the APR from 7.5% to 9.5% in Table 4.4 is that very little of the additional risk is captured by a decrease in the average credit score. The average score for booked loans declines by only a minus-

TABLE 4.4

*Good and bad loans booked at every credit score and the corresponding default rates for an example in which the price-response function for bad loans has a constant hazard rate of 1 and the price-response function for good loans has a hazard rate of 6*

| | POPULATION CHARACTERISTICS | | RATE = 7.5% | | | RATE = 9.5% | | |
|---|---|---|---|---|---|---|---|---|
| Score | Bad fraction | Approvals | Bads | Goods | Default rate | Bads | Goods | Default rate |
| 630 | .100 | 200 | 18.6 | 114.8 | 13.92% | 18.2 | 101.8 | 15.16% |
| 631 | .096 | 195 | 17.4 | 112.4 | 13.38 | 17.0 | 99.7 | 14.59 |
| 632 | .092 | 190 | 16.2 | 110.0 | 12.85 | 15.9 | 97.6 | 14.01 |
| 633 | .088 | 185 | 15.1 | 107.6 | 12.31 | 14.8 | 95.4 | 13.43 |
| 634 | .084 | 180 | 14.0 | 105.1 | 11.77 | 13.7 | 93.2 | 12.85 |
| 635 | .080 | 175 | 13.0 | 102.7 | 11.23 | 12.7 | 91.0 | 12.27 |
| 636 | .076 | 170 | 12.0 | 100.2 | 10.69 | 11.7 | 88.8 | 11.68 |
| 637 | .072 | 165 | 11.0 | 97.6 | 10.14 | 10.8 | 86.6 | 11.09 |
| 638 | .068 | 160 | 10.1 | 95.1 | 9.60 | 9.9 | 84.3 | 10.50 |
| 639 | .064 | 155 | 9.2 | 92.5 | 9.05 | 9.0 | 82.0 | 9.91 |
| 640 | .060 | 150 | 8.3 | 89.9 | 8.50 | 8.2 | 79.7 | 9.31 |
| 641 | .056 | 145 | 7.5 | 87.3 | 7.95 | 7.4 | 77.4 | 8.71 |
| 642 | .052 | 140 | 6.8 | 84.6 | 7.39 | 6.6 | 75.1 | 8.11 |
| 643 | .048 | 135 | 6.0 | 81.9 | 6.83 | 5.9 | 72.7 | 7.50 |
| 644 | .044 | 130 | 5.3 | 79.2 | 6.28 | 5.2 | 70.3 | 6.89 |
| 645 | .040 | 125 | 4.6 | 76.5 | 5.72 | 4.5 | 67.9 | 6.28 |
| 646 | .036 | 120 | 4.0 | 73.8 | 5.15 | 3.9 | 65.4 | 5.65 |
| 647 | .032 | 115 | 3.4 | 71.0 | 4.59 | 3.3 | 63.0 | 5.05 |
| 648 | .028 | 110 | 2.9 | 68.2 | 4.02 | 2.8 | 60.5 | 4.43 |
| 649 | .024 | 105 | 2.3 | 65.3 | 3.45 | 2.3 | 58.0 | 3.80 |
| 650 | .020 | 100 | 1.9 | 62.5 | 2.88 | 1.8 | 55.4 | 3.18 |
| **Totals/averages** | | | **189.6** | **1,878.2** | **9.17%** | **185.9** | **1,665.8** | **10.04%** |
| **Average score** | | | | **638.72** | | | **638.70** | |

cule amount—from 638.72 to 638.70—when the lender raises the rate. This reduction in credit score reflects *immediate price-dependent risk.* It is immediate in the sense that it can be measured by the lender at the time that loans are booked. If the lender anticipated the same default rate at every score as he had experienced at the old rate, he would anticipate a default rate of about 9.18%—only one basis point higher than the historical default rate of 9.17%. However, the default rate that he will actually experience is 10.04%, which is 121 basis points higher. The additional 120-basis-point increase in the default rate constitutes latent price-dependent risk. It is latent in that it cannot be observed by the change in FICO score from booked loans: the lender will learn about it only once the loans have already been booked and begin to default.

The situation illustrated in Table 4.4 is not uncommon: latent price-dependent risk is often greater than immediate price-dependent risk in the real world, especially in subprime lending. This means that relying on historical performance as measured solely by credit score (or any other statistical risk measure) may underestimate both the increase in risk that results from increased prices and the reduction in risk that results from lowering prices. Another implication of latent price-dependent risk is that the default rate implied by a credit score is a function of the historical price (or prices) of loans. In the example in Table 4.4, the average credit score for booked loans with an APR of 7.5% is 638.72 with a default rate of 9.17%. (This is consistent with the loss rates of 9.60% and 9.05% experienced for loans made at credit scores of 638 and 639, respectively.) In contrast, at an APR of 9.5%, the lender will experience a loss rate of more than 10%, which is significantly higher. When price changes, historical experience is no longer predictive of default rates at given credit scores—for a more accurate forecast, the lender would need to adjust expected default rates explicitly for latent price-dependent risk.

### Implications of Price-Dependent Risk

Price-dependent risk implies that the riskiness of a loan portfolio will depend on the prices at which the loans were issued. The magnitude of price-dependent risk depends on the proportion of goods and bads in the underlying population and the difference in price-response between goods and bads. Incorporating price-dependent risk into the calculation of the optimal price is much more important in more risky populations (e.g., subprime markets) than in less risky populations (e.g., superprime markets). Price-dependent risk rate also depends on the difference in price response between goods and bads. If price response (as measured by hazard rate) is the same or very similar for goods and bads, risk will not increase very much with rate. If, however, price response is very different between the two groups, then the risk of funded loans will increase much more rapidly as rates rise.

Understanding price-dependent risk is important for forecasting future defaults, especially for subprime loans. Price-dependent risk can also influence the optimal price to charge for a loan. Specifically, expected loss cannot be treated as fixed for a loan but rather should be represented as a function of price. For consumer lenders, the importance of price-dependent risk increases with the riskiness of the population being served. It is likely to be negligible for so-called superprime consumer segments with very low default rates. However, it can be quite important for subprime populations. We discuss how to incorporate price-dependent risk in the calculation of loan profitability in Chapter 5 and its influence on the optimal price in Chapter 7.

## SUMMARY

- The number of loans that a lender will fund will be determined by the number of consumers who are interested in the loan, the number of those consumers who apply to that lender, the number of those whom the lender deems creditworthy, and, finally, the fraction of accepted applicants who are willing to take the loan at the price the lender offers. This fraction will depend on which competing lenders customers have applied to, the rates offered by those lenders, and the preferences of customers for different lenders.

- The distribution of willingness to pay among consumers in a segment induces a price-response function for a particular loan offered by a lender. Typically different lenders will see different price-response functions for identical loans.

- In many cases, the price-response function faced by a lender for a loan with given characteristics can be modeled as the product of the number of accepted applications (which is not dependent on the price) and the fraction of accepted applications that take the loan as a function of the price. We call the fraction of accepted applications that take up the loan the *take-up rate*. The take-up rate is always between 0 and 1 and is a downward-sloping function of the price.

- The take-up rate as a function of price is the complementary cumulative distribution function (CCDF) of the willingness-to-pay distribution for the loan among consumers. This means that every price-response function is the CCDF of a probability distribution and vice versa.

- Price sensitivity refers to the magnitude of the change in demand resulting from a change in price. Three common measures of price sensitivity are the (absolute) slope, hazard rate, and elasticity of the price-response function. Larger values of each of these measures indicate higher sensitivity to price. These measures typically vary with price and, at a given price, can be calculated from the underlying price-response function.

- Low-risk consumers tend to be more price sensitive than high-risk consumers. A consequence of this fact is that as the price of a loan is increased, the expected loss rate from consumers who take the loan also increases. This phenomenon is termed *price-dependent risk*, and it is especially strong in subprime lending.

- Price-dependent risk can be classified as *immediate* and *latent*. Immediate price-dependent risk refers to the change in risk measures (e.g., the average credit score for funded loans) that are immediately observable when a loan is funded. Latent price-dependent risk refers to the increase in loss rate that is not immediately apparent in changes in risk measures when a loan is funded but manifests itself during the life of the loan. Both types of price-dependent risk should be considered when setting the price of a loan.

## NOTES

1. The use of the bar over the symbol $F$ is the standard way of denoting that $\overline{F}(p)$ is the complementary cumulative distribution function associated with the probability density function $f(p)$. $F(p)$ is typically used to denote the cumulative distribution function associated with $f(p)$ and $\overline{F}(p) = 1 - F(p)$ is the complementary cumulative distribution function.

2. More information on price-response functions and their properties and derivations can be found in van Ryzin (2012).

3. A discussion of the increasing hazard-rate property and which distributions possess it can be found in Lariviere (2006).

4. The discussion of price-dependent risk in this section is based on Phillips and Raffard (2011).

# 5 ESTIMATING PRICE RESPONSE

In Chapter 4 we introduced the concept of a price-response function that specifies how the take-up rate for a loan varies as a function of its price. Every lender who is looking to optimize prices would love to have an accurate price-response function available for every loan. This chapter describes a number of approaches for estimating price response. We focus primarily on *data-driven approaches* in which future price response is estimated on the basis of an analysis of historical data. A major benefit of data-driven approaches is that they are objective: if future customer behavior is similar to past behavior, then data-driven estimation will provide a good predictor of how demand will respond to price in the future. In addition, data-driven approaches facilitate ongoing evaluation and updating. As new observations of take-up are observed, they can be used to evaluate the predictive power of the current model and to update its parameters to reflect changes in market conditions or customer behavior.

The primary obstacle to using data-driven approaches to estimate price response is the availability of data. The ideal data set would contain a large number of observations specifying how past customers responded to a wide range of prices. If a lender does not have access to such a data set—if the number of historical observations is too small or does not include a sufficiently wide range of prices—then an alternative approach such as conjoint analysis or customer surveys needs to be used. Such data-free approaches do not require extensive historical data, but they can be limited in their ability to accurately represent price response across a large number of pricing segments.

In this section, we start by describing the type of data required to support a data-driven approach and some different ways that a lender can obtain the necessary data, such as randomized tests and A/B tests. Given the availability of an appropriate data set, there are two broad analytical approaches to estimating price response: regression-based approaches in which a functional form is chosen for the price-response function and nonparametric approaches in which no functional form is assumed. We illustrate the use of regression by going through the steps required to apply logistic regression to a real-world data set, the e-Car Data Set, which is available online. We discuss how the presence of field price discretion can introduce endogeneity into the data, and we discuss methods for detecting endogeneity and how a two-stage regression approach can be used to estimate unbiased parameters when endogeneity is present. We then discuss nonparametric approaches, how they can be applied, and their relative strengths and weaknesses relative to regression in supporting price optimization. Finally, we discuss the situation in which historical data is not available. In this case, alternative approaches such as surveys or conjoint analyses may be useful.

## DATA SOURCES FOR PRICE-RESPONSE ESTIMATION

Any data-driven approach to estimation requires a data set that includes information about the fate of a large number of approved loan applications. At a minimum, the data set needs to include the price at which the loan was offered and whether or not the loan was taken up, as well as characteristics of the loan such as term and amount. Ideally the data set would also include customer information such as risk score and geography along with information about the market environment such as a market rate (prime or LIBOR) and rates offered by competing lenders.

Two conditions are necessary for a data set of historical outcomes to support price-response estimation. First of all, there must be a sufficient number of approved applications for the resulting estimates to be statistically significant. Typically, this means at least several hundred (and ideally many thousand) observations. Second, there must be enough variation among the prices in the data to provide a basis for estimation. If the same price was always offered for the same type of loan to the same customer segment, then it is extremely difficult (if not impossible) to estimate a price-response function. If both conditions are not met by the data currently available, then the lender needs either to collect more data or to utilize a data-free approach.

There are several ways in which a lender might obtain data to support price-sensitivity estimation. The ideal is to perform a set of randomized price tests. If this is not possible, A/B tests are a good alternative. In cases where neither randomized tests nor A/B tests are feasible, a lender may need to rely on so-called natural experiments, in which different prices were offered to similar groups for reasons other than price testing. In addition, changes in price at either side of a pricing-segment boundary can be used as part of a regression discontinuity design. Finally, in many cases, field staff has the discretion to adjust the final prices offered to customers. In this case, different levels of discretion used for different deals will likely lead to a wide range of prices in the historical data. This variation can be used to estimate price sensitivity, with the caution that the use of local discretion is likely to bias the prices used. In this case, a two-stage estimation process may be required to eliminate endogeneity in the underlying data. In the remainder of this section, we describe each of these approaches to obtaining a data set to support price-response estimation.

### Randomized Price Testing

The gold standard for statistical inference is *randomized testing*. In a randomized test, members of the population are assigned to a *control group* and one or more *test groups*. The test groups receive different treatments while the control group does not receive any treatment. In a price test, the control group is quoted the current prices while the treatment groups are quoted alternative prices. The idea behind randomized testing is, as far as possible, to eliminate any systematic differences among the test groups and the control group that could influence the outcome. If this is done successfully, it is reasonable to infer that any statistically significant differences in outcome observed among the groups can be attributed to the differences in treatment.[1] In price testing, the inference is that any systematic differences in take-up rate among groups can be attributed solely to the different prices that they were quoted.

Ideally, a randomized test should meet four conditions:

1. Assignment to the treatment and control groups must be imposed—consumers cannot choose the group that they are assigned to. If individuals are allowed to select their group, then *selection bias* might influence the results: the fact that an individual chose a particular treatment could be correlated with her response.

2. The test and control groups must be balanced with respect to observable characteristics that might influence outcome. For price testing, this means that the control group and the test groups should have similar proportions of customers with different FICO scores, loans of similar size, and so on. Otherwise differences in response might be due to differences in group composition rather than differences in treatment. For example, if the control group happened to be 45% female while one of the test groups was 51% female, it is possible that an observed difference in take-up between the groups might be due to differential take-up by gender rather than to price response. For this reason, so-called randomized tests are often not truly randomized: individuals are often systematically assigned to the treatment and control groups in a way that ensures that the groups are balanced with respect to observable characteristics.

3. There must be a sufficient number of observations in each group for the differences in outcome to be statistically significant.

4. Differences in treatment should be the only differences in the way the two groups are treated.

In a price test with a single test group, customers who are approved for a loan are assigned either to the test group or to the control group according to the principles listed above. Customers assigned to the control group are quoted the control price $p_c$ while customers assigned to the treatment group are quoted a test price $p_t \neq p_c$. After a sufficient number of observations, the take-up rates for both the control group and the treatment group, which we label $\rho_c$ and $\rho_t$, respectively, are observed. Referring to Table 4.3, the elasticity of the price-response function can be estimated as $[(\rho_c - \rho_t)(p_c + p_t)]/[(\rho_c + \rho_t)(p_t - p_c)]$. Ideally, price testing would use multiple test groups, each with a different price quoted. These prices and corresponding take-up rates can be considered points on a price-response function, and a standard approach such as logistic regression can be used to estimate the corresponding parameters.

The Internet is generally well suited for randomized testing. In an online price test, each successful applicant can be randomly quoted a price chosen from a number of predetermined alternatives. The test ends when a sufficient number of responses has been obtained at each price. This assumes, of course, that the online lender has the technical infrastructure capable of performing such price tests. It is usually more difficult to perform randomized price testing in branches and call centers. In addition to the technical challenges, it may be difficult to explain randomized pricing to local staff. Finally, some banks are unwilling to perform randomized price testing as a matter of corporate policy. In this case, A/B testing may be the best alternative.

## A/B Testing

In an A/B test, customers with some characteristic are chosen to receive a control price and customers with a different characteristic are chosen to receive a test price. The difference with randomized testing is that selection into the treatment and control groups is not random. In a well-constructed A/B test, the characteristic used to separate customers into test and control groups is not correlated with the variable of interest—in this case, take-up rate.

Often, banks perform A/B price tests by offering test prices through a set of test branches. The remaining branches offer "pricing as usual." In evaluating the outcome, loan take-up at the test branches should not necessarily be compared to the overall take-up at all other branches. Rather, each test branch should be paired with a control branch such that members of each pair of branches are as similar as possible to one another in terms of characteristics such as demographics, loan mix, and competitive environment. This pairing should be done prior to running the test in order to avoid ex post selection bias. In addition, comparison should be performed not only at the branch level but also, to the extent possible, at the individual loan offer level. That is, each loan offer at the test price should be paired with the "closest possible" corresponding loan offer at the control price, where "closeness" is measured in terms of size of loan, term, customer FICO score, customer tenure with bank, and so on. The goal is to eliminate all other possible factors in order to isolate the influence of price on take-up.

The major problem with an A/B test is that, by definition, it is not randomized—changes in competition or the underlying economic environment can influence outcomes at the control branch but not at the test branches, or vice versa. These potential influences are the source of many of the objections that are often raised to the results of A/B tests, such as "The test branches performed better because those regions saw stronger economic growth than the control branches."

In the absence of true randomization, objections to A/B tests can be hard to answer. One approach to controlling for external influences in A/B tests is *difference-in-differences* (DiD). For a test-branch and control-branch pair, DiD compares the change in response in test branches before and after the price test to the change in response in control branches. The idea is that the magnitude of the price effect is best measured not by the difference in take-up between the test branch and the control branch during the test period but by the difference between the *changes* in take-up before and during the test period.

**Example 5.1: Difference-in-Differences.** A bank wishes to test the price sensitivity of an unsecured personal loan. It has been offering the loan at an annual percentage rate (APR) of 5%. As a test, it raises the APR to 5.5% at Branch A during the month of April while holding it constant at 5% at all other branches. To estimate the effect of the APR change on take-up, the bank compares the take-up observed at Branch A with the take-up observed at Branch B, which has similar demographics. The APRs and take-up rates observed at Branch A and Branch B for the months of March and April are shown in Table 5.1. Branch A saw a 2% decline in take-up from March to April, whereas Branch B saw a 3% increase. The difference-in-differences approach would estimate that the increase in APR from 5% to 5.5% resulted in a reduction of 5% in take-up rate—that is, the take-up rate at Branch A would have been 65% if the rate had remained constant at 5%.

The difference-in-differences approach is based on the so-called *parallel assumption*: in the absence of the treatment, it is assumed that the test group and the control group would have evolved "in parallel." For Example 5.1, this is equivalent to the assumption that take-up at Branch A would have increased by the same amount as Branch B if Branch A had continued to offered the same APR in April as in March. If the parallel assumption does not hold, then the results of an A/B test may be invalid.[2]

Another potential drawback of A/B tests is that they may be subject to the so-called *Hawthorne effect*, which occurs when the fact that a branch knows that it has been chosen for a test changes the behavior of the branch staff in a way that influences the outcome. If a branch knows that it is being used to test "special pricing" for a loan product, the local staff may increase the effort that they put into selling the product. This is particularly true if they believe that the results they achieve will be scrutinized more closely than usual. This change in behavior may in itself change the take-up rate, thereby confounding the results of the test. For this reason, a branch should be unaware that it is a "test branch" in an A/B test. If this is not possible, then both the test and the control branches should both be monitored to ensure that they are providing consistent treatment to customers.

Proper A/B tests can supply important information about price response, but they also have drawbacks. First of all, for any loan product, estimating the price-sensitivity function requires measuring response at more than just two points. Furthermore, lenders want to estimate price sensitivity not just for a single loan but for all of their loan products offered through all of their channels to all of their customer segments. This may mean estimating price-sensitivity functions for hundreds or thousands of price segments. In many cases,

TABLE 5.1
*Branch A and Branch B APRs and take-up rates in Example 5.1*

|  | TEST (BRANCH A) | | CONTROL (BRANCH B) | |
| --- | --- | --- | --- | --- |
|  | *APR* | *Take-up rate* | *APR* | *Take-up rate* |
| March | 5% | 62% | 5% | 58% |
| April | 5.5% | 60% | 5% | 61% |

information technology limitations or corporate policy may limit the ability of a lender to run a sufficient number of controlled price tests to cover all pricing segments.

## Natural Experiments

The term *natural experiment* refers to a situation in which different treatments—in our case, different prices—were offered to different groups of customers for reasons other than running a test or optimizing prices. If the differential treatments were imposed randomly, then a natural experiment can supply useful information about price response. An example of a natural experiment would be a software defect or data entry error that caused some customers to be quoted "erroneous" prices while others were quoted standard prices. If the erroneous prices were quoted to a random set of customers, then the difference in take-up between customers quoted the random prices and those quoted standard prices can be used to estimate price sensitivity. Another example of a natural experiment might be imposition of a local regulation that causes prices to be different in one jurisdiction from a neighboring jurisdiction. In this case, differences in take-up by similar customers on either side of the jurisdictional boundary might be used to estimate price sensitivity.

By definition, natural experiments cannot be planned, and they rarely provide ideal input for analysis. However, it is worthwhile for lenders to be aware of the possibility and to consider any situation in which different prices were offered to similar populations as an opportunity to better understand price response.

## Regression Discontinuity Design

A lender who has not varied prices much over time may be able to use a *regression discontinuity design* (RDD) to estimate elasticities at the boundaries of his pricing segments. In most situations, we would expect that price sensitivity varies continuously across a segment boundary while price jumps from one side of the boundary to the other. In this situation, we would expect that customers close to the boundary on either side should share similar price sensitivities, and we can use the price jump across the boundary as a sort of natural experiment to estimate price sensitivity.[3]

---

**Example 5.2: Regression Discontinuity Design.** A lender offers $100,000 35-year fixed mortgages to customers with FICO scores from 681 through 700 at an APR of 5.0% and to those with FICO scores from 701 through 720 at an APR of 4.5%. The take-up rate for customers with a FICO score of 700 is 63%, and that for customers with a FICO score of 701 is 68%. Applying the formula in Table 4.3, elasticity at the boundary between the two risk tiers would be estimated to be $\hat{\varepsilon} = (.045 + .05) \times (.68 - .63)/[(.05 - .045) \times (.68 + .63)] = .725$.

---

If the lender has varied prices across a large number of pricing segments, he can use RDD to estimate elasticity at each boundary and then use regression to fit a function that specifies how elasticity varies across all pricing dimensions.

## Discretionary Variation

As discussed in Chapter 1, in some markets, local staff have the authority to negotiate the final prices of loans, usually within specified limits. When local staff have such discretion, historical loan records will tend to show price variation reflecting different negotiated outcomes for similar loans. This variation can serve as a basis for estimating price response—however, a cautionary note needs to be sounded. Standard estimation techniques such as single-stage regression assume that the prices offered to customers are influenced by individual variations in willingness to pay only through variables that are recorded in the data. In randomized testing and well-designed A/B tests, independence of rate and individual willingness to pay is enforced by design. However, when prices are set (or influenced) by local staff, then it is likely that the final prices are not independent of individual variations in willingness to pay. This is a problem of *endogeneity*. When pricing variation is the result of field staff discretion, then the data needs to be tested for endogeneity and, if necessary, the estimation procedure needs to be modified to adjust for its presence. We discuss how this can be done later in this chapter.

### DATA-DRIVEN PRICE-RESPONSE ESTIMATION

Assume that the we have assembled a database of historical loan performance using one or more of the techniques described in the previous section. In this section, we describe how this data can be used to estimate price response. There are two basic approaches to doing this—in the first approach, a functional form is chosen for the price-response function, and we find the values of the parameters for the function that best fit the historical data. We call this a *regression-based* approach. An alternative approach is to use a supervised learning algorithm to find a classifier that can accurately predict take-up on the basis of price and other the features provided in the data without specifying a form for the price-response function. Over the past few decades, a large number of different approaches to this problem such as k-nearest neighbors, support vector machines, random forests, and neural nets have been developed. We call these *nonparametric* approaches because, in contrast to the regression-based approach, they are not based on estimating the parameters of a predefined price-response function.

In this section, we first describe how logistic regression can be applied to estimate the parameters of a price-response function. We illustrate the process of developing a model and choosing among different models using the e-Car data. We describe the problem of endogeneity in price-sensitivity estimation and show how a control function approach can be used to develop unbiased parameters in the presence of endogeneity. Finally, we discuss parameter estimation for a two-stage price quotation process.

## Regression

The general statistical estimation problem is to estimate the parameters of a function that predicts an outcome of interest based on the values of observed variables when there are many different observations to which the function can be fit. The outcome being predicted is called the *target variable*, and the variables used to predict the target variable are the *explanatory variables* or *features*. (The target variable is sometimes called the *dependent variable* and the explanatory variables the *independent variables*.)

In price-response function estimation, the target variable is take-up, and potential explanatory variables include price plus all of the customer, loan, and channel characteristics available along with any additional environmental variables to the lender. The goal of regression is to find a function of the explanatory variables that provides an accurate estimate of the probability that a customer will take up a loan. Whether or not a customer takes up a loan is represented by a variable that takes the value 0 if the customer does not take the loan and 1 if he does. In this case, finding the function that best predicts take-up is a problem of *binary regression*. Binary regression problems are common in many fields. For example, binary regression is used to estimate the probability that a customer with certain characteristics will click on an online ad. Binary regression is also used to estimate the probability that a patient suffering from a disease will be cured according to the characteristics of the patient, the severity of the disease, and the treatment regimen imposed. Because it is so widely used, binary regression has been intensively studied and there is a vast literature in how to apply it to different problems.

The first step in model estimation is to choose a form for the price-response function, which is equivalent to making an assumption about the underlying distribution of willingness to pay. For example, if we believed that the underlying distribution of willingness to pay were uniform, then the corresponding price-response function would be linear, and we could use linear regression to estimate the coefficients of the model. However, it is more common (and more realistic) to assume that willingness to pay follows a bell-shaped distribution such as the normal or logistic. The problem of fitting a cumulative normal distribution to binary outcomes is called *probit regression*, and the problem of fitting a cumulative logistic distribution to binary outcomes is called *logistic regression*. Both probit and logistic regression have been widely studied, both are easily implemented in R and SAS, and both give similar results when applied to take-up data. However, the logistic function is easier to work with and, as a result, is much more commonly used. For this reason, we focus on the application of logistic regression to historical data: probit regression would follow similar steps.

The logit price-response function has the form $\rho(p) = e^{a + bp}/(1 + e^{a + bp})$, where $\rho(p)$ is the probability that a customer will accept the loan at the price $p$ and $a$ and $b$ are parameters to be estimated. For a valid price-response function, we require that $b < 0$ so that price response is downward sloping. The parameter $a$ can be either positive or negative. When $p = -a/b$, $\rho(p) = .5$; that is, half of prospective customers will accept the loan. If $a < 0$, it implies that less than half of the approved applications would accept the loan at a rate of 0%. It is thus reasonable to assume that in most cases, we will have $a > 0$. Figure 5.1 shows the logistic price-response functions corresponding to three values of $a$ and $b$: $(a = 1, b = -20)$, $(a = 2.5, b = -50)$, and $(a = 5, b = -100)$. In each case, $-a/b = .05$, meaning that, at a rate of 5.0%, one half of approved customers would take up the loan. More negative values of $b$ are associated with higher levels of price sensitivity in the sense that, the higher the magnitude of $b$, the more the price-response function begins to resemble a cliff. At the critical price $\hat{p} = -a/b$, exactly half of the customers will take up the loan, which means that for $p < \hat{p}$,

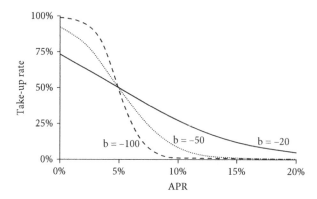

**Figure 5.1**   Logit price-response curves for three combinations of the parameters $a$ and $b$: $(a = 1, b = -20)$, $(a = 2.5, b = -50)$, $(a = 5, b = -100)$

most customers will take the loan, and for $p > \hat{p}$, most customers will not take the loan. For smaller values of $b$, the "cliff" becomes less pronounced and the price-response function begins more to resemble a gently sloping line. Changing $a$ while keeping $-a/b$ constant changes the location of the function but not its shape. For example, setting $-a/b = .10$ while holding $b$ constant would move the price-response functions to the right so that 50% of the customers would take up the loan at a rate of 10.0% but the shape of the function would remain the same. Logistic regression determines the values of $a$ and $b$ corresponding to the price-response function that best fits the underlying data.

### Segmented Versus Joint Estimation

So far we have assumed a simple form for the logistic model, namely $\rho(p) = e^{a + bp}/(1 + e^{a + bp})$, which has only two parameters, $a$ and $b$. This corresponds to a single price-response function for the entire population. However, in general, different pricing segments will have different price-response functions. One of the principles of price optimization is to take advantage of differential price response among segments in setting prices. To do this, we need to estimate a different price-response function for each segment.

There are two broad approaches to estimating price-response functions for multiple segments:

1. *Segmented estimation.* In segmented estimation, we independently estimate the parameter values for each segment. If we have $n$ pricing segments, then segmented estimation assumes that each segment $i$ has its own price-response function $\rho_i(p_i) = e^{a_i + b_i p_i}/[1 + e^{(a_i + b_i p_i)}]$, and we need to estimate the $2n$ parameters $a_i$ and $b_i$ for $i = 1, 2, \ldots, n$.

2. *Joint estimation.* In joint estimation, we create a single price-response function that incorporates all the explanatory variables within it (including price). In this case, we would have a single price-response function with the form $\rho(x_i, p_i, a_i, b_i, \theta) = e^{(a_i + b_i p_i + \theta^T x_i)}/[1 + e^{(a_i + b_i p_i + \theta^T x_i)}]$, where $p$ is the rate, $a$ and $b$ are parameters as before, $\mathbf{x}$ is a vector of pricing segmentation dimension values, and $\theta$

is a vector of coefficients. In this case, regression needs to determine the elements of $\theta$ along with $a$ and $b$.

Each of the two approaches has advantages and disadvantages. Segmented estimation is more flexible — it allows for the price-response function within each segment to be independent of the price-response functions in other segments, whereas joint estimation imposes relationships among the price-response functions. However, segmented estimation achieves this independence at the cost of a larger number of coefficients that need to be estimated, namely, two for each segment. For a lender with 10,000 segments, this means that 20,000 parameters need to be estimated. Segmented estimation requires sufficient historical data with significant price dispersion in each and every segment to support estimation of the price-response function for that segment. This condition is often not met. If there is a large number of segments, then many segments will have either not enough loan records or not enough historical price dispersion (or both) to support statistically significant price-response estimation. In this case, some form of joint estimation is required to create price-response functions for the sparse segments.

Joint estimation requires estimating a parameter for every explanatory variable rather than every segment. Because the number of explanatory variables is typically far smaller than the number of segments, it requires fewer historical observations to derive statistically significant estimates. Furthermore, as long as there is enough total data with price variation across all segments, joint estimation calculates coefficients that are applicable to all segments, including those with little or no historical data. However, joint estimation does this at the cost of requiring the modeler to specify the forms of the relationship among price sensitivity and continuous variables as well as the combinations of variables that need to be incorporated into the model. This requires an iterative process of model refinement, which we describe in the next section.

### The Estimation Process

Assume that we are using a joint estimation approach to estimating the coefficients of a price-response model. In this case, model estimation requires making three decisions:

1. *Variable selection.* Which explanatory variables should be included in the model?

2. *Variable transformations.* What mathematical transformations should be applied to the explanatory variables included in the model? For example, should we include *Amount*, *ln*(*Amount*), or *Amount*$^2$ or some combination of them in the model? (We follow the convention of italicizing and capitalizing the first letters of the names of variables used in a regression. Thus, *Amount* is the explanatory variable specifying the amount of a loan.) The process of choosing transformations for explanatory variables to be included in a model is called *feature engineering* in machine learning.

3. *Crossing variables.* Variables can be combined, or *crossed*, to create new variables. For example, if we believed that take-up depends not just on *Partner* and *Term* independently but also on the combination of *Partner* and *Term*, we could create a new variable, *Partner* × *Term*, that would allow for a different coefficient for each combination of *Partner* and *Term*.

**Example 5.3: Crossed Variables.** Consider a lender who classifies loans into five different risk tiers and three different terms and can offer a different price to each of the 15 possible combinations of risk tier and term. Let $x_i = 1$ if a loan falls into risk tier $i$ and $x_i = 0$ if it falls into some other tier, and let $y_j = 1$ if a loan has term $j$ and $y_j = 0$ otherwise. If the lender wishes to model term and tier independently, he would estimate eight total parameters— one of each risk tier and one for each term. However, if he believes that take-up varies as the combination of term and tier, then he could create the crossed variable $z_{ij} = x_i y_j$ such that $z_{ij} = 1$ if a loan is in risk tier $i$ and has term $j$ and $z_{ij} = 0$ otherwise. In this case, he would need to estimate 15 parameters, one for each possible value of $z_{ij}$. The question that the modeler needs to answer is whether creating additional variables by crossing existing variables provides improved predictive power for the model.

Answering these questions essentially requires structured "trial and error." The first step in fitting a model is to partition the historical data into a *training set* and a *test set*. The coefficients of the model are estimated using the training set and then the quality of the model is evaluated on the test set. This avoids the problem of *overfitting*, which occurs when some of the explanatory variables that have been included in the model actually reduce its accuracy. Adding additional explanatory variables, including more variable combinations, adding new transformations of existing variables, or creating and adding new crossed variables will always improve the quality of the model *as measured on the training set.* However, at some point, additional explanatory variables are being fit only to the noise in the data rather than the underlying relationships. The situation is illustrated in Figure 5.2—as more and more explanatory variables are added to a model, the "model error" on the training set—no matter how measured—will always decrease. However, at some point adding more explanatory variables begins to reduce the predictive power of the model—at this point the model is said to be *overfit*. If a model is overfit, adding more variables actually causes the predictive power of the model to degrade. The appropriate model to use is the one that minimizes the model error measured on the test data not on the training data.

Opinions differ on how much of the data set should be held out as a test set. For predictive applications—such as measuring price response, it is best to use the most recent data

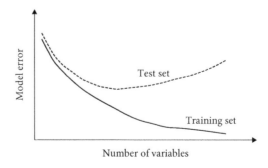

**Figure 5.2**    Typical behavior of model fit error measured on test and training data sets as the number of variables in the model is increased

for the test set. Which explanatory variables to include in the model—and which variable combinations and transformations to use—should be determined by estimating the parameters on the training set and measuring the quality of fit on the test set. This should be done for different combinations of explanatory variables and variable transformations.

To initiate the modeling process, we choose an initial model, apply logistic regression to estimate the coefficients of the model on the training set, and then measure the fit of this model on the test data set. This model is called the *champion*. Once we have established an initial champion, we can determine a final model using a *champion-challenger process*, which proceeds in five steps:

1.  Choose a set of explanatory variables and variable transformations that has not been tried before.

2.  Run a regression using the explanatory variables, variable combinations, and variable transformations chosen in Step 1 on the training set. The resulting model is called the *challenger*.

3.  Measure the performance of the challenger on the test data. If the challenger performs better than the champion, then the challenger becomes the new champion. If the champion outperforms the challenger, then the champion remains the champion.

4.  Go to Step 1 and continue until performance is no longer improving as new challengers are evaluated.

5.  Once a final champion has been chosen, reestimate the coefficients of the model using all of the available data (training data and test data).

This process is repeated each time a new challenger model is proposed. This means that, at any time, the current champion has demonstrated the best performance on the test data of all of the models that have been tested. In all cases, it is important to update the test data periodically with recent observations to ensure that model performance is measured against data that reflects the most current market conditions.

*Performance Measures*

Step 3 of the estimation process described above requires comparing the performance of a champion model with a challenger model and choosing the better performing model as the new champion. Three different measures of performance are commonly used:

1.  *Root mean squared error* (RMSE), which is also sometimes called the *root mean squared deviation* (RMSD) measures the standard deviation between the probability of take-up estimated by each model and the actual take-up. For a set of $N$ observations,

$$RMSE = \sqrt{\sum_{i=1}^{N}(\rho(x_i,p_i,a_i,b_i,\boldsymbol{\theta})-y_i)^2 / N}$$

    where $\rho(x_i, p_i, a, b, \boldsymbol{\theta})$ is the probability that transaction $i$ with characteristics given by the vector $x_i$ will be taken up at price $p_i$ given parameter values $a$, $b$, and $\theta$. The variable $y_i$ is *Outcome*, with $y_i = 1$ indicating that the loan was taken up and $y_i = 0$ indicating that it was not. For a binary model such as the ones that we consider, RMSE will be between 0 and 1, with a smaller value indicating a better-fitting model.

2. *Concordance* (also called area under the curve, or *AUC*) measures the frequency with which a model estimates a higher probability for loans that were taken up than those that were not taken up. A concordance of 1 means the model is a perfect predictor—that is, there is some value of $\hat{p}$ such that every loan with estimated probability $p \geq \hat{p}$ of being taken up was actually taken up and every loan with estimated probability $p < \hat{p}$ was not taken up. A concordance of .5 means that the model was no better than random chance—given a loan that was taken up and one that was not taken up, there is only a 50% probability that the loan that was taken up was assigned a higher probability of take-up than the loan that was not taken up. The higher the value of the concordance, the better job the model does of predicting loan take-up. Although concordances of less than .5 are possible, in practice concordance is typically between .5 and 1.0 with a higher value indicating a better-fitting model.

3. *Log-likelihood* measures the probability of observing the pattern of take-up and non-take-up in the test data set if the underlying model were correct. Log-likelihood is always less than 0, with larger values (i.e., less negative) indicating a better-fitting model.

---

**Example 5.4: Performance Measures.** Assume that our test data set includes only five loans (a woefully inadequate number) and that the predicted take-up $\hat{y}_i$ from our challenger model and the actual take-up $y_i$ are as shown in the second and third columns of Table 5.2. Then the squared error for each loans is equal to $e^2_i = (\hat{y}_i - y_i)^2$ and the likelihood for each loan is $L_i = \hat{y}_i \times y_1 + (1 - \hat{y}_i) \times (1 - y_i)$. The mean squared error of the model on the test data set is the average of the squared errors, which is .188, and the RMSE is the square root of this number, which is .44. The likelihood of the observed outcome is the product of the individual likelihoods: $L = L_1 \times L_2 \times \ldots \times L_5 = .069$; the log-likelihood is the natural logarithm of the likelihood, or $\ln(.069) = -2.67$. To calculate the concordance, we look at all pairs of loans in which one loan was taken up and the other was not. There are six such pairs in the data in Table 5.2. We call a pair in which the predicted take-up probability for the loan taken up was greater than or equal to the predicted take-up probability for the loan not taken up *concordant*. For example, the pair (1, 3) is concordant because the predicted take-up probability for Loan 1 (which was taken up) is greater than the predicted take-up probability for Loan 3 (which was not taken up). On the other hand, the pair (3, 4) is *discordant* because the predicted take-up probability for Loan 3 (which was not taken up) is higher than the predicted take-up probability for Loan 4 (which was taken up). Of the six disparate pairs, five were concordant and one was discordant so the concordance is 5/6 = .833.

TABLE 5.2

*Results for the test data set as described in Example 5.4, showing the predicted probability of take-up, actual take-up, and the corresponding squared errors and likelihoods for five loans*

| Number | Predicted take-up probability ($\hat{y}_i$) | Actual take-up ($y_i$) | Squared error | Likelihood |
|--------|------|------|------|------|
| 1 | .9 | 1 | .01 | .9 |
| 2 | .8 | 1 | .04 | .8 |
| 3 | .6 | 0 | .36 | .4 |
| 4 | .3 | 1 | .49 | .3 |
| 5 | .2 | 0 | .04 | .8 |

Each of these measures can be useful in comparing the performance of different models on the same test data set: in addition, concordance and RMSE can be useful in comparing models across data sets. Log-likelihood is not useful for comparing model performance on different test data sets because it depends strongly on the number of entries in the data set.

### Application to the e-Car Data

The e-Car Data Set is a CSV file that includes the prices, loan characteristics, customer characteristics, and outcomes for 50,000 approved loan offers extended by an online auto lender between April 17, 2005, and November 16, 2005. (The e-Car Data Set can be accessed online at https://info.nomissolutions.com/pricing_credit_products. To preserve anonymity, both the name of lender and some of the data have been changed.) During this period, e-Car determined the APR to quote to each successful applicant based on a single-stage process such as the one shown in Figure 1.3. A customer arriving at the e-Car website filled out a loan application that included enough information for e-Car to access her credit score and estimate her riskiness. Each application also specified the term and amount of the loan along with whether the loan would be used to purchase a new car, purchase a used car, or refinance an existing car loan.

If e-Car believed that an applicant was too risky, e-Car rejected her application. However, if e-Car judged an applicant to be creditworthy, e-Car offered her a loan and quoted her an APR. The customer then had 45 days to accept the loan. If the customer did not use the loan within 45 days, the offer expired and the customer was assumed to be "lost." There was no opportunity for the customer to negotiate a better rate from e-Car—the quoted APR was "take it or leave it." Of the customers who were offered a loan by e-Car during this period, about 32% accepted the loan, whereas the remaining 68% were lost sales—approved applications that did not book a loan.

The explanatory variables in the e-Car Data Set are shown in Table 5.3. These explanatory variables were either captured from the loan application or gathered from an outside source; for example, the competitive rate was taken from a competitor's website. The explanatory variables in the e-Car Data Set are typical of the data captured and stored by many lenders. We note that the data set does not include any variables specifying age, gender, or any other customer attribute that e-Car would not be willing to use in setting prices.

TABLE 5.3
*Data elements in the e-Car Data Set*

TABLE 5.3
*Data elements in the e-Car Data Set*

| Field | Type | Units | Description |
|---|---|---|---|
| Approval date | Numerical | — | Date application was approved (4/17/05 to 11/16/05) |
| Tier | Categorical | — | Risk segmentation defined by e-Car. Takes values 1, 2, 3, and 4, with 1 being least risky and 4 most risky |
| FICO | Numerical | — | FICO score |
| Term | Numerical | Months | Term of loan |
| Amount | Numerical | $ | Loan amount approved |
| Loan type | Categorical | — | N = new car finance, U = used car finance, R = refinance |
| Previous rate | Numerical | % | Previous APR for a refinance loan, only populated for *Loan Type* = R |
| Competition rate | Numerical | % | Competitive headline APR published on website |
| Cost of funds | Numerical | % | Cost of funds to the lender |
| Partner | Categorical | — | Indicator for the source of the inquiry: 1 = direct to e-Car website, 2 = click-through from a partner, 3 = click-through from a nonpartner website |
| Rate | Numerical | % | APR quoted to the customer by e-Car |
| Outcome | Binary | — | 1 if the customer took the loan; 0 otherwise |

The variables in the e-Car Data Set can be grouped into three types:

1. *Numerical* variables are those that take on meaningful numerical values. They include *FICO*, *Rate*, and *Amount*.

2. *Categorical* variables classify observations into a finite number of categories. Examples in the e-Car data include *Tier*, *Loan Type*, and *Partner*. Categorical variables must be mutually exclusive and collectively exhaustive—that is, each observation must fall into one category, no more and no less. Note that a categorical variable may take on a numerical value but this does not make it a numerical variable if the assignment of numbers to categories is arbitrary. Thus, the e-Car data have a variable partner that can take on the values 1, 2, or 3 depending on the source of the inquiry. However, the assignment of numbers to sources is completely arbitrary. This is in contrast to the FICO score, for which the values are proportional to the relative risk of different customers.

3. *Binary* variables can only take on the values 0 or 1. *Outcome* is a binary variable.

Table 5.3 lists the variables in the e-Car Data Set, the type of each variable, and a brief description. *Outcome* refers to the variable (which can either be 0 or 1) that specifies whether or not a customer took an offered loan. *Tier* is a risk category assigned by e-Car on the basis of FICO score and other information about the borrower. For customers who are refinancing, the APR of their current loan is recorded; for customers who are using the loan to purchase a car this field is not populated. *Loan Type* records whether the purpose of the loan is to finance a new car purchase (N), a used car purchase (U), or to refinance an existing loan (R). e-Car's major competitor published on their website the lowest APR available for each type of loan (i.e., the rate that they would charge to the lowest risk customers). The e-Car data captured this APR every day and recorded it as *Competition Rate*. The *Partner*

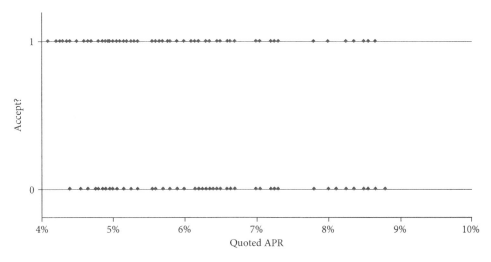

**Figure 5.3**   Loan acceptance (1) and nonacceptance (0) plotted as a function of APR for a portion of the e-Car data

field indicates how the customer arrived at the e-Car website. A value of 1 indicates that the customer came directly to the e-Car site. Also, e-Car had established a partnership with an auto sales website that would direct shoppers to the e-Car site if they indicated that they were interested in a loan. A value of 2 indicates that the customer came to e-Car's site from this partner site, and a value of 3 indicates that the customer was directed from some other (nonpartner) website.

Table 5.4 shows an extract of data from 10 quotes from the e-Car Data Set. Even this small extract shows that APR is not the only determinant of take-up—Loan 2 was not taken up at a rate of 4.45%, while Loan 3 was taken up at the higher rate of 5.45%. Figure 5.3 shows the outcome of each quote plotted against APR for a selection of similar loans from the e-Car Data Set. The horizontal axis is *APR*. The vertical axis is *Outcome*, which is equal to 1 if the customer took up the loan and 0 if the customer did not take up the loan. From the graph it is clear that as APR is increased, the fraction of customers taking the loan decreases. If auto loans were a commodity, then there would be a threshold APR, say, $\hat{p}$, such that all of the loans with $p \leq \hat{p}$ would have been taken up and all of those with $p > \hat{p}$ would not have been taken up. Instead of such a clean dividing line, Figure 5.3 shows the more typical pattern in which the take-up probability gradually decreases as price increases. The goal of our regression exercise is to find the coefficients of logistic function of the explanatory variables that best fits this data.

We illustrate how the model development process works using an extract from the e-Car Data Set. This extract includes 50,000 entries. We use the first 40,000 observations (found on the worksheet titled "Training") as the training set and the last 10,000 observations (found on the worksheet titled "Test") as the test set. We consider four models in increasing order of complexity:

• Model 1 includes only a constant term and *Rate* as explanatory variables.

TABLE 5.4

Extract of data elements from the e-Car Data Set

| No. | Approval date | Tier | FICO | Term | Amount ($) | Loan type | Prev. APR | Comp. rate | Cost of funds (%) | Partner | Rate | Outcome |
|---|---|---|---|---|---|---|---|---|---|---|---|---|
| 1 | 11/16/2005 | 1 | 750 | 60 | 37,000 | U | | 4.85 | 2.13 | 3 | 4.85 | 0 |
| 2 | 11/16/2005 | 1 | 804 | 60 | 21,000 | N | | 4.45 | 2.13 | 1 | 4.45 | 0 |
| 3 | 11/16/2005 | 1 | 805 | 60 | 19,315 | R | 10.0 | 5.55 | 2.13 | 3 | 5.45 | 1 |
| 4 | 11/16/2005 | 1 | 718 | 48 | 11,350 | U | | 4.85 | 2.13 | 2 | 4.85 | 1 |
| 5 | 11/16/2005 | 2 | 717 | 36 | 11,258 | U | | 4.35 | 2.13 | 3 | 4.35 | 1 |
| 6 | 11/16/2005 | 1 | 761 | 60 | 10,000 | U | | 4.85 | 2.13 | 1 | 4.85 | 1 |
| 7 | 11/16/2005 | 1 | 809 | 60 | 7,500 | U | | 4.85 | 2.13 | 3 | 4.85 | 1 |
| 8 | 11/16/2005 | 1 | 733 | 48 | 10,062 | U | | 4.85 | 2.13 | 3 | 4.85 | 1 |
| 9 | 11/16/2005 | 2 | 710 | 60 | 19,800 | R | 7.5 | 5.55 | 2.13 | 3 | 6.19 | 1 |
| 10 | 11/16/2005 | 1 | 767 | 60 | 22,975 | U | | 4.85 | 2.13 | 3 | 4.85 | 0 |

NOTE: Comp. rate is competition rate. Loan type U = used car, N = new car, and R = refinance.

- Model 2 includes a constant term and *Rate* plus *Previous Rate* (for refinance), *Competition Rate*, and *Cost of Funds*.

- Model 3 includes all of the variables in Model 2 as well as the logarithm of *FICO* and the logarithm of *Amount*.

- Model 4 includes all of the variables in Model 3 plus *Loan Type*.

Table 5.5 shows the coefficients of each model estimated on the training set along with an indication of the significance of the coefficient.[4] Significance is measured using the *p-value*, which gives the probability that the "true" value of the coefficient is 0. An explanatory variable with a coefficient of 0 has no influence on the target variable, and thus a high *p*-value means that there is a good chance that associated variable has no influence on *Outcome* and could possibly be excluded. The asterisks beside the coefficient indicate the level of significance according to the following convention:

- No asterisk means that the *p*-value is greater than .05.

- One asterisk means .01 < *p*-value < .05.

- Two asterisks mean .001 < *p*-value < .01.

- Three asterisks mean *p*-value < .001.

In all three models, all the coefficients have *p*-values less than .001 except for the constant for Model 1 and *Cost of Funds* for Models 2, 3 and 4. This means that they are significant at the .1% level, or there is a 99.9% probability that they are not 0.

Table 5.6 shows the RMSE, concordance, and log-likelihood for each of the four models. All three of these performance measures improve as more variables are added to the model. Model 4 has the best performance and is the champion among the four models. Performance improved most significantly from Model 2 to Model 3—when the logarithms of FICO and loan amount were added to the explanatory variables. This suggests that these two variables strongly influence the probability of take-up. It is notable that *Cost of Funds* is not significant in any of the models—this would suggest that a promising challenger would be a Model 5 based on Model 4 but excluding *Cost of Funds* as an explanatory variable.

A key element in model estimation is generating a plausible or believable model. Specifically, the sign of the coefficients in a model should be consistent with our understanding

TABLE 5.5

*Coefficients estimated for different model specifications on the e-Car Data Set*

| | | | | | | | | LOAN TYPE | |
| Model | Constant | Rate | Cost of funds | Competition rate | Previous rate | ln(Amt.) | ln(FICO) | U | N |
|---|---|---|---|---|---|---|---|---|---|
| 1 | .06 | −17.33*** | | | | | | | |
| 2 | −1.71*** | −25.71*** | −7.05 | 41.31*** | 11.60*** | | | | |
| 3 | 45.84*** | −42.19*** | 6.22 | 72.88*** | 3.03*** | −2.05*** | −4.21*** | | |
| 4 | 46.74*** | −51.61*** | 6.12 | 94.85*** | 22.31*** | −2.08*** | −4.67*** | 2.15*** | 1.84*** |

***p < .001; **p < .01.

TABLE 5.6

*Performance measures for the four models described in the text applied to the e-Car test data*

| Model | RMSE | Concordance | Log-likelihood |
|---|---|---|---|
| 1 | 0.422 | 0.602 | −5,395 |
| 2 | 0.414 | 0.670 | −5,208 |
| 3 | 0.378 | 0.797 | −4,458 |
| 4 | 0.373 | 0.804 | −4,378 |

of the market. In a logistic regression, the sign of the coefficient of the price variable—in our case, *Rate*—should be less than 0, indicating that take-up will go down with increasing price. All else being equal, customers with a high credit score will have lower take-up than those with a lower credit score: thus, we would anticipate that the coefficient on *FICO* (or ln(*FICO*)) should also be less than 0. Additionally, all else being equal, customers applying for larger loans should have a lower take-up rate than those applying for smaller loans. The coefficients of ln(*Amount*) in Models 3 and 4 are both less than 0, which implies that both models indeed predict that loan take-up decreases with loan amount. These sense checks on the model coefficients are always important because the modeler needs to understand her model and be able to stand behind it. The old maxim holds: "If a model doesn't correspond to our intuition, we need to either change the model or change our intuition."

The four models considered here would typically represent only the starting point of a more extensive process. Additional variables such as *Term* and *Approval Date* could be included in challenger models to determine whether they improved fit on the test set. Additional variable transformations could also be considered. Variables such as *FICO* and *APR* could be crossed to create new variables. Furthermore, numerical variables such as *FICO* and *Amount* could be binned to convert them into categorical variables. Such binning can reveal nonlinear relationships among explanatory variables and the target variable. For each set of variables to be considered, a new model would be fit using logistic regression. The performance of each of new model is then measured on the test data, and if it shows better performance than the current champion, it becomes the new champion. It is not unusual for tens or even hundreds of models to be tested before a final champion is chosen.

Many statistical packages such as SAS and R include routines that support the variable selection process. The process of testing various transformations and combinations of variables can also be automated by setting up batch runs that perform hundreds of regressions on the training set and calculate the performance of each one on the test data set. However, there remains a fair amount of art in model creation and evaluation. In particular, it is easy to conceive of a vast number of potential variable transformations and combinations. Among this vast number of combinations, the modeler needs to choose a much smaller number to actually test. The choice of which models to test will reflect both the modeler's experience and knowledge of the underlying market.

Because we are interested in setting prices, it is important that the coefficient of the price variable—*Rate* in the e-Car data—be as accurate as possible. At a minimum, the coefficient of price needs to be less than 0 for a model to exhibit sensible price response: the probability of observing *Outcome* = 1 should decrease as rate is increased. This de minimis condition is satisfied by all four models. Model 4 demonstrated the best performance of the four models tested, and it has a concordance greater than 80% on the test data set, which is impressively high. But the lack of stability in the coefficient of *Rate* among models is troubling: the coefficient changed from −42.19 to −51.61 from Model 2 to Model 3 when two new variables were added. In contrast, the coefficient of *Competition Rate* was much more stable — it changed by less than 1% from Model 3 to Model 4. Why is the coefficient of *Rate* less stable than the coefficient of *Competition Rate*?

Part of the answer is that *Rate* is correlated with the two variables added in Model 3: *Rate* depends on both the FICO score of the customer and the size of the loan. In addition, *Rate, Amount,* and *FICO* all influence take-up. Specifically, customers with higher FICO scores are less likely to take a loan, all else being equal, than customers with lower FICO scores, and customers applying for larger loans are less likely to take the loan than customers applying for smaller loans. The dependence of rate on FICO score and loan size can be confirmed by running a linear regression with *Rate* as target variable and ln(*FICO*) and ln(*Amount*) as explanatory variables. This regression shows that *Rate* = 1.78 − .26 × ln(*FICO*) −.001 × ln(*Amount*), with both coefficients significant at the 1% level. This confirms that e-Car was in fact offering lower prices to customers with higher FICO scores and to customers who applied for larger loans. Such correlation among explanatory variables is called *collinearity*. To the extent that *Rate* is correlated with variables in the data that also influence *Outcome*, those variables need to be incorporated into the model, otherwise the coefficient of *Rate* may be biased.

To estimate the coefficients of a price-response model that can support price optimization, we need an accurate estimate of the coefficient of price in the model. This is a more stringent requirement than simply requiring that a model accurately forecast take-up. In particular, to accurately estimate the price coefficient in a model we need to incorporate all the variables that might influence price in order to avoid collinearity. However, this is not enough to ensure that we have an accurate, unbiased estimate of the coefficient of price: there is also the possibility that there are unobservable variables that influence both price and take-up. This can occur if some of the historical variability in prices is based on adjustments made by field sales staff (or branch staff) who are setting or influencing prices based on characteristics of the customer or the economic environment that are not included in the data. This is the problem of *endogeneity*, which we address next.

## Endogeneity

As described in Chapter 1, there are markets in which the final price of a loan is determined through negotiation between the lender (or an intermediary) and the customer. For example, in auto lending in the United States and other countries, the final price of a loan is typically the result of a negotiation between the customer and a representative of the Finance and Insurance (F&I) department of a dealership.[5] In this case, the final price can be correlated with the customer willingness to pay through attributes or characteristics that are not recorded in the data. If this is the case, a single-stage approach to regression such as the one described earlier may result in biased estimates of the parameters of the price-response function. This phenomenon is called *endogeneity*.

To understand how endogeneity can influence the estimation of the price-response function, assume that a lender was endowed with the psychic power to determine the highest price that every customer would accept for a loan—that is, the lender could magically intuit the customer's willingness to pay. To maximize profitability, the lender would quote a price to each accepted applicant that was equal to her willingness to pay and each customer would accept the loan. (For simplicity, we have assumed that each customer's willingness to pay is high enough that the incremental profit of the loan to the lender would always be greater than 0.) In this case, a customer with a willingness to pay of 6.5% would be offered a loan at 6.5%, which she would accept, and one with a willingness to pay of 9.25% would be offered a loan at 9.25%, which she would also accept. The historical data would show a spread of prices and a 100% take-up rate at every price. In this case, a naïve analysis of the historical data would suggest that customers would accept any price for the loan up to the highest price offered. However, this conclusion is clearly incorrect and—if used as the basis for setting prices—would lead to drastic overpricing. This is the most extreme example of endogeneity.

The problem arises from the implicit assumption that the price historically offered to each customer depended on the customer's willingness to pay only through characteristics that were recorded in the data. This assumption is shown schematically in Figure 5.4. In this case, each customer's willingness to pay is a function of characteristics recorded in the data along with unobserved characteristics that might include the state of the consumer's household finances, her propensity to shop, her available alternatives, and so on. These unobserved characteristics are the source of the randomness observed in customer response and account for the fact that two customers who appear identical in the data may react differently to the same loan offer—one may take up the loan while the other does not. In the situation illustrated in Figure 5.4, willingness to pay and price are related only through recorded characteristics of the loan, channel, or customer. If this is the true situation, standard single-stage regression will provide unbiased estimates of price sensitivity.

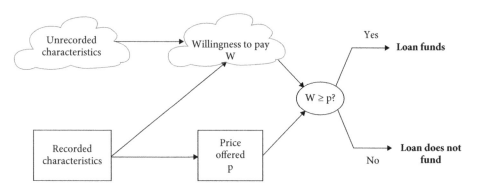

**Figure 5.4**   Relationships among recorded loan characteristics, unrecorded characteristics, willingness to pay, and price when endogeneity is not present

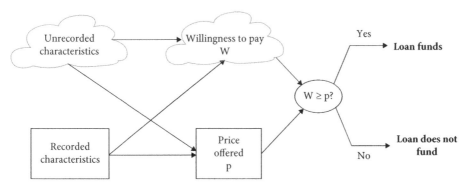

**Figure 5.5**  Relationship among recorded loan characteristics, unrecorded characteristics, willingness to pay, and price when the same unrecorded characteristics influence both price and customer willingness to pay

Trouble arises when unrecorded characteristics influence both the final price and the customer willingness to pay. This can happen when local staff has the authority to negotiate rates for individual deals. In this case, the local salesperson may observe customer attributes that are not recorded in the data and use those attributes in negotiating the final price. For example, a salesperson may notice that a particular customer seems very eager to take the loan and as a result holds the line on price, while another customer seems less eager to take the loan and the salesperson drops the price to close the deal. To the extent that the salesperson is correct in his estimation of customers' willingness to pay, the price offered depends on customer willingness to pay through variables not recorded in the data. This situation is illustrated in Figure 5.5. In this case, endogeneity may bias the coefficient estimates.

If this dependence among willingness to pay and unobserved characteristics is not accounted for in the estimation process, it is likely that the resulting price-sensitivity estimates will be biased. If sales staff are systematically adjusting prices toward the willingness to pay of customers (as they should do in order to increase profitability), then a naïve estimation procedure that ignores endogeneity will underestimate price sensitivity. If sales staff are using their pricing discretion on the average to adjust prices away from customer willingness to pay, naïve estimation will lead to price sensitivity being *overestimated*. If sales staff are varying prices in a way that is uncorrelated with customer willingness to pay, then endogeneity will not be present and the results of a single-stage regression will be unbiased.

When the variation of prices in historical data is due partially or entirely to sales force discretion, it is prudent to test for the presence of endogeneity and, if necessary, correct for it. The standard approach is to search for *instrumental variables* that are correlated with the explanatory variable of interest (in this case, *Rate*) but are not correlated with variation in the target variable (in this case *Outcome*).

In many cases, external instrumental variables can be identified and added to the explanatory variables as a method for clearing endogeneity. Unfortunately, in the case of lending, it is difficult or impossible to identify observable external variables that can serve as good instruments. In this case, a common alternative is to use a *control-function approach*, which proceeds in four steps:

1. Estimate an *expected price* for each offer. This is the price that would have been offered in the absence of local knowledge of unrecorded characteristics. One approach to estimate this expected price is to average the prices offered for "similar" deals during the same time period. For example, the expected price might be calculated as the average price of all offers for all loans of similar sizes and terms approved for similar customers during the same week.

2. Calculate the differences between the expected prices estimated in Step 1 and the actual prices offered for each approved loan.

3. Run a regression with *Outcome* as the target variable that includes the differences calculated in Step 2. If these differences enter the regression as significant, this indicates that endogeneity is present.

4. If endogeneity is present, then the difference between the actual price and the expected price should be included as an explanatory variable in the regression.

Although this may sound complicated, the basic idea is simple. In Step 1, we estimate the prices that would have been offered for each deal if the sales staff did not possess unobserved deal-specific information. This expected price is an instrumental variable because it is likely to be correlated with the price offered for an approved loan, but it is not correlated with the idiosyncratic willingness to pay of the customer for that loan. If the difference between expected price and the price actually offered is not significant, then the results of a regression using *Rate* as an independent variable will not be biased. If, however, the difference between predicted rate and actual rate is a significant predictor of *Outcome*, then this difference should be included as an explanatory variable in the regression. The coefficient of this variable will be a better estimate of price sensitivity than the coefficient of *Rate* estimated through simple regression.[6]

Ignoring endogeneity in parameter estimation can lead to significant misestimation of price sensitivity when discretion is present. A study of auto loans offered by dealerships in which the finance and insurance (F&I) staff negotiated price with customers found that ignoring endogeneity resulted in underestimation of the hazard rate of price sensitivity by a factor of 2 or more. Fortunately for both the dealers and lenders, the same study showed that local staff were, on the average, negotiating prices that were closer to customer willingness to pay than the list price, therefore increasing overall profitability.

The finding that local sales staff use price discretion to improve profitability may not be too surprising: after all, that is what they are paid to do. However, local pricing discretion does not always leads to higher profitability. A proprietary Nomis study showed that local staff at a Canadian unsecured lender systematically adjusted rates away from customer willingness to pay: they were offering higher rates to more price-sensitive customers and lower rates to less price-sensitive customers. Specifically, field staff tended to offer higher rates to new customers (who are more price sensitive) than to existing customers (who are less price sensitive). In doing so, they reduced overall profitability by about 2%. The key difference between the auto lender and the unsecured lender was the underlying incentive structure—bonuses for the F&I staff at the dealer were based on profit, whereas staff bonuses at the unsecured lender were based on a formula that emphasized net promoter score, which measures the likelihood of existing customers to recommend the bank to others. Staff in this case apparently felt that offering lower prices to existing customers would lead to higher net promoter scores and they negotiated prices accordingly. While the directions of the underlying biases were different, in both cases, two-stage regression was required to obtain unbiased estimates of the price-response coefficients.[7]

## Nonparametric Approaches

We have described in some detail how logistic regression can be used to estimate the parameters of a price-response function. Logistic regression has many advantages—it is widely used for binary regression, it corresponds to a "realistic" price-response function (the logit), and the sign of the estimated coefficients can be checked for reasonability (e.g. the price coefficient should be negative in all cases). However, requiring a logit price response for all segments is a strong assumption—what if customers respond to prices in a way that is not well captured by the logit function?

If we had a specific alternative to the logit—say, the probit—in mind for the price-response function for a particular segment, there would be little difficulty: we would use regression to estimate the parameters of the probit price-response function on the training data and estimate performance on the test data. If the probit price-response function performed better than the current champion on the standard performance measures, it would become the new champion. However, this approach is not completely satisfying. First of all, if we want to test one or more alternative functional forms, it requires going through the variable selection and transformation procedure described earlier for each candidate function, potentially vastly expanding the amount of work required. Ultimately, this raises the question of why we should have to specify a candidate function at all. Why shouldn't we allow the data itself to tell us how customers respond to prices without imposing a specific functional form?

How to use historical data to predict future outcomes without postulating an underlying functional form has been one of the most active research topics in business analytics over the past decade. This research has been motivated by the increasing availability of massive amounts of data ("big data") and the plummeting cost of computation, which together have allowed for much more complex algorithms to be applied to increasingly vast volumes of data. Many of the techniques developed through this research have been lumped under the terms *machine learning* and *artificial intelligence*. Rather than trying to impose a precise meaning on these somewhat slippery terms, we will consider a class of machine-learning algorithms that have been developed to address the problem of supervised learning. We introduced the concept of supervised learning in Chapter 2 in the context of predicting the probability of default associated with an application. We use it here to denote the problem of determining the probability that an approved customer will take up a loan.

Supervised learning starts with an outcome of interest, called the *target variable*, and a vector of characteristics or features. The idea is to predict the target variable given particular values of the features. In case of default prediction the target variable is the probability that an applicant will default on a loan, and the features are all of the entries in the applicant's credit file plus the characteristics of the loan plus all other information that is useful for prediction. For price-response estimation, the features are all of the characteristics of the loan, borrower, and channel that can be used in pricing *plus* the price of the loan. The target variable is the probability of take-up. Logistic regression is one approach to supervised learning; however, we are interested in algorithms that do not require specification of a functional form.

An example of a supervised learning approach that does not require specifying an underlying functional form is the *k-nearest neighbors* (kNN) algorithm. The kNN algorithm is based on the idea that, given a candidate feature vector $\mathbf{x}$ and a corresponding target value $y$ that can either take the value of 0 or 1, the estimated probability $Pr\{y = 1 | \mathbf{x}\}$ should be based on the outcomes of historical observations with feature vectors that are "close" to $\mathbf{x}$. In terms of lending, this means that the predicted probability of take-up for a candidate loan at a given rate would be based on the historical take-ups seen for similar loans offered to similar customers at similar rates. Formally, we denote the distance between two vectors $\mathbf{x}_1$ and $\mathbf{x}_2$ as $d(\mathbf{x}_1, \mathbf{x}_2)$. If the elements of $\mathbf{x}$ are all numeric, then we can use the standard Euclidean distance, namely:

$$d(\mathbf{x}_1, \mathbf{x}_2) = \sqrt{\sum_i (x_{1,i} - x_{2,i})^2}.$$

If some of the features are categorical or discrete, then the difference metric needs to be modified accordingly.

The k-nearest neighbors algorithm starts by calculating the distance of every historical observation to the candidate loan. It then estimates the probability that the candidate loan will be taken up as the fraction of the $k$ historical loans that are closest to the candidate loan that were taken up. Thus, if the lender were using the 15-nearest neighbors algorithm, he would find the 15 historical loans that were closest to the candidate loan. If nine of those loans were taken up, the lender would estimate the take-up probability for the candidate loan to be $9/15 = .6$.

---

**Example 5.5: 3-Nearest Neighbors Algorithm.** A lender offers loans of $10,000 to applicants with FICO scores between 700 and 710. The APRs and outcomes of 10 historical loans are shown in Table 5.7. On the basis of this data, the lender wants to use the 3-nearest neighbors algorithm to estimate the probability that a customer with a FICO score of 709 will accept a loan if offered an APR of 6.2%. The distance from the candidate loan to each of the historical loans is shown in the fifth column of Table 5.7. The three closest loans to the candidate loan are Loan 4 ($d = 1.04$), Loan 9 ($d = 1.64$), and Loan 3 ($d = 1.80$). Since two of these loans (Loan 4 and Loan 9) were taken up, the 3-nearest neighbors algorithm would predict a two-thirds probability that the candidate loan would be taken up.

---

TABLE 5.7

*FICO scores and APRs for 10 historical loans referred to in Example 5.5*

| Loan | FICO score | APR | Outcome | Distance from candidate loan |
|------|-----------|-----|---------|------------------------------|
| 1 | 700 | 8.0 | 1 | 9.18 |
| 2 | 702 | 7.5 | 1 | 7.12 |
| 3 | 710 | 7.7 | 0 | 1.80 |
| 4 | 708 | 6.5 | 1 | 1.04 |
| 5 | 705 | 7.9 | 0 | 4.35 |
| 6 | 702 | 8.1 | 0 | 7.25 |
| 7 | 706 | 7.7 | 1 | 3.35 |
| 8 | 707 | 6.8 | 0 | 2.09 |
| 9 | 710 | 7.5 | 1 | 1.64 |
| 10 | 704 | 8.1 | 0 | 5.35 |

NOTE: The fifth column shows the standard Euclidean distance of each loan from a candidate loan with FICO score of 709 and APR 6.2%.

The application of the 3-nearest neighbors algorithm in Example 5.5 is highly simplified. To be a serious competitor for logistic regression in predicting take-up in a real-world setting, it would require modification and tuning. In particular, the distances between different features need to be weighted—it could be that differences in APR are twice as important as differences in FICO score in predicting take-up. In this case, the best set of weights to use can be determined by regression. Furthermore, the value of $k$—the number of neighbors to consider—also needs to be determined. And, of course, additional variables chosen from those listed in Table 5.4 should be included in the determination of distance.

Although Example 5.5 is highly simplified, it illustrates some of the potential strengths and weaknesses of nonparametric approaches relative to regression. The great strength of a nonparametric approach such as kNN is that it does not require specification of a functional form. This enables the relationship between the features (e.g., APR and FICO score) and take-up to be much more flexible and determined entirely by the data rather than restricted to follow a particular functional form.

One of the drawbacks of many nonparametric approaches such as kNN is that they do not specify in general how the probability of take-up will vary for a particular loan as a function of price. However, the relationship between price and probability of take-up is exactly what we need to optimize price. This means that an additional step may be required to convert the output of a nonparametric approach into a price-response function. One way to do this is to use the nonparametric approach to predict the probability of take-up of the same loan at a range of different prices. A function can then be fitted to the results. This, however, requires an additional step between estimation and optimization.

Another issue is that the price-response function implied by many nonparametric approaches may not possess desirable qualities such as continuity or monotonicity. For example, kNN estimates of take-up probability are typically not continuous in price—the take-up probability predicted by kNN can jump discontinuously for a small change in price. In addition, it can be difficult with some nonparametric approaches to determine whether a property such as monotonicity holds everywhere, and it is often not clear what to do when it does not hold. These can be serious problems for price optimization. As we discuss in detail in Chapter 7, standard approaches to price optimization require price-response functions that are everywhere continuous and decreasing in price. While it is possible to impose conditions of monotonicity and continuity on nonparametric supervised learning approaches, this can be at the cost of predictive power. Finding ways to harness the predictive power of advanced nonparametric approaches such as neural nets and random forests while meeting the needs of effective optimization is a topic of ongoing research.

## Price Response in Two-Stage Price Quotation Processes

The discussion so far has assumed a single-stage price quotation process as shown in Figure 1.3, in which the lender quotes a price that a customer either accepts or reject. However, some lenders employ a two-stage process as shown in Figure 1.4, in which a borrower receives an initial quote prior to application and a final price only after her application is approved. The initial quote is based on limited information about a customer at the point of inquiry, whereas the final price can be based on additional information obtained from her application or other sources. Intuitively, the initial quote should always be lower than the final quote: otherwise the lender would be discouraging some customers from filling out an application by quoting an unnecessarily high price. This means that pricing in a two-stage process requires determining two quantities: an initial price to quote upon inquiry and a *loading* greater than or equal to 0 that is added to the initial quote once an application is accepted.

The initial price in a two-stage process should be the lowest price that would be offered to any customer based on the information available at inquiry. Thus, if no information is available about the creditworthiness of a customer at inquiry, the initial price should be the price that would be offered to the lowest-risk customers qualifying for that loan. If a customer decides to apply after receiving the initial price, then her actual risk can be estimated with the information on her application. If she qualifies for the loan, a loading may be added to the initial price to determine the final price. In the case of a two-stage process, price optimization requires estimates of customer response both to the initial price and to the loading.

Let $\mathbf{x}$ be the information available about a customer at the initial quote, and let $p(\mathbf{x})$ be the initial price based on that information. Let $\mathbf{y}$ represent the additional information obtained about a customer post-application, and let $\Delta p(\mathbf{x}, \mathbf{y}) \geq 0$ be the loading to be applied once $\mathbf{y}$ is known. A two-stage pricing-quotation process involves five steps:

1. A customer makes an inquiry and reveals information $\mathbf{x}$.
2. On the basis of $\mathbf{x}$, the lender quotes an initial price $p(\mathbf{x})$.
3. The customer either abandons the process (a *lost quote*) or fills out an application.
4. From the information in the application, the lender may decide that the customer is too risky and decide not to offer a loan. Alternatively, he could offer the loan at the original price $p(\mathbf{x})$ plus a loading $\Delta p(\mathbf{x}, \mathbf{y})$.

5. A successful applicant is quoted the final price $p(\mathbf{x}) + \Delta p(\mathbf{x}, \mathbf{y})$ and decides whether to take the loan.

If customers are only interested in the final price, $p(\mathbf{x}) + \Delta p(\mathbf{x}, \mathbf{y})$, then we can estimate price sensitivity at that price and determine the appropriate loading accordingly. It is possible, however, that customers have different levels of sensitivity to the initial price and the loading. In this case, the sensitivity to the loading needs to be estimated as a function of $\mathbf{y}$ and incorporated explicitly in optimization.

## Updating

The coefficients of a price-response function cannot simply be estimated once and then held constant for all time. Rather, the coefficients need to be updated over time in response to changing market and competitive conditions. Most lenders periodically update the coefficients of their price-response functions, typically quarterly or every six months. However, it is also important to reestimate coefficients whenever there has been a significant change in market or competitive conditions. It is particularly important to reestimate when market rates rise above or fall below levels that have been seen in the past. The estimation techniques described in this chapter are valid only near the range of prices in the historical data. For example, assume that, for the past five years, market rates for a loan have ranged between 5.00% and 7.00%. Now assume that, due to a rise in the federal funds rate, the market rate has jumped to 10.00% in the course of two months. In this case, it is likely that estimates of price response based on the historical data will not be valid in the new environment. The lender should monitor take-up carefully and reestimate price-sensitivity coefficients as soon as practical.

In addition to periodic updates, a prudent lender will continually compare actual loan take-up to the predictions of his model. This approach is part of the closed-loop pricing process shown in Figure 1.5. If the price-response model is predicting that take-up in a particular pricing segment should be 85% but actual take-up is only 65%, this is a signal that the price-sensitivity coefficients for that segment should be updated. However, it can be the case that price sensitivity within a segment may change in a way that is not reflected in changes in take-up rate. To the extent that it is feasible, the most prudent approach for a lender is to perform periodic price tests to ensure that current estimates of elasticity are still valid and, if not, to reestimate the coefficients of the price-response function.[8]

## DATA-FREE APPROACHES TO ESTIMATION

The approaches to price-sensitivity estimation that we have discussed so far rely on the existence of a database containing the outcome of a large number of loans offered at different rates. In some cases this data may not be available either because the product is too new to have generated a significant number of observations or because there is insufficient price variation in the data to support estimation. Some lenders are unable or unwilling to run price tests. In this case, it may be impossible to use data-driven approaches to estimate price sensitivity and alternative "data-free" approaches must be used. The most popular of these approaches include the following:

- *Surveys and focus groups*: Both surveys and focus groups can be used to elicit information about the importance of price relative to other aspects of a loan. Both rely on extrapolating information from a relatively small group to an entire population.

- *Conjoint analysis*: Conjoint analysis is a systematic method for eliciting customer trade-offs among price, brand, and other features. Each participant in a conjoint analysis study is given a series of choices between two different possible offerings with different features and prices. For example, a particular choice might be "Would you prefer a 20-year fixed mortgage of $100,000 at an APR of 5.5% or a 25-year $100,000 mortgage with an initial fixed APR 3.5% for a year converting to a variable rate mortgage at prime plus 2% after the first year?" For each choice presented, participants specify either which alternative they prefer or that they are indifferent between the two alternatives. To estimate price sensitivity, price must be included along with other attributes such as term, brand, and channel. The idea behind conjoint analysis is that, by structuring the alternatives and the sequence of choices appropriately, the preference structure of each participant can be determined with a relatively small number of questions. If a study includes a sufficient number of participants with backgrounds representative of the population as a whole, the results can be used to construct a price-response function for the entire population. Conjoint analysis has been widely used in designing and pricing new products across a wide range of industries, and there is extensive literature on how to conduct effective conjoint analyses.[9]

Data-free approaches to price-sensitivity estimation have one important strength: they can be used to elicit information about combinations of features and price that the lender has not previously offered. This is relevant for an entirely new product and may be important if market conditions have changed so dramatically that past customer behavior is not a reliable predictor of future behavior.

In contrast, data-free approaches have clear drawbacks. Surveys are subject to *response bias*: recipients who return a survey may not be representative of the population as a whole. For conjoint analyses, it may be difficult to obtain results from groups of participants who are both representative of the population as a whole and large enough to provide statistically reliable results. In addition, participants in surveys and focus groups often give the answer that reflects the choice that they think they should make rather than the choice that they actually would make in the real world. Finally, surveys and conjoint analyses typically present choices in a structured manner ("How important is service to you in choosing a bank?" or "Would you prefer Loan X to Loan Y?") that does not necessarily reflect the way in which financial decisions arise and need to be addressed by consumers in the real world. As a result, mortgage preferences elicited through the highly structured process of conjoint analysis may not predict how a customer will actually choose a mortgage during the stressful and somewhat chaotic process of purchasing a new house. For these reasons, focus groups, surveys, and conjoint analysis can give a lender an idea of the general level at which prices should be set but optimization of the prices across a number of pricing segments typically requires a data-driven approach.

## SUMMARY

- The "gold standard" for estimating price response is the randomized price test. The goal of randomization is to isolate the effect of price on take-up by choosing test and control populations that are equivalent in terms of all other variables that might influence take-up. Ensuring this balance may require assigning participants to groups in a fashion that is not truly random.

- Many lenders find price testing to be difficult or impossible. As a result, the data used to estimate price response is usually derived either from (nonrandomized) A/B price tests and/or from "natural" dispersion in the pricing of historical loans. This dispersion might result from so-called natural experiments (accidents), from pricing discontinuities, or from field pricing discretion.

- Fitting a price-response function to the results of A/B price tests and/or historical take-up data is a problem of *Bernoulli* or *binary* regression. Many techniques have been developed for fitting response functions to binary data—the most common is *logistic regression*, which fits an S-shaped logistic price-response function to the data.

- To fit a price-response function to a data set on historical loan take-up, the data is divided into a *training set* and *test set*. For a particular set of candidate variables, regression is performed using the training set. The fit of the resulting model is measured on the test set using measures such as root mean squared error, concordance, and log-likelihood. Candidate models are tested by adding, transforming, combining, and removing predictive variables. Each time a new model is estimated, its performance on the test data is compared to the current champion. If the new model is more predictive, it becomes the new champion. This process continues until new models are no longer demonstrating improved performance.

- *Nonparametric approaches* do not require specification of a functional form—rather, they estimate take-up probability based entirely on the data. Some well-known nonparametric approaches to the supervised learning problem include neural nets, support vector machines, and k-nearest neighbors. While these approaches can be effective at predicting take-up, the outputs can be hard to interpret and their predictions do not necessarily follow the properties of continuity and monotonicity that are highly desirable for optimization.

- In estimating a price-response function, it is important to understand the underlying pricing process—in particular, how the price dispersion in the data was generated. If price dispersion is due to local price discretion, then the historical data should be tested for endogeneity; if endogeneity is present, a two-step process should be used to ensure that the price coefficient in the take-up model is unbiased.

- If historical data is not available or there is no price dispersion in historical data, then data-free methods such as surveys or conjoint analysis can be used. It is generally advisable that price testing be used to supplement these approaches moving forward so that price response is ultimately based on actual market observations.

## NOTES

1. The requirement that the treatment is the only difference between the test and control groups is enforced in medical research by the use of triple-blind trials in which neither the patient nor the administering physician nor those evaluating the results know which individuals belong to which group. This prevents patients from changing their behavior according to whether they are receiving the treatment or the placebo. It also prevents physicians from unconsciously providing a different level of care to a patient on the basis of whether that patient has been assigned to the treatment or control group. Finally, it prevents researchers from evaluating outcomes differently depending on whether a patient was in the control or test group.

2. Two instructive examples of the use of the difference-in-differences (DiD) method in retailing are Gallino and Moreno (2014), who use DiD to evaluate the effect of a "buy online, pickup in store" program for a retail chain, and Blake, Nosko, and Tadelis (2015), who use DiD to estimate the effectiveness of online advertisement purchases.

3. A good example of regression discontinuity design applied to price-sensitivity estimation can be found in Cohen et al. (2016), who use discontinuities in the surge multiplier that Uber applied to its base prices from time to time in order to estimate price elasticity at the discontinuity points.

4. The coefficients for the various models in Table 5.5 and the performance measures in Table 5.6 were calculated using a proprietary Excel add-in for logistic estimation developed by Columbia Business School. Coefficients and performance measures calculated using different programs may vary slightly from the values reported in the text.

5. Here, we use the term *negotiation* somewhat loosely. The F&I representative determines which price to offer and has the authority to negotiate, but the customer may assume that the first price offered is "take it or leave it" and may not counteroffer. Thus, the interaction between the lender and the customer may not include the give-and-take usually associated with the term *negotiation*.

6. Testing for endogeneity and developing estimation approaches that produce unbiased coefficient estimates in the presence of endogeneity has been one of the most active areas of research in econometrics and applied statistics over the past few decades. The control function approach was proposed by Rivers and Vuong (1988) and was applied to auto-lending data by Phillips, Simsek, and van Ryzin (2015). A survey of the literature found that the treatment of endogeneity was the primary source of difference among estimates of price sensitivity in similar industries (Bijmolt, Heerde, and Pieters 2005). A good overview of approaches to estimation in the presence of endogeneity is the book *Mostly Harmless Econometrics: An Empiricist's Companion,* by Angrist and Pischke (2009).

7. The comparison of endogeneity in auto lending and unsecured lending is from Phillips (2014).

8. Considerable research has been devoted to the topic of how often price tests should be performed to reestimate price-response curves. There is consensus that periodic price testing is important even when the take-up predictions of the current price-response estimators are accurate. For a discussion of the issues and references to the literature, see Özer and Phillips (2012).

9. A good, high-level introduction to conjoint analysis is *Getting Started with Conjoint Analysis*, by Bryan Orme (2009). For a survey of applications in marketing, see the article by Green and Srinivasan (1990).

# 6 PRICING SEGMENTATION

In marketing, the term *segmentation* generally refers to a classification of customers into categories based on their propensities for some behavior of interest such as clicking on an online ad or responding to a promotion. We use the term *pricing segmentation* to refer to a classification of *transactions* into pricing segments such that transactions within the same segment are assigned the same list price. Pricing segments can be based not only on customer attributes (e.g., FICO score) but also on loan attributes (e.g., term) and on the channel through which the transaction takes place. Thus, one pricing segment might consist of loans between $10,000 and $25,000 offered to customers with FICO scores between 700 and 750 who apply through the Internet, whereas another pricing segment might consist of loans above $35,000 offered to customers with FICO scores between 650 and 700 who applied through a branch. A *customer dimension* refers to any attribute of the customer (e.g., geography, FICO score) that is used as a factor in setting price, and a *product dimension* is any characteristic of the loan (e.g., term or size of loan) that is used as a factor in setting price. The collection of all customer and product dimensions plus channel (if it is considered in setting price) constitute the *pricing dimensions* for a lender.

Pricing dimensions may be discrete by nature, such as branch versus Internet or a new-car loan versus a used-car loan, or they may be numerical, such as FICO score or loan amount. Lenders typically divide continuous dimension into discrete ranges—called *buckets* or *tiers*—for purposes of segmentation. Examples of buckets include "all customers with FICO scores above 750" or "all loans between $20,000 and $39,999." A *pricing segment* is a combination of buckets. Every approved loan application can be mapped into exactly one pricing segment. The lender can quote a different list price to each pricing segment at the same time, and in the absence of field discretion, all approved applicants in the same pricing segment will be quoted the same price. The total number of pricing segments will be equal to product of the number of buckets along each dimension.

**Example 6.1: Pricing Segments.** An unsecured personal lender differentiates pricing by ten risk categories, five loan tiers, three channels, and four different terms. This lender needs to set prices for $10 \times 5 \times 3 \times 4 = 600$ pricing segments.

Multiplying the number of buckets in each pricing dimension together gives only an upper bound to the number of actual pricing segments because loans may not be offered to every combination of pricing dimension. For example, a lender may offer only loans less than $50,000 to customers with FICO scores below 680 while offering loans up to $100,000 for customers with higher FICO scores.

Determining which dimensions to use in pricing and how to bucket the numerical dimensions are key decisions for a lender. Increasing the number of pricing segments by adding new pricing dimensions or by dividing existing dimensions into smaller buckets will provide more opportunity to increase revenue and profit by enabling more targeted pricing. However, increasing the number of pricing segments increases complexity and requires more effort to maintain, update, and communicate prices. The logical limit of adding more and more dimensions and dividing them into finer and finer buckets is the market of one, in which a price is calculated individually for each customer. We discuss some of the issues associated with market-of-one pricing later in this chapter.

In practice, most lenders stop well short of market-of-one pricing. Rather, they divide each dimension into a relatively small number of buckets. However, if there are a large number of pricing dimensions, the number of pricing segments can become quite large. For example, a lender in the United States varied home-equity prices with customer risk, geography, loan-to-value ratio, term, size of loan, lien position, and relationship, among other dimensions, resulting in more than two million pricing segments.

A lender should consider three factors when choosing a pricing segmentation:

1. Pricing segments can be based only on information that is known to the lender when the price is quoted.

2. Each pricing dimension should be correlated either with price sensitivity or with incremental profitability, or both.

3. Pricing dimensions should include only characteristics that the lender is willing to use in setting prices.

Different lenders set different pricing segmentations for the same product. Furthermore, a lender typically sets different pricing segments for different products: a lender will usually use different pricing segments for mortgages than for auto loans. Typically, lenders change their pricing segmentations quite infrequently: a pricing segmentation may stay in place for years. For this reason, it is important for a lender to think carefully about his pricing segmentation. A lender should have a set of pricing segments in place for a product that allows him to target prices effectively without incurring undue complexity.

In this chapter we show how pricing segmentation can generate additional profit compared to "one price fits all" pricing. We discuss the dimensions most commonly used in lending and how each of these dimensions is correlated with price sensitivity or incremental profit (or both). We discuss the challenges involved in moving from segmented pricing to market-of-one pricing. Finally, we discuss how pricing segmentation can be used to create strategic advantage in a competitive environment.

## THE ECONOMICS OF PRICING SEGMENTATION

There are three reasons a lender might want to offer different prices to different pricing segments:

1.  Different segments have different levels of incremental profitability at the same price. All else being equal, a lender should charge lower prices to a segment with higher incremental profit per funded loan than one with lower incremental profit per funded loan.
2.  Different segments demonstrate different levels of price sensitivity. All else being equal, a segment that is more price sensitive should be quoted a lower price than a group that is less price sensitive for the same loan.
3.  The lender might wish to offer a lower rate to some customers in order to meet a business goal other than maximizing expected profitability. For example, a lender might offer a lower rate for customers who apply via the Internet because the lender wishes to encourage the use of that channel.

In this section, we focus on the first two reasons—improving profitability by setting prices based on systematic differences in incremental profitability and/or willingness to pay among pricing segments. How prices can be used to achieve alternative goals for different segments is described in Chapter 7.

In Chapter 5 we showed how the variation of willingness to pay among customers gives rise to a price-response curve. One purpose of pricing segmentation is to separate customers with a higher willingness to pay from those with a lower willingness to pay and to target prices accordingly. To see how this can generate additional profit, consider the case of a lender who can offer only a single price to a population with a linear price-response curve $d(p) = mp - b$ and a unit cost of $c$. A profit-maximizing lender will choose the price $p^*$, shown in the left-hand graph in Figure 6.1. His profit will be proportional to the area of the shaded rectangle. This is the most profit that can be generated using a single price.

A "one price fits all" policy always leaves money on the table. In Figure 6.1, there are some customers who would have paid more than $p^*$ for the loan but were happy to take it

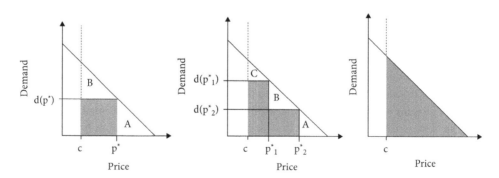

**Figure 6.1**   Three levels of pricing segmentation: a single price (*left*), two prices (*center*), and a different price for each customer (*right*)

at $p^*$. The profit that could have realized had these customers been charged their individual willingness to pay rather than $p^*$ is equal to the area of triangle $A$ in Figure 6.1. In addition, there are customers whose willingness to pay is greater than $c$ but less than $p^*$. These customers would be willing to take the loan at a rate higher than the cost, but they are not willing to pay $p^*$. If the lender were able to offer the loan to these customers at their individual willingnesses to pay, he would realize additional profit equal to the area of triangle $B$ in Figure 6.1.[1]

Assume that the lender can offer two prices $c < p_1^* < p_2^*$ and that he can perform perfect segmentation—that is, when a customer arrives, the lender can ascertain that customer's exact willingness to pay and can offer her the price $p_1^*$ or $p_1^*$ that is closest to her willingness to pay without exceeding it. This situation is illustrated in the middle graph in Figure 6.1. The lender's profit is proportional to the shaded area, and the money left on the table is the sum of the three triangles $A$, $B$, and $C$. By choosing the right values of $p_1^*$ and $p_2^*$, the lender can clearly realize higher profit than with a single price. However, with any finite number of prices, the lender will still leave money on the table. The ideal case from the lender's point of view occurs when he can determine the willingness to pay of each customer and can quote a different price to each customer—market-of-one pricing. In this case, a profit-maximizing lender will charge each customer a price exactly equal to her willingness to pay and each customer will accept. (For simplicity, we consider only customers whose willingness to pay is greater than the cost of the loan.) The result is shown on the right-hand graph in Figure 6.1, in which the lender is able to suck up all of the available profit and no money is left on the table.

The benefits from segmentation can be substantial. A lender facing a linear price-response curve such as the one shown in Figure 6.1 can increase his profit by 33.33% by establishing two segments and charging two prices relative to charging a single price to the entire population. If the lender were able to price each customer according to her willingness to pay—market-of-one pricing—then he could double his profits relative to charging a single price. This provides a strong economic motivation for retailers of all kinds—including lenders—to segment their customers according to willingness to pay and charge a different price to each segment.

So why do all sellers not utilize market-of-one pricing all of the time? One important reason is that it is impossible for a seller to determine the exact willingness to pay of each customer. Second, a seller may not be able to charge a different price to every single customer because of regulations, business considerations, or limitations in the price quotation system. Third, for many sellers, the possibility of *arbitrage* limits the opportunity for price segmentation: customers who are charged a lower price could resell to customers who were quoted a higher price and pocket the difference.

Retail lenders typically do not need to worry too much about arbitrage. However, even with all of the data that might conceivably be available, the willingness to pay of a particular customer for a particular loan is impossible to determine with certainty—and probably always will be. In addition to observable attributes such as credit score and geography, the willingness to pay of a particular customer depends on—among other things—her level of financial sophistication, whether or not she likes dealing with a particular lender, her urgency to obtain the loan, other sources of credit available to her, and many other factors that are unobservable.

Regulatory, business, and infrastructural constraints also limit the extent to which many lenders can segment their transactions. In most countries, regulatory agencies have specified that certain characteristics cannot be used in pricing and/or underwriting decisions. In the United States, the Equal Credit Opportunity Act (ECOA) prohibits disparate treatment based on race, national origin, gender, and religion, among other factors. Furthermore, even if a customer characteristic could be used as a pricing segmentor, a lender may choose not to use it. For example, strength of relationship is a logical customer dimension to use in pricing segmentation—customers with a stronger relationship to a lender will be less price sensitive. The logical implication is that loyal customers should be charged higher rates than new customers. However, many lenders may choose not to set higher prices for their loyal customers.

Despite these limitations, lenders still have considerable opportunity to segment prices. Some of the most commonly used segmentation dimensions are shown in Table 6.1. In the following three sections, we discuss the most common pricing dimensions in lending and how they are used to differentiate prices.

## CUSTOMER DIMENSIONS

Customers vary dramatically both in cost to serve and price sensitivity. Many of these differences are systematic and correlated with observable customer characteristics. However, taking advantage of these differences through differentiated pricing is often difficult, not only in lending but also in many retail businesses. In many cases it is illegal, inadvisable, or both to vary price directly on certain characteristics such as race, gender, or religion. As discussed in Chapter 1, lenders typically face more stringent antidiscrimination regulations than other retailers because access to affordable credit is considered a social good and many governments believe that regulation is necessary to provide equal access to affordable credit

TABLE 6.1
*Common pricing segmentation dimensions*

| Category | Dimension | Comment |
|---|---|---|
| Customer | Risk | Less risky customers tend to be more price sensitive and have lower expected cost than more risky customers. |
| | Age | Older customers tend to be more price sensitive than younger customers. |
| | Geography | Customers in areas with more competition tend to be more price sensitive. |
| | Relationship | Customers who have a longer relationship with a lender or have more products with that lender tend to be less price sensitive than new customers. |
| Product | Loan size | Customers applying for large loans tend to be more price sensitive than those applying for smaller loans. |
| | Term | Longer-term loans tend to be more price sensitive than shorter-term. |
| | Loan-to-value ratio | Higher loan-to-value (LTV) and combined loan-to-value (CLTV) loans are riskier and borrowers tend to be less price sensitive. |
| Channel | Channel | Customers applying for a loan through the Internet tend to be more price sensitive than those applying through other channels. |

for minorities or other disadvantaged groups. However, even in the absence of regulation, lenders can be sensitive to perceptions of unfair pricing. The issue of perceived fairness in pricing is discussed in more detail in Chapter 8.

The combination of regulatory scrutiny and customer sensitivity means that, in practice, opportunities for direct price segmentation in lending are limited. Risk, age, geography, and lender relationship are the mostly commonly used customer pricing dimensions. We discuss each one in some detail.

## Risk

The risk associated with a loan is a major component of its variable cost. As a consequence, many lenders have adopted risk-based pricing to charge higher prices to more risky customers. As discussed in Chapter 2, lower-risk customers are not only more profitable on an incremental profit basis; they are also more price sensitive. The correlation between price sensitivity and risk can also be measured and used to inform pricing.

We can illustrate the effect of risk on customer price sensitivity using the e-Car data. Note that the logarithm of FICO score, ln(*FICO*), enters as a significant explanatory variable of take-up in the e-Car data in the champion Model 4. As shown in Table 5.5, the coefficient of ln(*FICO*) is less than 0, which means that, all else (including price) being equal, customers with high FICO scores are less likely to take up a loan than customers with lower FICO scores. Figure 6.2 shows the take-up rate predicted by Model 4 as a function of FICO score for a new-car loan of $20,000 offered at a 7.0% rate, assuming that the cost of funds is 1.8% and the competition rate is 6.0%. Predicted take-up declines from about 69% at *FICO* = 600 to about 31% at *FICO* = 840. In this case, risk has a dramatic effect on expected take-up. This relationship between risk and price sensitivity is also responsible for the phenomenon of price-dependent risk as discussed in Chapter 4.

Because low-risk customers are less costly and more price sensitive than higher-risk customers, it is optimal for a profit-maximizing lender to charge a smaller margin to the low-risk customers, all else being equal.

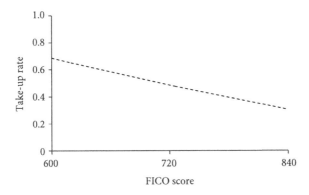

**Figure 6.2** Predicted take-up as a function of FICO score for a new-car loan of $20,000 at a 7.0% rate, assuming a cost of funds of 1.8% and a competition rate of 6.0%, as predicted by Model 4 in Table 5.5

## Age

In many markets, including lending, the price sensitivity of customers varies with age in a predictable fashion. All else being equal, customers younger than approximately 25 and customers older than approximately 60 tend to be more price sensitive than customers between those ages. This pattern has been observed in a wide range of markets and provides one explanation for the common use of student discounts and senior discounts in a variety of different markets.

The relationship between age and price sensitivity is probably due in part to differences in propensity to shop. Younger people, especially students, tend to be willing to spend more time shopping for lower prices because the opportunity cost of their time is low. As people grow older and take on jobs and the responsibility of raising children, the opportunity cost of their time goes up and they may spend less time price shopping. After retirement, the opportunity cost of a customer's time decreases and customers are willing to spend more time shopping for rates. An alternative (or additional) explanation for the greater price sensitivity displayed by those older than 60 is that customers become more savvy in dealing with financial institutions as they gain life experience and learn to shop more effectively for better rates. A Nomis Solutions analysis of unsecured consumer loans in the United Kingdom found much higher rate sensitivity in customers older than 60 years of age than those between 35 and 60.

Consistent variation in price sensitivity with age has been observed in many different loan products across different countries. The ability of a lender to take advantage of these differences through age-based segmentation varies across jurisdictions. In the United States, it is illegal to set different loan prices based on age. For this reason, *Age* is not included as an explanatory variable in any of the e-Car models listed in Table 5.5. In the United Kingdom and other countries it is legal to differentiate prices on the basis of age and lenders routinely do so.

## Geography

Geography is a common pricing dimension. International banks offer different rates in different countries reflecting national differences in cost of capital and inflation rates. Loan prices also can also vary among regions within a country. As an example, Table 6.2 shows the different average market rates for different home equity loans in different regions of the United States in June 2015. In addition to differences among regions, loan prices may also vary between rural and urban areas. Geographical price variation typically reflects variation in competitive intensity as well as differences in demographic makeup and average risk for regions.

Differences in the prevailing rates among regions such as those shown in Table 6.2 are sufficient motivation in themselves for a lender to include geography as a pricing dimension. However, there is an additional reason regional pricing can be important—namely, the fact that a lender is likely to have different competitive positions in different regions. A lender may have a strong brand and branch presence in some regions and a weaker brand and branch presence in others. In the regions in which the lender's position is strong, he can

TABLE 6.2
*Average rates for a 30-year fixed $250,000 home-equity loan at
80% LTV for a customer with a 740 FICO score for four states on
June 24, 2015*

| State | Rate (%) |
| --- | --- |
| California | 4.215 |
| Illinois | 4.194 |
| New York | 4.163 |
| Texas | 4.206 |

SOURCE: ICON Advisory Group.

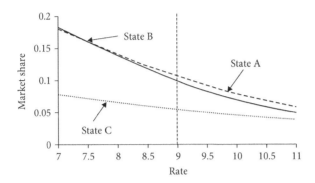

**Figure 6.3**   Market share as a function of price for a home-equity loan offered by a lender in three different states

SOURCE: Nomis Solutions.

generate the same level of business at higher prices than in regions in which his competitive position is weak.

Figure 6.3 shows the estimated price-response for an American home-equity lender in three different states. This lender was long established in states A and B and had a strong branch presence in those states. However, the lender had only recently entered state C through the acquisition of a small bank and had a much smaller branch presence and brand recognition in that state. Not surprisingly, the lender could achieve a higher market share in states A and B than in state C at the same rate—this is one of the benefits that the lender realized for investing in his brand and his branch network in those states.

The variation in price response shown in Figure 6.3 can be explained by the lender's competitive position in each of the three states. In shopping for a home-equity loan, many people consider their primary bank first—in fact, many customers apply only to their primary bank for a loan. Customers who apply to more than one lender are likely, at least in part, to be price shopping. Because the lender in Figure 6.3 had a relatively small market presence in state C, it is likely that most of its loan applicants were already customers of that lender. However, the lender's stronger presence in states A and B means that a larger proportion of those who applied for loans in those states were considering the lender as their second or third alternative in addition to their primary bank. These customers may actually be more price sensitive because they are considering multiple options and the lender is not their primary bank.

Regulation often limits the extent to which lenders can differentiate prices within a region. In the United States, the practice of using neighborhood in underwriting decisions—so-called *redlining*—was prohibited because it was deemed discriminatory against minorities and other protected groups. The Federal Financial Institutions Examination Council (FFIEC 1999, i) specifies that mortgage lenders cannot "discriminate on a prohibited basis because of . . . the neighborhood or other area where property to be financed is located." In addition to regulation, lenders often wish to maintain consistent pricing among branches within a region to prevent the same customer from getting quoted different prices for the same loan at different branches. For these reasons, lenders often choose not to differentiate prices at the lowest possible geographical level. Rather, they may vary prices at a higher geographical level—for example, by rural versus urban locations or by Canadian province. The US Census Bureau has classified urban areas into 388 metropolitan statistical areas, or MSAs. Some lenders differentiate loan prices at the MSA level. This enables them to set prices that take account of competitive differences among different metropolitan regions without running the risk of being viewed as discriminating against individual neighborhoods within a city.

## Relationship

Customer loyalty is highly correlated with price sensitivity. Simply put, a lender's loyal customers are his least price sensitive. This holds true whether loyalty is measured by tenure (years as a customer), number of products, number of renewals, or any other metric. The correlation between loyalty and price sensitivity should not be too surprising: customers are loyal for a reason—there is something they like about their favorite lender that keeps loyal customers coming back. There are at least six reasons a customer might display loyalty to a lender:

1. *Quality.* A customer may rate the quality of a lender's product or service higher than competing alternatives. This may be due to the lender's brand strength or to real (or perceived) aspects of the lender's offering. To the extent that a customer values higher quality, they are likely to be less sensitive to price.

2. *Uniqueness.* A lender may have an offering that is not available elsewhere. Customers who value this offering will appear to be loyal simply because they have no alternative.

3. *Convenience.* A lender may be the most convenient alternative for a customer (e.g., nearest branch).

4. *Loyalty program.* A customer might be a member of a loyalty program that rewards her for repeat business.

5. *Inertia.* A customer might appear loyal simply because she has not taken the time or effort to research alternatives.

6. *Switching costs.* The cost or effort required to switch lenders—perhaps paying off a loan and taking out a new one—may be sufficiently high to encourage a customer to remain with her current lender, even if the price is higher than some competitors.

Nomis analysis of certificate of deposit (CD) renewal data from banks in the United Kingdom, Canada, and the United States has shown that the number of times that a customer has previously renewed a CD is negatively correlated with price sensitivity. Customers who have renewed a CD many times are far less price sensitive than new customers or those who have renewed only once or twice. This dependence is quite strong and is consistent across countries. The relationship also holds for lending: studies of loan customers in Canada have shown that customer price sensitivity is strongly correlated both to tenure (the length of the customer's relationship with the bank) and to depth of relationship (number of products the customer had with the bank). Customers with longer tenure and deeper relationships are less price sensitive than those with short tenure or those who hold fewer products.

Customers can be divided into three broad groups based on loyalty:

1. *Defectors.* Those who were previously customers of a lender but are no longer using any products from that lender.

2. *New customers.* Those who have never used a lender's services before.

3. *Existing customers.* Active customers.

Defectors are the most price-sensitive group. In all likelihood, a customer defected for a reason and will require especially low prices to be lured back. New customers fall into two categories. The first category consists of those who are shopping for a financial service provider for the first time. These customers are likely to be comparison shopping and require a lower rate to be captured. The second category consists of current customers of competing banks. All of the factors that make these customers less sensitive to their current lender's prices make them more sensitive to another lender's. Finally, existing customers are less price sensitive than either defectors or new customers.[2]

The implication of the relationship between loyalty and price sensitivity is that a lender who wants to maximize short-term profit should charge higher prices to loyal customers and lower prices to new customers and defectors. Yet charging higher rates to loyal customers flies in the face of the idea held by most customers (and many bank employees) that loyalty should be "rewarded" with lower prices rather than "punished" with higher prices. This is the *paradox of loyalty.*

There are a number of ways that lenders—like other retailers—deal with the paradox of loyalty. A common approach is to offer an introductory low rate for 6 months or a year. Promotions can be specifically targeted to new customers or defectors—"We want you back and are willing to prove it!" These promotions may be in the form of a lower initial rate, waived fees, or even cash. All of these approaches are ways to offer lower rates to new customers or defectors than to existing customers. While the overall effect of such introductory discounts is that existing customers pay higher rates than new customers, the fact that the difference is framed as a discount means that it is generally not perceived as unfair. This shows the importance of proper *framing*, which we discuss in more detail in Chapter 8.

### Other Customer Dimensions

Without much difficulty, most lenders could name additional customer characteristics that are correlated with price sensitivity. However, for many of these characteristics, it is impossible, illegal, or unwise (or some combination of the three) to use the characteristic as a pricing dimension. For this reason, lenders—like most retailers—perform additional customer segmentation *indirectly*, by targeting promotional offers to groups on the basis of price sensitivity. Thus, a promotional credit card offer could be mailed to neighborhoods with certain demographics. Or online advertising for a broadly available promotion could be targeted to a certain demographic—such as married couples between the ages of 30 and 50. The messaging in the advertising campaign could be tailored to appeal to that group and the lender could purchase online impressions specifically for that group. Thus, although the promotion might be available to everyone, the lender drives higher awareness and, ideally, greater take-up from the targeted group.

Recently, there has been considerable interest in the potential to use social network data such as Facebook messages and Twitter feeds to better segment customers and thereby target product and promotion offers with more precision. The online lender Kreditech uses social network data to evaluate the creditworthiness of loan applicants from regions where traditional credit scoring and other measures are not widely available—the "4 billion people without credit scores" as their website describes. Part of the evaluation relies on Facebook friends, the idea being that someone whose friends are all creditworthy is likely to be creditworthy herself. It may be the case that a similar phenomenon holds for price sensitivity: a customer whose "friends" are highly price sensitive is likely to be more price sensitive than a customer whose friends are less press sensitive. The extent to which such correlations can be detected in social network data and, more importantly, if they could be utilized to differentiate loan prices remains to be seen.

### PRODUCT DIMENSIONS

Charging different prices for different products is far less controversial than charging different prices to different customers for the same product. For that reason, product differentiation plays a major role in loan pricing. In this section, we discuss three common lending product segmentation dimensions—loan size, term, and loan-to-value ratio—and how they influence optimal pricing. We also discuss the potential for virtual products in lending.

### Loan Size

It is common practice for lenders to offer lower rates for larger loans. In part, this reflects cost differentials—servicing costs are a smaller fraction of the loan amount for a larger loan. However, in most cases servicing costs are a very small fraction of variable lending costs. The primary reason that lower rates are offered for larger loans is that customers applying for large loans tend to be more price sensitive than those applying for smaller loans. This is intuitive—customers naturally tend to spend more time rate shopping for a larger loan than a smaller one.

Differential take-up as a function of loan size can be seen in the coefficients of ln(*Amount*) in Model 4 in Table 5.5. The coefficient of the logarithm of the loan amount is both significant and negative. This indicates that, everything else being equal, the take-up rate will be lower for larger loans than smaller loans. Figure 6.4 shows expected take-up as a function of interest rate for three different sizes of loan: $10,000, $25,000, and $50,000 as predicted by Model 4. At every rate, the take-up for the $10,000 loan is higher than for the $25,000 loan, which is in turn higher than the take-up rate for the $50,000 loan. The effect of loan size on take-up can be quite significant: at an interest rate of 6.0%, the take-up rate for a $10,000 loan is estimated to be 82%, compared to a take-up rate of only 14% for the $50,000 loan. The strength of this relationship provides a strong motivation for lenders to charge lower rates for larger loans.

## Term

Everything else being equal, customers applying for longer-term loans will tend to be more sensitive to rate than customers applying for shorter-term loans. There are at least two reasons for this:

1. For the same price and initial balance, the monthly payment for a longer-term loan is lower than for a shorter-term loan. As a result, everything else being equal, more price-sensitive customers will be attracted to longer-term loans. This is a *selection effect*.

2. A fractional change in the APR of a longer-term loan results in a higher fractional change in monthly payment than the same change in a shorter-term loan. Both the absolute change in monthly payment and the percentage change are smaller for the shorter-term loan. Customers who are focused on monthly payment will respond more strongly to the same fractional change in the rate of a long-term loan than in the rate of a shorter-term loan. This is a *leverage effect*.

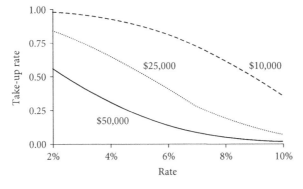

**Figure 6.4**   Take-up for new-car loans of size $10,000, $25,000, and $50,000 as a function of price, as predicted by Model 4 in Table 5.5, for a customer with a FICO score of 700, assuming a cost of funds of 1.8% and competitor rate of 6.0%

The *payment elasticity* of a simple loan is the percentage increase in monthly payment resulting from a 1% increase in APR. Thus, if a loan with an APR of 6.0% has a payment elasticity of .5, it means that increasing the rate by 1% (from 6.0% to 6.6%) will result in a 0.5% increase in the monthly payment.

**Example 6.2: Payment Elasticity and Term.** The monthly payment for a 1-year simple loan of $10,000 with an APR of 6.00% is $860.66. The monthly payment for the same loan at the same rate is $193.33 if the term is increased to 5 years. If we raise the APR from 6.0% to 7.0% (a 16.67% increase), the monthly payment for the 5-year loan increases by $4.68 to $198.01 (a 2.42% increase) while the payment for the 1-year loan increases by $4.60 to $865.27 (only a .54% increase). The payment elasticity for the 1-year loan is .54/16.67 = .03, whereas the payment elasticity for the 5-year loan is 2.42/16.67 = .15.

Payment elasticity is very small for short-term loans and increases with both rate and term. Table 6.3 shows the payment elasticities for a simple loan at different annual rates and terms. (Payment elasticity for a simple loan depends only on rate and term—it does not depend on the balance). As can be seen, payment elasticity depends very strongly on term: it is more than 10 times as high for a 30-year loan than for a 1-year loan for the range of APRs shown. This means that, everything else being equal, an equal percentage change has a greater relative impact on the monthly payment of a long-term loan than a shorter-term loan. To the extent that customers base their loan choice on monthly payment, they will appear to be more sensitive to changes in the price of long-term loans than short-term loans.

Because customers applying for longer-term loans are more price sensitive than those applying for shorter-term loans, everything else being equal, it is logical to quote them lower prices. However, this is counterbalanced by the fact that longer-term loans tend to be more risky than shorter-term loans. Long-term loans are risky partly because the longer term means a greater likelihood that the borrower will be subject to an adverse circumstance leading to default during the term of the loan. However, longer-term loans are also subject to adverse selection: customers who choose longer-term loans tend to be riskier than those choosing shorter-term loans. Part of the challenge of price optimization is to balance these two effects to find the price that maximizes expected profitability for each term.

TABLE 6.3
*Payment elasticities for different combinations of term
and APR*

| APR | TERM (MONTHS) | | | |
|---|---|---|---|---|
| | *12* | *60* | *120* | *360* |
| 1 | 0.01 | 0.03 | 0.05 | 0.14 |
| 5 | 0.03 | 0.12 | 0.23 | 0.57 |
| 10 | 0.05 | 0.23 | 0.39 | 0.84 |
| 20 | 0.09 | 0.42 | 0.69 | 0.98 |

## Loan-to-Value Ratio

The *loan-to-value ratio* (LTV) is the amount of a secured loan divided by the value of the collateral. If a customer holds multiple loans secured with the same collateral, then the *combined loan-to-value ratio* (CLTV) is the sum of the loan balances divided by the value of the collateral.

---

**Example 6.3: LTV and CLTV.** A $50,000 mortgage on a property valued at $100,000 has a loan-to-value ratio of 50%. A $50,000 mortgage and a home equity loan of $10,000 both collateralized with the same property valued at $100,000 corresponds to a CLTV of 60%.

---

Both LTV and CLTV are typically used in estimating the risk associated with a loan: higher-LTV and higher-CLTV loans are riskier. However, LTV and CLTV are also correlated with price sensitivity: customers with a higher LTV or CLTV tend to be less price sensitive than those with a lower LTV or CLTV. This is consistent with the hypothesis that customers with a higher LTV or CLTV need the loan more badly and are willing to leverage their assets to a greater extent to obtain the money. For the same reason, high LTV or CLTV borrowers also tend to be riskier. Because higher LTV or CLTV customers are both riskier and less price sensitive than customers with lower LTV or CLTV, it is profitable to charge them more.

## Product Differentiation and Virtual Products

As we have seen, loan characteristics such as size, term, and loan-to-value ratio influence price sensitivity in consistent and predictable fashions. Furthermore, it is generally easier and less controversial for lenders to differentiate prices along product dimensions than customer dimensions. For this reason, it makes sense for lenders to differentiate pricing along product dimensions, and in fact, most consumer lenders do so. However, it is important to realize that, in many industries, differentiating prices by product is, in reality, a mechanism for segmenting *customers* according to their willingness to pay or, more accurately, how their willingness to pay is influenced by product features. Specifically, price differences among products should reflect the different price sensitivities of the customers for those products as much (or more) than differences in product costs. This means that *product differentiation* can be an effective approach to customer segmentation.

To see how retailers use product differentiation, consider the case of a car rental company that offers three types of cars for rent: compact, midsize, and full size. It is likely that the daily unit operating cost of each of these cars is roughly the same—say $12 a day. The full-size automobile may have cost more to purchase, but its purchase cost is sunk at the time of rental and is irrelevant to the rental price. However, the car rental company might charge $70 per day for the full-size car, $50 per day for the midsize, and $25 per day for the compact. Since there are very little or no differences in incremental cost among the three options, the differences in price must be due to differential price sensitivity. The full-size car appeals to customers who need a full-size car because of the number of passengers and those who value the perceived higher quality of the larger car. For this reason, customers who prefer the full-size car are likely to be less price sensitive than those choosing the compact car, and rental car companies accordingly charge more.[3]

The first step in product differentiation is to create a menu of products for customers to choose from. The products may have similar or identical unit variable costs—however, the margin applied reflects the differential price sensitivity of the customers attracted to a particular alternative. Since customers choose the product they wish to purchase, this approach seems fairer than pricing differentiation based directly on customer attributes. Product segmentation is also appealing to lenders because it is less likely to draw regulatory scrutiny than customer segmentation.

The logical conclusion of product differentiation is the creation of *virtual products*, for which the difference in products is artificially imposed by the seller and does not reflect any difference in costs. Airline pricing is a classic example: to compete with discount carriers, traditional airlines differentiated their base product—air transportation from point A to point B—into business-class and discount-class products. The discount-class product was sold at a low price but required booking two weeks in advance and a Saturday-night stay, whereas the business-class product had no such restrictions but was sold at a higher price. The distinction between the two products was not based on differences in variable cost but was imposed primarily as a way to differentially price highly price-sensitive leisure travelers who could meet the early booking and Saturday-night stay restrictions and price-insensitive business travelers who often needed to book closer to departure and were not willing to stay over Saturday night. Creating these virtual products enabled airlines to realize the primary goal of price differentiation: charging lower prices to customers who are more price sensitive and higher prices to customers who are more price sensitive without directly differentiating prices among customers.[4]

How might a lender create virtual products? Consider the fact that almost a quarter (23%) of respondents to a 2015 survey on mortgage satisfaction said that they would be willing to pay a premium for a speedier process. On average, these customers were willing to pay $1,448 extra for faster processing of their mortgage applications. A lender that could reliably process loan applications more quickly could potentially charge more—at least to some customers. The virtual product strategy would be to offer "premium processing" for an extra fee. This would allow customers to segment themselves into the price sensitive who prefer to save money and don't mind waiting longer and the speed sensitive who are willing to pay more for faster service.[5]

Offering a premium processing product would pose an operation challenge for many lenders. For a premium processing strategy to succeed, a lender would need to sustain a real difference in processing time between standard and premium service. This may require that the lender deliberately delay processing of some standard applications. Otherwise, the distinction between the virtual products will disappear. Freight carriers offering expedited services have faced a similar dilemma—operationally, it is often most efficient (and seems fairest to customers) to ship everything on hand as quickly as possible. However, a freight carrier that wants to maintain a price difference between standard and expedited shipping may need to leave some standard packages on the terminal dock even when there is capacity to carry them in a departing truck—otherwise, the quality differential between the two levels of service would disappear.

## CHANNEL

The channel through which a customer approaches a lender is an indicator of price sensitivity. Everything else being equal, customers who approach through the Internet are more price sensitive than customers who call into a call center. Call-center customers are in turn more price sensitive than customers who approach through a branch. Such variations in channel price sensitivity are likely due to a combination of a *selection effect* and a *switching cost effect*. The selection effect arises from the fact that more price-sensitive customers are likely to do more price shopping than less price-sensitive customers, and the Internet and telephone are easier ways to comparison shop than is visiting different branches. The switching cost effect is due to the fact that refusing the current offer and finding an alternative is easiest on the Internet, slightly less easy via telephone, and most difficult at a branch.

Differential price sensitivity across channels implies that, all else being equal, the profit-maximizing rate to offer a customer on the Internet is lower than the profit-maximizing rate to offer to an identical customer in a branch. This may or may not be consistent with the channel strategy of the lender—if the lender wishes to encourage online interaction to reduce branch costs, then he should price Internet loans more cheaply. Some lenders, however, would like to encourage branch visits or maintain channel neutrality with respect to pricing. In this case, a lender can specify in the optimization process that identical loans offered to identical customers should be priced the same on the Internet as in a branch. Alternatively, a lender could simply not include channel as a pricing dimension.

Customers who use a mortgage broker tend to be more price sensitive than those who approach a bank directly. This is probably due to both a selection effect (more price-sensitive customers tend to use brokers) and a loyalty effect—at least some customers who apply directly to a lender have a preference for that lender while customers who apply through a broker are likely to be indifferent to the choice of lender. On the Internet, customers who arrive directly to a lender's website tend to be less price sensitive than those who arrive to the website through a third-party site or via an online aggregator. For example, in the e-Car data, customers who approach through e-Car's online partner (*Partner* = 2) or from another website (*Partner* = 3) have significantly lower take-up, all else being equal, than customers who come directly to the e-Car website (*Partner* = 1).

The implication of differential channel price sensitivity is that, all else being equal, lenders should quote lower rates to customers who arrive through more price-sensitive channels such as the Internet than those who arrive through less price-sensitive channels such as a branch. The lower variable and handling costs associated with the Internet may be an additional reason for offering lower prices through that channel.

## MARKET-OF-ONE PRICING

The logical limit of adding more and more pricing dimensions and more and more buckets in each dimension is *market-of-one pricing*, in which all the information available for a loan application that can be used for pricing is used. In market-of-one pricing there are no pricing segments. Instead, when an application is accepted, the information from the application and all other available sources is used to estimate the price sensitivity and expected profitability for the transaction. An optimal price is then calculated for each transaction in real time. Under market-of-one pricing, three customers who are otherwise identical but have slightly different FICO scores—say 719, 720, and 721—could conceivably be quoted three different rates for exactly the same loan through the same channel. Market-of-one pricing represents the most granular level of pricing possible and, at least in theory, should provide a higher level of expected profit than any finite price-segmentation scheme.

Figure 6.5 shows optimal market-of-one prices compared to historical prices for the e-Car data; e-Car had based its historical pricing segmentation on credit score, size of loan, and term, resulting in a total of 32 pricing segments. The horizontal axis in Figure 6.5 is the rate that e-Car offered to each approved application, and the vertical axis is the optimal (profit-maximizing) price calculated for each transaction using every piece of information in the e-Car Data Set. Entries below the 45-degree line were priced too high relative to the market-of-one price, and those above the 45-degree line were priced too low. Each vertical "column" in the figure corresponds to accepted applications in one of the existing pricing segments—all of which were quoted the same price.

Figure 6.5 reveals several interesting insights. First of all, in this case, market-of-one pricing did not greatly increase pricing dispersion. With the exception of a few outliers, the optimal rates ranged from about 5.0% to about 14.25%, while e-Car had actually quoted rates ranging from about 3.75% to about 11.25%. Second, there was very significant variation in optimal rates within each pricing segment, indicating that the pricing segments that were being used by e-Car were not well aligned with the market. Finally, e-Car was systematically underpricing Tier 1 and Tier 2 (low-risk) loans while somewhat overpricing Tier 7 (high-risk) loans.

By calculating the optimal price for each transaction, market-of-one pricing has the potential to generate higher profits than any finite segmentation scheme. However, market-of-one pricing requires a significantly different pricing and quote architecture than most

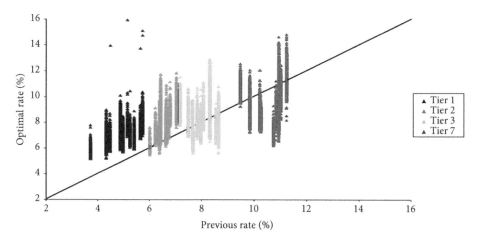

**Figure 6.5**   Actual quoted prices and optimal market-of-one prices for all approved loans quoted by e-Car during one month

SOURCE: Nomis Solutions.

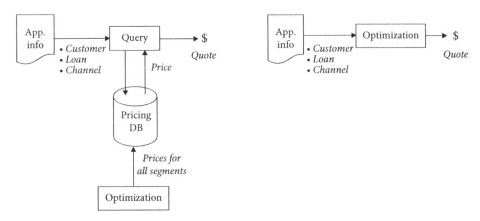

**Figure 6.6**    Conceptual architectures for a price-optimization system based on segmentation (*left*) and one enabling market-of-one pricing (*right*)

lenders have in place. Figure 6.6 shows the high-level conceptual architecture of a system based on pricing segmentation (left) and the architecture of a market-of-one pricing system (right). Under a pricing-segmentation approach, prices for each segment are stored in a database. When a price needs to be quoted, the system gathers information about the customer, product, and channel. This information is used to determine the corresponding pricing segment and the appropriate price is retrieved from the database and communicated to the customer. Price optimization is a process that runs periodically offline and populates the database with the optimized price for each segment.

In contrast, the market-of-one pricing system uses customer, loan, and channel information to calculate the optimal price for each transaction. This requires running a price-optimization algorithm in "real time" each time an application is accepted. The resulting price is then communicated to the customer.

Although the architecture of the market-of-one pricing approach may appear simpler than the pricing segmentation approach, it can be more difficult to implement and may entail more operational risk. There are four reasons for this:

1. In market-of-one pricing, the optimal price is calculated each time a request for a quote is received. It may be impossible to perform the extensive computations required to determine the optimal price for each customer in the time while the customer is waiting for the quote. In this case, a simpler computation may be required to calculate a near-optimal price, reducing the benefits.

2. Under the market-of-one pricing architecture shown in Figure 6.6, the algorithm for price optimization is "mission critical": if it fails for any reason, the lender is unable to quote a price. This means that a backup pricing system needs to be in place.

3. Most lenders currently use a segmentation-based pricing architecture such as that shown on the left side of Figure 6.6. Replacing this existing architecture with a real-time pricing system usually requires significant investment in new information technology infrastructure.

4. Under a pricing segmentation scheme, a lender can scan the prices in the database and satisfy himself that the prices are reasonable. If a lender is not comfortable with a price, he can override that price in the database before it is released to the market. This provides a level of comfort that is harder to achieve with market-of-one pricing in which there is no price list that can be reviewed and overridden—there is only an algorithm. This lack of "reviewability" and control has been cited by some lenders as a reason for their reluctance to move to market-of-one pricing.

These objections notwithstanding, it is likely that lending will move increasingly toward market-of-one pricing. Other industries—notably the airlines and online retailers such as Amazon—have adopted increasing levels of dynamic optimization in their pricing. Increasingly reliable software architecture has largely eliminated concerns about the use of real-time algorithms in pricing. The success of dynamic pricing within a number of industries has eliminated the belief that every price offered to a customer needs to be reviewed and vetted by a human being. Tools have been developed that enable pricing to be controlled and reviewed at a higher level while allowing individual prices to be determined based not only on customer and transaction characteristics but also the current state of the market and the current competitive environment.

There has been some movement within consumer lending toward market-of-one pricing. At least one unsecured lender in the United Kingdom uses a real-time algorithm to set the prices for approved applications. The Nomis Deal Manager (NDM) software is used by a number of banks in Canada as well as Australia and New Zealand to calculate recommended ranges for mortgage prices on a quote-by-quote basis.[6] Given the potential benefits and the pattern in other industries, it is likely that lending will move more and more toward market-of-one pricing over the coming decade.

## SEGMENTATION AS A COMPETITIVE ADVANTAGE

We have seen that lenders can increase expected profitability by establishing a set of pricing segments and charging different prices to each segment. However, increased profit is only one of the benefits of pricing segmentation. Properly segmented pricing not only benefits a lender by attracting more profitable customers; it can hurt competitors by leaving them customers who are less profitable. This is easy to demonstrate in the case of risk-based pricing. Consider two lenders offering loans of $10,000 to a population of 1,000 customers with an expected loss rate of 1.5%. Assume that both lenders have a common cost of capital of 2.0% and a target margin of 2.0%. Under uniform pricing they will both charge a price of 5.5% and (assuming equal market strength) they will split the market. Each lender will realize expected profit proportional to $500 \times \$10,000 \times 2.0\% = \$100,000$.

Now assume that one lender (Lender A) institutes risk-based pricing and divides the 1,000 customers into two risk-tiers of 500 customers each, such that the high-risk tier has a probability of default of 2.0% and the low-risk tier has a probability of default of 1.0%. Lender A charges the low-risk customers a 5.0% rate and the high-risk customers a 5.5%

TABLE 6.4

*Market share, net interest income (NII), and loss rate experienced by each lender in a market in which Lender A uses risk-based pricing while Lender B uses uniform pricing*

|  | RATE (%) | | SHARE (%) | | NUMBER OF LOANS | | | Normalized NII ($) | Loss rate (%) |
|---|---|---|---|---|---|---|---|---|---|
|  | High risk | Low risk | High risk | Low risk | High risk | Low risk | Total | | |
| Lender A | 6.0 | 5.0 | 46.3 | 57.4 | 231.3 | 287.2 | 518.5 | 103,701 | 1.45 |
| Lender B | 5.5 | 5.5 | 53.7 | 42.6 | 268.7 | 212.8 | 481.5 | 93,502 | 1.56 |

rate. If the second lender (Lender B) cannot distinguish customers by risk, he will continue to charge a uniform rate of 5.5% to all customers. If we assume a typical pattern of differential price response between high-risk and low-risk customers, the resulting market shares, normalized net interest income, and loss rate experienced by each lender will be as shown in Table 6.4.

By implementing risk-based pricing, Lender A realizes profits 11% higher than Lender B. Furthermore, with risk-based pricing Lender A enjoys a lower loss rate than Lender B. Risk-based pricing enables Lender A to increase his own profitability by about 3.7% while reducing his competitor's profit by 6.5%. This illustrates how even a simple pricing segmentation scheme not only increases expected profit for a lender but can also reduce profit for the competition.

In fact, the situation is even more favorable to Lender A. Because Lender B's loss rate increased, he will ultimately need to increase his price from 5.5% to 5.56% to maintain his target margin. This creates an additional price advantage for Lender A, which means that he will gain even more market share. And since the customers he gains from lowering his price again are disproportionately low risk, his loss rate will decrease while Lender B's increases. The result is that, even using very simplistic risk-based pricing, Lender A can capture 52.5% of the market while enjoying profitability 10.7% higher than Lender B along with a lower loss rate.

The risk-based pricing scheme adopted by Lender A to achieve the results shown in Table 6.4 is very simple. In particular, Lender A did not optimize his prices: he simply estimated differential risk and applied a common margin. How much better might he do if he actually optimized prices? To address this question, we simulated a market in which two competing lenders can each choose among three levels of pricing sophistication:

1. *Optimal single price.* The lender charges a single price that maximizes profit to all customers.

2. *Risk-based pricing.* The lender segments the population into five risk segments and determines the optimal common margin to charge. The rate charged for each segment is the common cost of funds plus the expected loss rate for the segment plus the optimal common margin.

3. *Optimized pricing.* The lender determines the rate to charge to each segment that maximizes expected profitability from that segment.

We consider the case of two competing lenders in which each lender chooses one of these three strategies. The profitabilities achieved by each lender for each possible combination of the strategies chosen by both lenders is shown in Table 6.5. Each row in the table corresponds to a pricing strategy chosen by Lender A and each column corresponds to a pricing approach taken by Lender B. The numbers in parentheses in the table represent the expected profit achieved by Lender A and by Lender B, respectively. Thus, if Lender A chooses optimized pricing and Lender B chooses optimal single price, then Lender A receives expected profit of $1,657, whereas Lender B receives expected profit of $1,067. The payoffs are symmetrical because the two lenders are identical and indistinguishable.

In the case shown in Table 6.5, increased pricing sophistication always leads to higher profits. Thus, if both lenders are setting an optimal single price, Lender A can increase his profit from $1,084 to $1,419 by implementing risk-based pricing and to $1,657 by implementing optimized pricing. The fact that increasing pricing sophistication increases profitability in the face of a passive competitor is not particularly surprising. However, it is interesting that when both lenders increase their level of sophistication, profits increase for both lenders. This can be seen by moving up the diagonal from the lower-right corner to the upper-left corner of the payoff matrix in Table 6.5: the profit for each lender increases from $1,084 if they both set an optimal single price to $1,257, if they both adopt risk-based pricing to $1,588, and if they both implement optimized pricing. This suggests that improved pricing sophistication is not simply an arms race in which simultaneous investment in improved pricing technology by both lenders leaves them both in the same position. This is consistent with the experience of the airline industry, which found that increased revenue management sophistication led to higher overall profits for the industry.[7]

Another interesting observation from Table 6.5 is that increased sophistication on the part of one lender does not always lead to decreased profits for his competitor. If Lender B is using optimized pricing and Lender A moves from an optimal single price to risk-based pricing, then Lender B's profit will drop from $1,657 to $1,459. However, if Lender A then moves from risk-based pricing to optimized pricing, Lender B's profit will increase from $1,459 up to $1,588. This indicates that when a lender improves pricing sophistication it may not necessarily reduce the profitability of competing lenders. More sophisticated pricing by a set of competing lenders may benefit all of them.[8]

Table 6.5 will look familiar to readers who have studied game theory: payoffs to the two lenders are presented in the *normal form* representation of a two-person game. In the terminology of game theory, Lender A and Lender B are the players, the three levels of pricing

TABLE 6.5
*Payoffs to Lender A and Lender B based on the level of pricing sophistication adopted by each*

| | LENDER B STRATEGY | | |
|---|---|---|---|
| LENDER A STRATEGY | *Optimized pricing* | *Risk-based pricing* | *Optimal single price* |
| Optimized pricing | ($1,588, $1,588) | ($1,459, $1,355) | ($1,657, $1,067) |
| Risk-based pricing | ($1,355, $1,459) | ($1,257, $1,257) | ($1,419, $978) |
| Optimal single price | ($1,067, $1,657) | ($978, $1,419) | ($1,084, $1,084) |

sophistication represent their possible *actions*, and the pairs of profit numbers in the table represent the *payoffs* to the players for each combination of actions. The two-person game with the payoff matrix shown in Table 6.5 has a unique Nash equilibrium in which both of the players choose optimized pricing. This is true because, for each player, the payoff from choosing optimized pricing is always the highest no matter which other action the other player chooses. If this game represented all the costs and benefits faced by the two lenders for each strategy, we would expect both lenders to adopt optimized pricing. However, the game as specified does not include the costs that would be required for a lender to move from one level to a more sophisticated level. If these costs are small relative to the improvement in profitability, choosing optimized pricing on the part of both players would still be the unique Nash equilibrium. If investment costs are high relative to the gains, then the game could have a different equilibrium. This is particularly true if the payoffs and costs are not the same for the two lenders, which is likely to be the case in the real world. We found that, under a wide range of assumptions about price response and market position, increased pricing sophistication always generates additional profit for the adopting lender and usually (but not always) reduces profit for the competitor.

The analysis in this section suggests that pricing sophistication is not a zero-sum game: increased pricing sophistication can lead to increased profitability for the industry as a whole. The analysis is highly stylized and more work needs to be done. However, it is fair to conclude that improving pricing sophistication will always lead to increased profitability for a lender. Furthermore, lenders who are slow to adopt more sophisticated approaches are vulnerable because adoption of more sophisticated pricing by a competitor may lead to reduced profit.

## SUMMARY

- *Pricing segmentation* refers to the classification of potential transactions into distinct pricing segments for the purpose of offering different prices to different segments. In lending, transactions can be segmented based on characteristics of the loan such as term and amount (product dimensions), characteristics of the customer such as FICO score or loyalty (customer dimensions), and channel (branch versus Internet). Typically, each dimension is divided into a finite number of discrete buckets (e.g., risk tiers). A feasible combination of buckets is a *pricing segment*: every potential transaction can be mapped into a single pricing segment and every pricing segment can be quoted a different price.

- The choice of pricing dimensions and how to partition the dimensions into buckets are key decisions for a lender. Typically, more buckets will provide more opportunity for increasing profitability by differentiating pricing at a finer level. The cost of additional buckets is added complexity.

- Typical customer dimensions used in pricing segmentation include risk, geography, loyalty, and (sometimes) age. The ability to use additional customer dimensions in segmenting prices is limited by customer acceptance, regulation, and (often) lender policy.

- Typical product dimensions used in pricing segmentation include term, amount, and loan-to-value ratio.
- Which channel a customer uses to approach a lender—Internet, branch, or call center—is also correlated with price sensitivity. Internet customers are typically more price sensitive than call-center customers, who are more price sensitive than customers who approach through a branch.
- The logical conclusion of more and more granular pricing segmentation is *market-of-one* pricing, in which the price quoted for a transaction is based on all the information available at the time of quote. Implementing market-of-one pricing requires a real-time pricing algorithm to generate a price for every quote in real time. For most lenders this would require investment in additional IT capabilities to support the underlying pricing and quoting processes. Market-of-one pricing is still uncommon in lending; however, the experience of airlines and online retailers indicates that it is likely to become more common in the future as lenders become more sophisticated in pricing.
- In addition to increased expected profitability, there is also a strong competitive incentive for a lender to establish a set of pricing segments and determine a different price for each segment. Specifically, targeting pricing more accurately to more granular pricing segments can reduce the profitability of the loans issued by less sophisticated competitors.
- A simple game-theoretic analysis shows that increased pricing sophistication by a lender increases profitability for that lender and may reduce the profitability of a competitor. Increased sophistication by all competitors within a market can lead to improved profitability for all of them—price optimization is not necessarily a zero-sum game.

## NOTES

1. The area of Triangle A is called the *consumer surplus* and the area of Triangle B is called the *deadweight loss*. Consumer surplus is the total additional amount that customers who took the loan would have been willing to pay. The deadweight loss measures the surplus lost by not being able to sell to customers who are willing to pay more than the cost but are not willing to pay the price that the seller is charging. Both the customers and the seller would be better off if the seller had a way to sell to these customers at a lower price without cannibalizing customers who were willing to pay the higher price.

2. The same relationship has been found in newspaper subscriptions—the longer a subscriber has been a customer, the less price sensitive she is. New newspaper customers are also much more price sensitive than existing customers and defectors (Lewis 2005).

3. The rental car example is from Phillips (2005, 83–84).

4. For more details on airline pricing segmentation, see Barnes (2012) and chapter 6 in Phillips (2005).

5. The figures on faster processing are from J. D. Power and Associates (2015) and Martin (2016). The idea of artificially creating an inferior substitute that costs more but

sells at a lower price is called a *damaged-product* strategy, a term introduced by Deneckere and McAfee (1996).

6. Information on the usage of the Nomis Deal Manager can be found in Bretzke (2016).

7. For a discussion of the effect of more sophisticated customer segmentation and improved revenue management on airline industry profits, see Gorin and Belobaba (2004).

8. The analysis of two competing lenders choosing different levels of pricing sophistication was adapted from Kuckuk and Phillips (2010). The market-response function used in the analysis was calibrated using data from the unsecured lending market in the United Kingdom.

# 7 OPTIMIZING PRICES

In the preceding chapters we discussed how to divide a population of customers into pricing segments, how to estimate the price sensitivity of each segment, and how to calculate the expected incremental profitability (including risk) of different loans offered at different prices. Although these topics are important in themselves, our interest is primarily in how they can support better pricing. The goal of optimization is to use estimates of price sensitivity and incremental profit in different segments to determine the set of prices that will best meet a lender's business goals.

In this chapter, we first show how to calculate the prices that maximize expected profitability and revenue for a single loan under a simplifying set of assumptions—notably the absence of price-dependent risk. These assumptions make it easy to show the relationships among the failure rate of the price-response function, the incremental profitability of the loan, and the prices that maximize profitability and revenue. We then extend the analysis to the case in which price-dependent risk is significant and then to the problem of optimizing prices for multiple segments simultaneously. Determining the optimal solution for multiple segments is complicated by the fact that lenders typically apply constraints to ensure that the final prices meet various conditions. The presence of such constraints significantly complicates price optimization because it introduces dependencies among the prices that can be offered to different segments. We note that optimization assumes a single objective, but lenders—like many other businesses—are often interested in simultaneously pursuing multiple objectives such as maximizing profitability and minimizing risk. We show how the trade-off between two competing objectives can be visualized using an efficient frontier.

## PRICE OPTIMIZATION FOR A SINGLE LOAN

In this section, we consider the problem of finding the price that maximizes expected profit and expected revenue for a single loan. We first consider a simple model of loan profitability that considers only net interest income, cost of funds, and expected loss and use that simple model to introduce the basic concepts of price optimization. We then extend that simple model to the case of price-dependent risk and to a more realistic nonlinear model of expected profit.

Consider a two-period loan with an initial balance of $B = 1$ offered at a rate of $p$ with a cost of capital of $c$. If the loan does not default, in period 2 the lender receives a profit of $p - c$. If the loan defaults, the lender loses the loss given default plus the cost of capital, which we denote by $\ell = LGD + c$. Let the probability of default be $PD$. Then, the expected incremental profit if the loan funds is $(1 - PD) \times (p - c) - PD \times \ell$. Assume that the probability the loan will be accepted as a function of $p$ is given by the price-response function $\bar{F}(p)$. Then, the expected profit that the lender will realize from offering the loan at price $p$ is given by the following:

$$E[\pi(p)] = \bar{F}(p)[(1 - PD) \times (p - c) - PD \times \ell]$$

$$= \bar{F}(p)(1 - PD)\left( p - c - \frac{\ell}{o} \right), \tag{7.1}$$

where $o = (1 - PD)/PD$ is the odds that the loan will not default. A price-taking lender would set an underwriting criterion of

$$o^* = \frac{LGD + c}{p - c},$$

and would accept any loans for which the expected odds are greater than $o^*$ and reject any loans with odds less than $o^*$. (Note that this is simply an extension of the risk-cutoff criterion in Equation 2.6 to the case in which $LGD \leq 1$.)

---

**Example 7.1: Optimal Underwriting.** A price-taking lender has a cost of capital $c = .01$. He is considering a one-period loan with an associated price $p = .03$ and loss given default of 50%. On this basis, it is profitable for him to accept the loan only if the odds are greater than $o^* = (.5 + .01)/(.03 - .01) = 25.5$, which is equivalent to a probability-of-default criterion of $PD < 1/26.5 = 3.7\%$.

---

We are primarily interested in the case in which a lender has the power to set prices. In this case, a risk-neutral profit-maximizing lender would charge the price $p^*$ that maximizes expected profit as defined by Equation 7.1. The fundamental trade-off faced by the lender is between the incremental profit of funded loans, which increases as $p$ increases, and the number of customers who will accept the loan, which decreases as $p$ increases. This trade-off is illustrated in Figure 7.1 for an example loan. The dashed line is the expected profit if the loan funds, and the solid line is the probability that the customer will accept the loan as a function of the rate $p$. The take-up rate decreases from about 86% at a rate of 0% to about 5% at a rate of 10%. The expected profit—represented by the dotted line—is the product of these two functions. Expected profit is less than 0 when the price is less than the cost of funds plus the normalized loss rate. Expected profit initially rises with price as the increase in incremental profit from each funded loan outweighs the reduced take-up probability. Expected profit reaches a peak at a rate of 5.8% and then begins to decline as the business lost from increasing the price further outweighs the additional incremental profit from funded loans. A risk-neutral, profit-maximizing lender would set $p^* = 5.8\%$, yielding an expected profit of about $193 per accepted application.

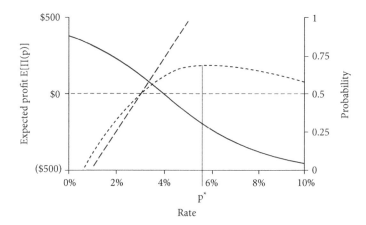

**Figure 7.1** Expected incremental profit (*dashed line*), price response (*solid line*), and expected profit (*dotted line*) as a function of rate for an example loan with cost of funds of 2% per year, a probability of default of 5%, and a loss given default of 50%

One way to calculate the profit-maximizing price for the two-period loan is to differentiate $E[\pi(p)]$ in Equation 7.1 with respect to $p$ and set the derivative equal to 0. The derivative of Equation 7.1 with respect to $p$ is $dE[\pi(p)]/dp = (1 - PD)[\overline{F}(p) - f(p)(p - c - \ell/o)]$, using the fact that the derivative of $\overline{F}(p)$ with respect to $p$ is equal to $-f(p)$. By setting the derivative equal to 0 and rearranging terms, we can derive the condition for the profit-maximizing price $p^*$:

$$h(p^*) = \frac{1}{p^* - c - \dfrac{\ell}{o}}, \tag{7.2}$$

where $h(p) = f(p)/\overline{F}(p)$ is the failure rate associated with the price-response function $\overline{F}(p)$.[1] Equation 7.2 says that, at the optimal price $p^*$, the failure rate is equal to the inverse of the expected price minus the cost of funds and the normalized loss.

Using the fact that the elasticity at any price is equal to the price times the hazard rate, we can show that an equivalent condition for a price to be optimal is that

$$\epsilon(p^*) = \frac{p^*}{p^* - c - \dfrac{\ell}{o}}. \tag{7.3}$$

As noted in Chapter 4, most common price-response functions including the linear, probit, and logit have continuous and increasing failure rates. For any price-response function with a continuous and increasing failure rate, the expected profit function $E[\pi(p)]$ possesses three highly desirable properties:

1. There exists a unique profit-maximizing price $p^*$ satisfying Equation 7.2 that maximizes expected profit.
2. $p^* > c + \ell/o$. This means expected profit for the loan at the profit-maximizing price will be greater than 0.

3. $p^*$ is increasing in both $c$ and $\ell/o$. That is, everything else being equal, if the cost of funds increases or lending risk (measured either by loss given default or probability of default or both) increases, the optimal price will also increase.

These properties of $p^*$ are illustrated in Figure 7.2. The horizontal axis in Figure 7.2 is the price $p$. Two curves are shown: the failure rate $h(p)$, which increases in $p$, and the curve $1/(p - c - \ell/o)$, which decreases from infinity at $p = c + \ell/o$ toward 0 as $p$ increases. The two curves cross at the profit-maximizing price $p^*$. Since $h(p)$ is increasing by assumption and $1/(p - c - \ell/o)$ is decreasing, the two curves must cross at a single point, which means that $p^*$ is unique. It is clear from Figure 7.2 that $p^*$ must be greater than $c + \ell/o$, so expected profit at $p^*$ will be positive. Increasing $c + \ell/o$ would move the curve $1/(p - c - \ell/o)$ to the right, and the crossing point with $h(p)$—and thus $p^*$—would increase, which means that $p^*$ is an increasing function of $c$ and $PD$.

Equation 7.2 can be solved to find $p^*$ for any price-response function $\overline{F}(p)$ and any values of $c$, $l$, and $o$. Example 7.2 shows how this optimal price can be calculated analytically when the price-response function is linear; however, this is not generally the case: there is no closed form solution for $p^*$ when the price-response function is logit or probit. Nonetheless, if the parameters of the underlying price-response function are known, it is straightforward to calculate $p^*$ using standard numerical techniques such as line search or gradient descent.

---

**Example 7.2: Profit-Maximizing Price with Linear Price-Response Function.** A lender with a cost of funds of $c = .03$ faces a linear price-response function with parameter $b = .1$ for a loan with normalized loss of $\ell/o = .01$ so that $\overline{F}(p) = \max(1 - p/b, 0)$. From Table 4.2, the failure rate associated with a linear price-response function is $h(p) = 1/(b - p)$, and the profit-maximizing price must solve $1/(b - p^*) = 1/(p^* - c - \ell/o)$ or $p^* = (b + c + \ell/o)/2 = .14/2 = .07$.

---

## Revenue Maximization

In some cases, a lender may seek to maximize total expected revenue rather than expected profit from his loans. This could be the case, for example, when a lender is entering a new

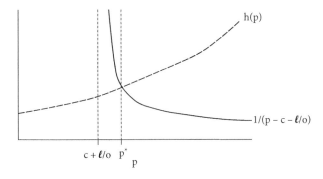

**Figure 7.2**    The failure rate $h(p)$ and the function $1/(p - c - \ell/o)$ shown as a function of price for a simple loan with a continuous increasing failure rate

market and wishes to gain market share. In this case, the lender would want to find the price that maximizes total bookings, which means that, for a loan with balance $B$, he would want to maximize $R(p) = B\overline{F}(p)p$. Setting the derivative of $R(p)$ to 0 and solving gives us the first-order necessary condition for the revenue-maximizing price $\breve{p}$:

$$h(\breve{p}) = \frac{1}{\breve{p}}, \qquad (7.4)$$

which means that the failure rate at the revenue-maximizing price is equal to the reciprocal of the price. The similarity to Equation 7.2 is obvious, and indeed, maximizing revenue is equivalent to maximizing profit assuming that the cost of funds $c$ and the risk $\ell/o$ are both equal to 0.

By multiplying both sides of Equation 7.4 by $\breve{p}$, we can derive the condition on elasticity for a price to maximize expected revenue, namely $\epsilon(\breve{p}) = 1$; the elasticity of price response at the revenue-maximizing price must be equal to 1. An implication of this condition is that a realistic price-response function cannot have a constant elasticity over all prices: if the elasticity were greater than 1 everywhere, then revenue could always be increased by reducing price; if the elasticity were less than 1 everywhere, then revenue could always be reducing price. Since these conditions don't seem to occur in the real world, it is safe to say that constant-elasticity price response is not a good global assumption.

The relationship of the revenue-maximizing price to the profit-maximizing price is illustrated in Figure 7.3. At the revenue-maximizing price $\breve{p}$ the failure-rate curve intersects $1/p$. Since $1/p$ is a decreasing function of $p$, the two curves must cross and therefore there is a unique revenue-maximizing price. If $c + \ell/o > 0$, as is usually the case, $\breve{p} < p^*$; that is, the revenue-maximizing price is generally less than the profit-maximizing price. The only exception would be the case in which the cost of funds is not only less than 0 but also sufficiently negative to entirely outweigh the loss rate. In this highly unusual situation, the revenue-maximizing price could be higher than the profit-maximizing price.

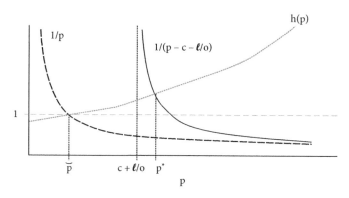

**Figure 7.3**    Relationship between the revenue-maximizing price $\breve{p}$ and the profit-maximizing price $p^*$

---

**Example 7.3: Revenue-Maximizing Price with Linear Price-Response Function.** Consider the loan in Example 7.2 and assume that the lender wants to maximize expected revenue rather than expected profit. In this case, the lender would find the price $\tilde{p}$ such that $1/(b-\tilde{p})=1/\tilde{p}$ or, equivalently, $b-\tilde{p}=\tilde{p}$, which means that $\tilde{p}=.05$, which is less than the profit-maximizing price of .07 calculated in Example 7.2.

---

We can see from Figure 7.3 that there is no guarantee that expected profit at the revenue-maximizing price is greater than 0. In fact, it can be the case that $\tilde{p}<c+\ell/o$ or even $\tilde{p}<c$, in which case the lender should expect to lose money if he charges the revenue-maximizing price. As an alternative, the lender might wish to maximize expected revenue received over the life of the loan, including the possibility that the borrower might default. In that case, the lender would maximize $\overline{F}(p)(p-\ell/o)$, and the optimal price would solve $h(\tilde{p})=1/(\tilde{p}-\ell/o)$. In this case the resulting optimal price would satisfy $\tilde{p}>\ell/o$, but it would still be possible that $\tilde{p}<c+\ell/o$ and that the loan would have an expected profit less than 0.

## Optimization with Price-Dependent Risk

The discussion so far has assumed that neither the probability of default nor the loss given default depends on the price of the loan. This is a reasonable assumption for low-risk loans, but as we saw previously, for riskier loans, the probability of default and loss given default both increase with price for risky loans. To see how this influences the profit-maximizing price, consider a population consisting of $D_g$ good customers who will not default and $D_b$ bad customers who will default if they are extended a loan, and assume that these two populations have price-response functions $\overline{F}_g(p)$ and $\overline{F}_b(p)$, respectively.

We can express expected profit at price $p$ as

$$E[\pi(p)]=\overline{F}_g(p)D_g(p-c)-\overline{F}_b(p)D_b\ell. \tag{7.5}$$

The first-order necessary condition for the profit-maximizing price $p^*$ can be found by taking the first derivative of Equation 7.5 and setting it to 0, which gives this condition:

$$h_g(p^*)=\dfrac{1}{p^*-c-\left(\dfrac{f_b(p^*)}{f_g(p^*)}\right)\left(\dfrac{\ell}{o_0}\right)}, \tag{7.6}$$

where $h_g(p)=f_g(p)/\overline{F}_g(p)$ is the failure rate for the price-response function of goods and $o_0=D_g/D_b$ is the population odds. (See Chapter 2 for a definition of population odds.) Let $o(p)$ be the odds at price $p$. If the price-response functions are identical for goods and bads, then $f_b(p)=f_g(p)$ for all $p$ and there is no price-dependent risk. In this case, Equation 7.5 is equivalent to Equation 7.2. However, if $\overline{F}_g(p)<\overline{F}_b(p), D_g>0$, and $D_b>0$, the population will display price-dependent risk. As shown in Chapter 2, if the difference between $\check{F}_g(p)$

and $\hat{F}_b(p)$ is greater than some constant and/or $D_b$ is too large relative to $D_g$, then there may be no price at which it is profitable to lend to this population, and a profit-maximizing lender would not offer the loan.

Assume that the conditions for price-dependent risk hold and that there is some price at which the loan is profitable. Consider two pricing policies. Under the first policy, the lender sets the optimal price $p^*$ incorporating price-dependent risk according to Equation 7.6. Under the second policy, the lender can observe the odds at every price $\bar{F}_g(p)D_g / \bar{F}_b(p)D_b$ but assumes that the odds will not change if he changes the price—that is, he can measure the risk accurately but ignores the possibility of price-dependent risk. In this case, the lender would set the price $\hat{p}$ that satisfies

$$h_g(\hat{p}) = \frac{1}{p - c - (\dfrac{\bar{F}_b(\hat{p})}{\bar{F}_g(\hat{p})})} = \frac{1}{\hat{p} - c - \ell / o(\hat{p})}. \tag{7.7}$$

The fact that goods have a higher failure rate than bads means that $f_g(p) / \bar{F}_g(p) > f_b(p) / \bar{F}_b(p)$, implying that $f_b(p) / f_g(p) < \bar{F}_b(p) / \bar{F}_g(p)$ for all $p$. Applying this inequality to Equations 7.6 and 7.7, we see that we must have $p^* < \hat{p}$; that is, a lender who is able to accurately estimate risk but does not consider the influence of price on risk will set a price that is higher than the price set by a lender who explicitly incorporates price-dependent risk into determining the optimal price. In addition, the first lender will experience higher losses and will realize lower profit than the second lender. This suggests that estimating the price-dependent risk rate and incorporating it explicitly into price optimization can be important, especially in subprime lending.

## AN ADAPTIVE APPROACH TO PRICE OPTIMIZATION

One question is whether the optimal price for a loan can be determined—or at least closely approximated—if the underlying price-response function is unknown. The (perhaps surprising) answer is yes, *if* the underlying price-response function has a continuous increasing failure rate *and* the lender is willing to perform price testing. In this case, the price can be adjusted sequentially in a way that enables the lender to approach the optimal price $p^*$ without postulating a form for the price-response curve, much less estimating parameters. Such an *adaptive* approach is illustrated in Figure 7.4, which shows the failure rate—which we assume is unknown to the lender—and the function $1/(p - c - \ell/o)$ for a loan. (For simplicity, we ignore price-dependent risk and assume that $o$ is constant.)

In the adaptive approach, the lender starts by choosing some test price, $p(0) > c + \ell/o$. He then updates the price over time in a way that ideally moves it closer and closer to $p^*$ using the following steps:

1. Define an iteration counter $k$ and set $k = 0$. Choose a stopping criterion $\varepsilon > 0$ and a set of price adjustments $\alpha(0) > \alpha(1) > \alpha(2) > \ldots > 0$.

2. Use price testing to estimate the failure rate around the current price, $p(k)$. This involves observing demand at a set of prices close to $p(k)$ and using the resulting

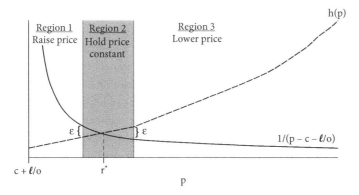

Region 1
Raise price

Region 2
Hold price
constant

Region 3
Lower price

$h(p)$

$\epsilon\{$

$\}\epsilon$

$1/(p - c - \ell/o)$

$c + \ell/o$

$r^*$

$p$

**Figure 7.4** Sequential adjustment approach to finding $p^*$ when the underlying price-response function is unknown

observations to estimate the failure rate. For example, $D_1$ approvals could be priced at $p(k)$ with $d_1$ approvals taking up the loan, and $D_2$ approvals could be priced at some nearby price $p(k) + \delta$ with $d_2$ taking up the loan at that price. In this case, the failure rate can be estimated by $\hat{h}(p(k)) = 2(d_1D_2 - d_2D_1)/[\delta(d_1D_2 + d_2D_1)]$ using the estimator in Table 4.3.

3. Calculate the gap at the current price $p(k)$ by $g(p(k)) = \hat{h}(p(k)) - 1/(p(k) - c - \ell/o)$.

4. If $-\epsilon \le g(p(k)) \le \epsilon$, set $p^* = p(k)$ and stop.

5. If $g(p(k)) < -\epsilon$, set $p(k+1) = p(k) + \alpha_k$, set $k = k+1$ and go to step 2.

6. If $g(p(k)) > \epsilon$, set $p(k+1) = p(k) - \alpha_k$, set $k = k+1$ and go to step 2.

As shown in Figure 7.4, this approach sequentially runs a set of price tests around the current price, uses the results of those price tests to estimate the local failure rate, and—based on the relationship of the failure rate to the inverse margin—adjusts the price to move toward the optimal price. The gap $g(p(k))$ is the distance between the estimated failure rate and $1/(p(k) - c - \ell/o)$. The $\alpha(k)$s are adjustment factors. They gradually decrease so that $p(k)$ is changing by smaller amounts each time. If the estimated failure rate at the current price $p(k)$ is significantly less than $1/(p(k) - c - \ell/o)$, then the price is adjusted upward. If the estimated failure rate is significantly higher than $1/(p(k) - c - \ell/o)$, then the price is adjusted downward. If the gap $g(p(k))$ is less than the stopping criterion $\epsilon$, the algorithm terminates because the current value of $p(k)$ is "close enough" to the true value of $p^*$.

---

**Example 7.4: Adaptive Price Adjustment.** A two-period simple loan has cost $c = .02$ and normalized risk $\ell/o = .01$. The profit-maximizing price must satisfy $h(p^*) = 1/(p^* - .03)$. The lender currently sets a price $p = .05$ and uses price testing to estimate that the failure rate at that price is $\hat{h}(.05) = 35$. The current inverse margin is $1/(.05 - .03) = 50$. Because the estimated failure rate is less than the inverse margin at the current price, the lender could increase profit by raising the price.

This adaptive approach to pricing is an example of a "learning and earning" (or some-times, "exploration and exploitation") approach. It is similar to the dynamic pricing algo-rithms used by a number of online retailers. It is called a nonparametric approach because it does not make any assumption about the form of the underlying price-response function other than that is continuous and has an increasing failure rate.

One disadvantage of the adaptive approach is that it can require a considerable amount of price testing—demand response must be tested at a number of prices close to the cur-rent price $p(k)$ in order to approximate the failure rate. A sufficient number of price tests needs to be performed to ensure that the estimate of hazard rate, $\hat{h}(p(k))$, is statistically significant before the next adjustment is made. This requires that the lender has the ability (and the appetite) to perform price testing on a regular basis. Hybrid approaches are also possible—a lender may have an estimate of the parameters of the price-response function $\hat{F}(p)$ but use price testing to determine that the gap $g(p(k))$ is indeed close to 0 at the cal-culated price $p^*$. If the gap is not close to 0, then the lender needs to update the parameters of the price-response function and choose a new value of $p^*$.[2]

## SENSITIVITY TO COST AND PRICE RESPONSE

Equation 7.2 implies that the profit-maximizing price is a function of three components: the failure rate of the underlying price-response curve $h(p)$, the incremental loan cost $c$, and the risk $\ell/o$. An interesting question is how the profit-maximizing price would change if one or more of these components is either increased or decreased. Everything else being equal:

1. If the incremental cost associated with a pricing segment increases, then the profit-maximizing price will increase.

2. If the risk associated with a pricing segment as measured by either loss given default or probability of default (or both) increases, then the profit-maximizing price will increase.

3. If the failure rate at the optimal price $h(p^*)$ increases, then the profit-maximizing price will decrease.

These three properties are intuitive. Incremental cost and risk are both "costs" of a loan—and increasing the cost of a product always leads to an increase in its optimal price. If cus-tomers become more price sensitive—perhaps as a result of aggressive price cutting on the part of a competitor—we would expect the optimal price to be lower.

We can also compare the optimal prices for two different pricing segments:

1. If two pricing segments have the same price-response curve but different incremen-tal costs and/or risks, then the segment with the higher incremental cost plus risk will have the higher profit-maximizing price.

2. If two pricing segments have the same incremental cost and risk but the price-response curve for one segment has a higher failure rate than the other at every price then the segment with the higher failure rate will have a lower profit-maximiz-ing price.

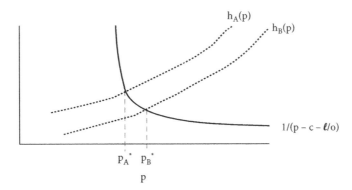

**Figure 7.5** Profit-maximizing prices for two price-response functions when the failure rate of price-response function A is greater than the failure rate of price-response function B for all values of $p$

The first property follows from the fact that the profit-maximizing price is an increasing function of cost and risk. The second property is illustrated in Figure 7.5. In this figure, the failure rate for segment $A$ is always higher than the failure rate for segment $B$. In this case it is clear that the intersection of the failure rate for segment $A$ with the inverse margin curve $1/(p - c - \ell/o)$ at the profit-maximizing price must be at a lower price than that of segment $B$. This will be the case for all possible values of $c$, $l$, and $o$.

## OPTIMIZATION WITH MULTIPLE SEGMENTS

In the previous section we considered the problem of finding the price that maximizes the expected profit from a single loan. However, in practice, lenders need to set the prices for many different pricing segments simultaneously. If the segments are independent, then the prices can be calculated by simply calculating the optimal price for each segment individually. The problem becomes more complex when the lender wishes to enforce conditions on the prices or to impose limits on total fundings, risk, or other quantities. These conditions can be incorporated into the determination of the optimal prices by the use of constraints. If constraints are imposed on the optimal solution—and in practice they always are—finding the optimal prices requires solving a multivariable nonlinear optimization problem.[3]

The problem of finding the profit-maximizing price for a single loan can be written as follows:

$$p^* = \arg \max_{p} D\overline{F}(p)\pi(p), \tag{7.8}$$

where $D$ is the demand in the segment, $\overline{F}(p)$ is the price-response function, and $\pi(p)$ is the incremental profit function, noting that $x^* = \arg \max[f(x)]$ indicates that $x^*$ is the value of $x$ that maximizes the function $f(x)$.

In the parlance of optimization theory, the price $p$ is the *decision variable*, and the expected profit $D\overline{F}(p)\pi(p)$ is the *objective function*. Equation 7.8 is classified as an *unconstrained* optimization problem because there are no constraints specified. As discussed in the previous section, the optimization problem in Equation 7.8 is quite well behaved providing that $\overline{F}(p)$ is continuous and demonstrates an increasing failure rate. In this case, the log-concavity of the incremental profit function $\pi(p)$ guarantees the existence of a unique maximizer to $\overline{F}(p)\pi(p)$. The optimal price in this case is independent of $D$ so that we can set $D = 1$ without loss of generality.

Now consider the case in which the lender needs to set the prices for $N$ pricing segments indexed by $i = 1, 2, \ldots, N$. The corresponding optimization problem is

$$\mathbf{p}^* = \arg\max_{\mathbf{p}} \sum_{i=1}^{N} D_i \overline{F}_i(p_i)\pi_i(p_i) \tag{7.9}$$

where $\mathbf{p}^*$ is the vector of optimal prices $(p_1^*, p_2^*, \ldots, p_N^*)$, $D_i$ is the market demand in segment $i$ and $F_i(p)$ and $\pi_i(p)$ are the price-response and incremental profit functions respectively for segment $i$. The decision variables are the prices to charge for all pricing segments and the objective function is total expected profit. The optimization problem in Equation 7.9 is *separable*, which means that it can be solved by solving the single-loan problem in Equation 7.8 separately for each segment.

In a similar vein, a lender could find the prices that maximize expected revenue by solving:

$$\check{\mathbf{p}} = \arg\max_{\mathbf{p}} \sum_{i=1}^{N} D_i \overline{F}_i(p_i)R_i(p_i),$$

where $R_i(p)$ is the expected revenue for loan $i$ as a function of price $p$. The lender could also pursue a mixed goal in which he sets prices to maximize revenue in some pricing segments and to maximize expected profit in the others. Assume that the lender wants to maximize expected profit in segments $1, 2, \ldots, n$ and expected revenue in the remaining segments $n + 1, n + 2, \ldots, N$. In this case, he would solve the problem:

$$\mathbf{p}^* = \arg\max_{\mathbf{p}} \left[ \sum_{i=1}^{n} D_i \overline{F}_i(p_i)\pi_i(p_i) + \sum_{i=n+1}^{N} D_i \overline{F}_i(p_i)R_i(p_i) \right].$$

In the absence of constraints, the lender could apply a single-loan optimization procedure to determine the optimal price to charge for each segment. However, in most real-world situations, lenders apply constraints to guarantee that the optimal prices satisfy conditions that the lender deems necessary or desirable.

## CONSTRAINTS

Restrictions that lenders need (or want) to place on the prices that they put into the market are specified as constraints in the optimization problem. Some constraints are imposed in order to meet regulatory restrictions, such as an upper bound on prices required to conform to usury laws. Other constraints reflect the desire of the lender to maintain a "logical" price structure. For example, a lender may want to set a constraint such that less risky customers are never charged more than more risky customers for the same loan. Finally, some constraints result from business requirements: for example, a desire that the total revenue not fall below a lower limit or that total risk not exceed a specified maximum.

Adding constraints transforms the lender's problem from an unconstrained to a constrained optimization problem. Typically constrained problems are harder to solve than unconstrained problems because constraints tie prices together so that we can no longer solve for the optimal price in each segment independently. Furthermore, constraints can make the prices generated by the optimization harder to interpret because the optimal value for each price is potentially influenced by the values of all the other prices. Finally, imposing too many constraints can lead to a situation in which the optimization problem has no feasible solution. This means that constraints should be added judiciously and carefully managed.

In the remainder of this section we discuss the types of constraints that are typically used in price optimization and how they are formulated. Finally, we discuss some of the issues involved with overconstraining and how the chances of overconstraining can be reduced or avoided.

## Bounds

Lenders commonly apply upper and lower bounds to prices. A lower bound for segment $i$ has the form $p_i \geq p_i^-$ and an upper bound has the form $p_i \leq p_i^+$, where $p_i^-$ and $p_i^+$ are the lower and upper bounds, respectively. In addition, bounds may be used to guarantee that a new price does not deviate too greatly from a previous one, in order to avoid excessive price swings from period to period. A lower bound of 0 may be necessary for business reasons and may even be binding if the cost of funds drops significantly below 0. An upper bound may be required to satisfy usury laws.

Another reason for imposing bounds is that the estimate of the price-response function $\bar{F}_i(p)$ may be statistically significant only within some range. This will be true if the parameters of $\bar{F}_i(p)$ were estimated using historical observations. In this case, the estimates of the coefficients of the price-response function are reliable only in the range of prices experienced in the past. Bounds can be used to ensure that recommended prices are within the range of statistical reliability of the price-response coefficient estimates.

## Structural Constraints

Structural constraints are used to enforce relationships among prices that lenders considerable necessary or desirable. For example, many lenders believe that, all else being equal, lower-risk customers should never be quoted a higher price than higher-risk customers for the same loan. In a similar vein, most lenders believe that, all else being equal, a higher price should not be quoted for a larger loan than a smaller loan to the same customer.[4] If prices did not follow this pattern, a customer seeking to borrow $100,000 might receive a better price by applying for two $50,000 loans.

Relationships such as those described above can be enforced using *monotonicity constraints* that guarantee that prices consistently increase or decrease along some pricing dimension. As an example, consider a lender who classifies customers into six risk tiers such that lower tiers represent lower risk, and the lender wants to ensure that lower-risk customers are always quoted the same price as or a lower price than higher-risk customers for the same loan. Assume that the same lender has five loan-size buckets for a total of 30 pricing segments. Let $p_{ij}$ be the price that he offers to loans in risk tier $i$ and loan-size bucket $j$. Then the lender would solve an optimization problem with the objective function of Equation 7.9 but with 35 constraints of the form:

$$p^- \leq p_{11}; \quad p_{11} \leq p_{21}; \quad p_{21} \leq p_{31}; \quad p_{31} \leq p_{41}; \quad p_{41} \leq p_{51}; \quad p_{51} \leq p_{61} \quad p_{61} \leq p^+$$
$$p^- \leq p_{12}; \quad p_{12} \leq p_{22}; \quad p_{22} \leq p_{32}; \quad p_{32} \leq p_{42}; \quad p_{42} \leq p_{52}; \quad p_{52} \leq p_{62} \quad p_{62} \leq p^+$$
$$\vdots \qquad\qquad\qquad\qquad\qquad \vdots \qquad\qquad\qquad\qquad\qquad \vdots$$
$$p^- \leq p_{15}; \quad p_{15} \leq p_{25}; \quad p_{25} \leq p_{35}; \quad p_{35} \leq p_{45}; \quad p_{45} \leq p_{55}; \quad p_{55} \leq p_{65} \quad p_{65} \leq p^+.$$

The number of structural constraints can grow quite rapidly—for example, if the same lender wanted to ensure that lower prices were quoted for larger loans than smaller loans for borrowers in the same risk tier, he would need to add an additional 30 constraints of the form: $p_{11} \geq p_{12}, p_{12} \geq p_{13}, \ldots, p_{64} \geq p_{65}$. A total of 65 constraints are required to ensure monotonicity along just two segmentation dimensions. Structural constraints can easily number in the hundreds or even thousands for a lender with many pricing dimensions.

Structural constraints can be used to enforce other desired relationships among prices. For example, a lender may wish to encourage borrowers to use the Internet rather than branches for their borrowing. In this case, the lender could impose a series of structural constraints to ensure that the price quoted through the Internet for a loan was always lower than the price quoted for a similar loan to a similar customer through a branch. Structural constraints can also be used to ensure that loyal customers—however defined—are always quoted prices at least as low as new customers for the same loans.

### Business Performance Constraints

Business performance constraints ensure that prices are consistent with specified performance requirements on business metrics such as revenue, expected profitability, or risk. Business performance constraints may be imposed on a single pricing segment, on a set of pricing segments, or on the entire portfolio. A lender may wish to maximize profit subject to the constraint that total revenue from new fundings exceeds some target $R^*$. In this case, he would maximize profit according to the objective function in Equation 7.9 but with the added constraint

$$\sum_i D_i \bar{F}_i(p_i) R_i(p_i) \geq R^*,$$

where $D_i \bar{F}_i(p_i) R_i(p_i)$ is the expected revenue from offering price $p_i$ to segment $i$. This constraint pertains to the entire portfolio; however, minimum revenue from a single segment $j$ could be imposed with the constraint $D_j \bar{F}_j(p_j) R_j(p_j) \geq R^*$. A lower bound on expected revenue from a combination of pricing segments, say, $j = 1$, 2, and 3, could be imposed using the constraint $E[R_1(p_1)] + E[R_2(p_2)] + E[R_3(p_3)] \geq R^*$. It is equally easy to specify constraints on expected loss—let us assume that $EL_i$ is the expected loss rate in segment $i$ and that $L$ is the maximum expected losses that the lender will accept for the portfolio as a whole. Then, the lender would solve Equation 7.9 subject to the constraint

$$\sum_i EL_i \times D_i \overline{F}(p_i) \leq L$$

Business performance constraints can also be specified to ratios. For example, a lender, may wish the expected loss rate from his portfolio to be less than some specified fraction $L^*$. In this case, he could add the constraint

$$\sum_i EL_i \times D_i \overline{F}(p_i) \leq L^* \sum_i D_i \overline{F}(p_i).$$

Again, constraints of this form could be specified for the portfolio as a whole or for individual pricing segments or for arbitrary combinations of pricing segments.

---

**Example 7.5: Optimization with a Risk Constraint.** Assume that a lender has established five pricing segments with different levels of risk and price response. The lender has estimated that price response in each segment is logistic, so that $\overline{F}_i(p_i) = e^{a_i + b_i p_i} / (1 + e^{a_i + b_i p_i})$. The total demands, expected loss rates, and parameters for each segment are shown in Table 7.1. Expected profit from segment $i$ at price $p_i$ can be approximated by $\pi_i(p_i) = D_i \overline{F}_i(p_i)(p_i - c_i - \ell_i)$, where $\ell_i$ is the normalized loss rate for the segment and $c = .02$ is the cost of capital. If the lender maximizes total expected profitability, at the optimal prices he will achieve a total profit of $717.00 but will have an expected loss rate of 4.1%.

Now assume that the lender decides that he does not want an expected loss rate higher than 3.0% for his portfolio. If he restricts lending to the two segments with a loss rate less than or equal to 3.0% and charges the optimal prices, his profit will drop to $231.90 and his expected loss rate will be 2.52%. If, however, he allows lending to all the segments but sets a constraint on the portfolio, he can achieve a profit of $466.63 with an associated expected loss rate of 3.0%.

---

## Rate Endings

In many cases, lenders want to publish only rates that end with certain digits, such as 0, 5, or 9.[5] Thus, a lender might wish to offer loans at rates of 4.85% and 6.7% rather than 4.83% and 6.72%. Such rate ending requirements can be enforced as constraints; however, doing so makes the underlying optimization problem much more difficult to solve. Because of

TABLE 7.1
*Logistic parameters, loss rates, and demands by segment used in Example 7.5*

| Segment | PARAMETERS | | Loss rate | Demand |
| | a | b | | |
|---|---|---|---|---|
| 1 | .64 | −8 | .06 | 5,000 |
| 2 | .72 | −9 | .05 | 4,500 |
| 3 | .80 | −10 | .04 | 4,000 |
| 4 | .88 | −11 | .03 | 3,500 |
| 5 | .96 | −12 | .02 | 3,000 |

this, in most cases, optimal prices are determined without any price-ending constraints and then rounded afterward. For example, if the optimization recommended a price of 4.83%, the post-processor might round the price to 4.85%, which has a more acceptable ending. Because this approach is applied as a post-processor, the prices that result are not guaranteed to be optimal or even feasible (i.e., meet all the constraints). However, in practice, adjusting rate endings after optimization makes only a trivial difference in the objective function while requiring far less computational effort than including additional constraints in the optimization.

## The Dangers of Overconstraining

Constraints are usually necessary to ensure that the final set of prices makes structural sense, meets regulatory requirements, and satisfies all of the lender's business performance targets. However, while constraints are unquestionably necessary, lenders often have a tendency to add too many constraints. In the extreme, adding too many constraints can lead to *infeasibility*—a situation in which no set of prices exists that meets all of the constraints. This is a particular danger when multiple business performance constraints are imposed, such as simultaneously requiring that fundings be greater than some target while expected losses are below another target. It may the case that there is no set of prices that can simultaneously meet both requirements. In this case, the optimization problem is infeasible and no solution can be found.

Infeasibility can be the result of an input error: for example, a constraint may have been entered as "less than or equal to" when it should have been "greater than or equal to" or a bound was entered as $p_i \leq .5\%$ when it should have been $p_i \leq 5\%$. Input errors of this sort are usually relatively easy to detect and fix. The more difficult case is when the constraints have been entered correctly but cannot be simultaneously satisfied by any set of prices. Resolving this situation requires careful consideration of what the constraints were designed to achieve and which ones should be removed or relaxed. A good starting point in this process is to consider which constraints would be violated by the set of prices currently in place.

Infeasibility is not the only danger of overconstraining. Constraints impose costs: adding a constraint can never improve the optimal result and in most cases will make it worse. This means that constraints should be added only if they are required to satisfy real business needs or regulatory requirements. Unfortunately, lenders sometimes add constraints to steer the model toward generating "better" prices. If an optimization model produces a set of prices that does not correspond to the user's expectations, the first step for the user should be to try to understand why the model recommended these prices. If the recommendations are based on incorrect data or faulty assumptions, these should be fixed and the model should be rerun. If constraints are truly needed to enforce a real business need or meet regulations, then they should be retained. However, constraints should not be added simply to force a solution in a desired direction.

Constraints make the prices generated by a model harder to interpret. The question of why the model is recommending price $p$ for segment $i$ becomes harder to answer the more constraints that are imposed. When there are relatively few constraints, the price set for each pricing segment will tend to be close to its unconstrained optimal value. As more and more constraints are imposed, the prices are likely to be pushed farther and farther from their unconstrained optimal values. For example, a constraint that specifies that loan fundings must be greater than or equal to a certain level may force some prices lower than their profit-maximizing level in order to drive total fundings toward the desired level. As more constraints are added, more and more prices will be forced away from their optimal levels. When many constraints are in play, it can become difficult or impossible to pinpoint why a given price was recommended.

A final danger is that, without a good process for periodic review and validation, constraints tend to accumulate over time. It is good practice for a lender to periodically review all the constraints that are imposed in any model to ensure that they are all still relevant and to remove constraints that have become outdated and do not reflect the current business reality.

## Existence and Uniqueness of Solutions

We have seen that a unique profit-maximizing price and a unique revenue-maximizing price always exist in the case of a single loan under the condition that the price-response function has an increasing failure rate and the expected profit function for the loan is continuous and log-concave. This is a happy state of affairs because it means that the price that satisfies the first-order condition in Equation 7.2 is guaranteed to be the unique maximizer. Things are not so simple once constraints are applied, particularly in the case of multiple pricing segments. If the underlying problem is feasible and has reasonable parameters, there is almost certainly a set of prices for all the segments that maximizes the objective function. In other words, *existence* of a solution is not typically an issue. However, *uniqueness* of the solution is not necessarily guaranteed. There may be multiple *local maxima* at which the first-order necessary condition is satisfied. Most approaches for solving constrained nonlinear optimization are so-called hill-climbing algorithms, which start from some initial feasible set of prices and then move in a direction that improves the value of the objective function, changing directions as necessary, until they find a set of prices at which there is no feasible direction to move in which the objective function continues to improve. Such a set of prices is called a *local maximum*. Unfortunately not every local maximum is a global maximum, and in fact there may be multiple local maxima. Multiple local maxima may occur because the objective function has multiple maxima, or it may arise from the structure of the constraints. We discuss both cases.

---

**Example 7.6: Multiple Maxima.** A single loan with multiple maxima is shown in Figure 7.6, which shows the expected profitability as a function of price of a pricing segment that consists 50% of customers with a price-response function of $\overline{F}(p) = e^{1-20p} / (1 + e^{1-20p})$ and 50% with a price-response function $\overline{F}(p) = e^{10-200p} / (1 + e^{10-200p})$. Each loan has an initial balance of \$10,000, a term of 5 years and a monthly cost of capital of .17%. The annual probability of default is 5.0% and the expected loss given default is 50%. The expected profit function has two local maxima: one at $p_1^* = 4.8\%$ and the other at $p_2^* = 9.9\%$, with expected profits of \$230.22 and \$225.63, respectively.

---

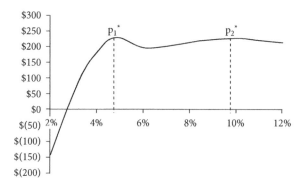

**Figure 7.6**  Expected profit for a pricing segment consisting of an equal mixture of two populations, as specified in Example 7.6

The objective function in Example 7.6 has two maxima because the segment contains a mixture of two subpopulations with very different price-response functions. While the price-response function for each individual subpopulation has an increasing failure rate, the mixture of the two subpopulations does not have an increasing failure rate. More generally, mixing populations with increasing failure rate price-response functions does not necessarily result in a single population with an increasing failure rate. Without an increasing failure-rate price-response function, there may be multiple profit-maximizing or revenue-maximizing prices. An obvious solution is to "unmix" the populations into different segments, each of which has an increasing failure-rate price-response function and to allow each segment to be charged a different price. Dividing a population in this way not only solves the problem of multiple maxima but also increases profit relative to charging the mixed populations the same price. In this case of the loan described in Example 7.6, by dividing the population into two segments and charging each segment its profit-maximizing rate, the lender could increase his expected profit from \$230.22 (the maximum for the mixed population) to \$341.06.

The objective function in Figure 7.6 has multiple maxima, which is clearly problematic. However, even if the objective function has a single maximum, adding constraints can lead to multiple maxima. Figure 7.7 shows a contour map of expected profit as a function of two prices: higher elevations correspond to higher expected profit. The unconstrained problem has a single maximum at the highest point. Now assume that the problem is constrained so that only the shaded region is feasible. Point C is the constrained maximum value to the problem. However, most optimization algorithms started at point A would climb the hill and end up at point B. Point B is a local maximum for the constrained problem because there is no *feasible* direction to move from B in which expected profit improves.

Multiple maxima are problematic for several reasons. The first reason is that the lender would like to be confident that the prices recommended by the algorithm are really the prices that maximize his objective function. If the algorithm stops at a local maximum that is not the global maximum, this will not be the case. In Figure 7.7, point C generates higher expected profit than point B—a lender who used the prices corresponding to point

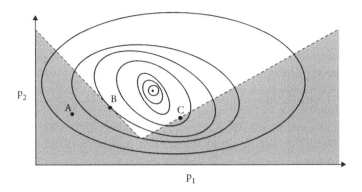

**Figure 7.7**   Expected profit as a function of the prices offered to two pricing segments $p_1$ and $p_2$

NOTE: The data is shown as a contour map with higher elevations on the contour map representing higher levels of expected profit. The shaded area is the feasible region. The optimal prices are represented by the point at the top of the hill. Point C is the constrained maximum; however, many algorithms started at point A would end up at point B, which is a local maximum but not a global maximum.

B would realize less expected profit than was actually available in the market. A second reason that multiple maxima can be problematic is credibility of the model: a user may understandably lose faith in a model that gives different answers to the same problem depending on the starting point. Finally, one of the most common uses of optimization models is to understand the cost of constraints. The cost of imposing a constraint can be determined by solving the optimization problem with and without the constraint and comparing the resulting objective function values. If the constrained problem has a single maximum, this approach will work. If there are multiple maxima, however, the comparison may be misleading—the user might compare a local maximum for one problem with the global maximum of the other.

It is usually difficult, if not impossible, to impose conditions on a price maximization problem that entirely eliminate the possibility of multiple maxima. Fortunately, there are a number of ways that a lender can minimize the probability of multiple maxima. The first way is to ensure that the price-response function for each pricing segment is decreasing, continuous, and satisfies the increasing failure rate property. In addition, the incremental profit function for each pricing segment should be continuous and log-concave. With price-dependent risk, profit may not always increase with price—this is not a problem, as long as the profit function is continuous and log-concave. These conditions on the price-response functions and the expected profit functions guarantee that a unique profit-maximizing price exists for each pricing segment, which is a necessary condition for a unique set of prices to exist for all segments. These conditions can easily be checked using a preprocessor prior to optimizing.

Another good practice is to bound the prices for each pricing segment to ensure that they are within the region of predictive accuracy of the price-response function. This is a good idea in itself, but it also reduces the probability of multiple solutions by restricting the range of prices that is considered.

From the point of view of optimization, more pricing buckets along a continuous dimension such as loan size or credit score are better than fewer. Adding buckets along a segment can reduce the probability of multiple maxima arising from subpopulations with very different price responses being lumped together as in Example 7.6. Separating heterogeneous populations into different pricing segments reduces the risk of multiple maxima.

Finally, it is good practice to choose constraints in a way that ensures that the feasible region is *convex*. Convexity means that, if any two sets of prices—say, $\mathbf{p}_1$ and $\mathbf{p}_2$—are both in the feasible region, then all sets of prices on the line between $\mathbf{p}_1$ and $\mathbf{p}_2$ are also in the feasible region: that is, all points $\alpha\mathbf{p}_1 + (1 - \alpha)\mathbf{p}_2$ are feasible for $0 \leq \alpha \leq 1$. This is clearly not the case in Figure 7.7 because points B and C are both in the feasible region, but the line joining them passes through the infeasible region. Convexity of the feasible region guarantees that, if the constrained problem has a unique global optimum, a hill-climbing algorithm will find it.

Even with these precautions, the possibility of multiple solutions cannot be entirely eliminated. The most common approach to dealing with multiple maxima is simply to solve the same optimization problem several times starting from different points. If there are multiple local maxima, it is likely that the global optimum will be reached from at least one of the starting points. If the algorithm finds more than one local maxima, the lender should choose the one with the highest objective function value. There are a number of procedures for systematically choosing starting points to maximize the probability of finding a global optimum while minimizing the number of starting points tested. Of course, solving the optimization problem multiple times in this fashion requires additional time and computational resources relative to solving it once.

While the possibility of multiple maxima needs to be acknowledged, it should not be overstressed. The probability of multiple maxima can be reduced by following the practices described above. It is also good practice to initiate the optimization from a set of prices that are being considered for implementation. This set of prices should be feasible. By using them as a starting point, an optimization algorithm will always find a set of prices that improves performance. This provides value even if the recommended prices are not a global maximum. Finally, the expected profit function often tends to be fairly flat around the global maximum, and multiple maxima, when they exist, all tend to be within the "flat" region. This means that the global maximum price tends to occur in a region in which small variations from the global maximum result in very small changes in expected profitability. When this is the case, choosing any of the local maxima will result in profitability very close to the maximum attainable.

## OPTIMIZATION WITH COMPETING OBJECTIVES: THE EFFICIENT FRONTIER

Lenders—like other businesses—sometimes want to pursue different and even conflicting goals: "We need to maximize expected profit and originations while minimizing risk." However, optimization can only maximize (or minimize) a single quantity such as revenue or profit. When multiple objective functions are being considered, an *efficient frontier* provides a way to understand the trade-offs among them.

Consider a simple loan with expected profit function $E[\pi(p)] = \bar{F}(p)(1-PD)$ $\times (p - c - \ell/o)$. Denote the revenue-maximizing price for this loan by $\check{p}$ and the profit-maximizing price by $p^*$ by $\check{p} < p^*$. The expected revenue and profit for such a loan as a function of price are shown in Figure 7.8. As the price is increased from 0, both revenue and expected profitability initially increase. Revenue reaches a maximum at $\check{p}$, after which it begins to decline while expected profit continues to increase until it reaches a maximum at $p^*$. For prices higher than $p^*$, expected profit and revenue both decline.

Faced with the expected profit and revenue curves shown in Figure 7.8, a lender who only cared about maximizing revenue would set the price to $\check{p}$, while a lender who cared about only maximizing expected profit would set the price to $p^*$. A lender who cared about both revenue and profit would choose some price between $\check{p}$ and $p^*$. He would never choose a price higher than $p^*$ or lower than $\check{p}$ because he could improve both revenue and profit by choosing a price between $\check{p}$ and $p^*$.

An *efficient frontier* for a single loan is given in Figure 7.9. Here, the horizontal axis is expected revenue and the vertical axis is expected profit. The curve represents all combinations of expected revenue and profit that could be achieved by the lender at some price. The

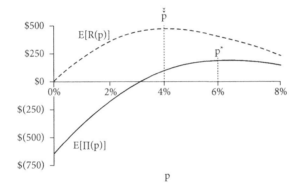

**Figure 7.8**  Revenue and profit for a simple loan as a function of price

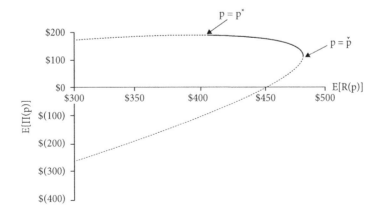

**Figure 7.9**  Efficient frontier for a single loan

portion of the curve shown with a solid line is the efficient frontier—it represents the combinations of expected profit and revenue that the lender could achieve by choosing a price between $\bar{p}$ and $p^*$. A lender concerned about only profit and revenue would never choose to operate on the dashed part of the curve because he could increase both profit and revenue by choosing a point on the efficient frontier.

For a single loan, all possible combinations of revenue and profit lie on a curve such as the one in Figure 7.9. The situation is more complicated when a lender sets prices for many pricing segments. In this case, the possible combinations of expected revenue and profit fall into a two-dimensional region such as the shaded area in Figure 7.10. Assume $N$ pricing segments and let $\mathbf{p} = (p_1, p_2, \ldots p_N)$ be a vector of prices for the segments. Each feasible value of $\mathbf{p}$ will generate an expected revenue $E[R(\mathbf{p})]$ and an expected profit $E[\Pi(\mathbf{p})]$. Each feasible pair $(E[R(\mathbf{p})], E[\Pi(\mathbf{p})])$ is a point in the shaded region in Figure 7.10. Points outside the shaded region are not the result of any feasible combination of prices and are thus not achievable without violating one or more constraints. The efficient frontier in Figure 7.10 is the thick dark curve marking the upper-right-hand border of the feasible region. This segment corresponds to all of the undominated feasible price combinations. If the lender sets prices that fall anywhere but on the feasible region, he could increase both profit and revenue by changing prices to correspond to a point on the efficient frontier. For example, a lender who had set prices that achieved the expected revenue and profit combination represented by point A could increase revenue while keeping profit the same by moving to point B. He could increase profit while keeping revenue the same by moving to point C. He could increase both revenue and profit by moving to a point on the efficient frontier between A and B.

A lender who cares only about revenue and profit will choose a price on the efficient frontier: but what price should he choose? If he could quantify his trade-off between revenue and profitability, then he could specify the appropriately weighted sum as his objective function and solve the resulting optimization problem. For example, a lender who valued a dollar of profit 10 times more than a dollar of revenue would maximize $10 \times E[\Pi(\mathbf{p})] + E[R(\mathbf{p})]$. However, in many cases, a lender is not able to be that precise about his preferences. In this

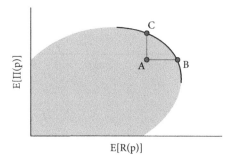

**Figure 7.10**   Efficient frontier when a lender is setting prices for a large number of different loans

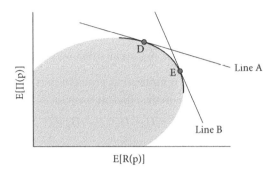

**Figure 7.11**    Points on the efficient frontier that might be chosen by two different lenders

N O T E : A lender choosing point D weights profit more highly relative to revenue than a lender choosing point E. The (negative) slope of the tangent line through any point on the efficient frontier is equal to the ratio of the value of profit to the value of revenue at that point.

case, an efficient frontier enables him to visualize the trade-offs he faces. The point on the efficient frontier that a lender chooses reveals his trade-off between the two goals. Say that a lender facing the efficient frontier shown in Figure 7.11 chooses the point D. The slope of the line tangent to the efficient frontier at D is the ratio of the lender's value of revenue to his value of profit. In this case, the slope of the corresponding tangent line (Line A) is about .33. This means that the lender values a dollar of profit about 3 times as much as a dollar of revenue. The slope of the tangent line through point E is about 2.5. A lender choosing that point values each dollar of revenue about 2.5 times as much as a dollar of profit. A lender who cared only about revenue would pick the rightmost point on the efficient frontier. The tangent line at that point is vertical, corresponding to a profit value of 0. A lender who cared only for profit would choose the highest point in the efficient frontier corresponding to a horizontal tangent line and a value of 0 for revenue.

The efficient frontier can be a valuable visualization tool because it enables decision makers to understand how far they are from the efficient frontier and allows them to choose prices that satisfy their trade-off between the two goals. However, generating the efficient frontier requires solving multiple optimization problems. Assume that a lender needs to price loans in $N$ different pricing segments. Let $\mathbf{p}^{*} = (p_1^{*}, p_2^{*}, \ldots, p_N^{*})$ be the vector of prices that maximizes expected profitability and $\breve{p} = (\breve{p}_1, \breve{p}_2, \ldots, \breve{p}_N)$ be the vector of prices that maximizes expected revenue, both subject to the same constraints. Define $\Pi^{*} = E\left[\pi(\mathbf{p}^{*})\right]$, $\breve{\Pi} = E\left[\pi(\breve{p})\right]$, $R^{*} = E\left[R(\mathbf{p}^{*})\right]$, and $\breve{R} = E[R(\breve{p})]$. Then, $\Pi^{*} \geq \breve{\Pi}$ and $\breve{R} \geq R^{*}$.[6]

Three different approaches can be used to calculate points on the efficient frontier:

1. Define a set of $M$ weights $0 = \alpha_1 < \alpha_2 < \ldots \alpha_M = 1$. Solve the $M$ optimization problems with objective function max $\alpha_i E[R(\mathbf{p})] + (1 - \alpha_i)E[\Pi(\mathbf{p})]$. Let $\mathbf{p}_k$ be the solution to the problem with weight $\alpha_k$. Then each of the pairs $(E[R(\mathbf{p}_k)], E[\Pi(\mathbf{p}_k)])$ is a point on the efficient frontier.

2. Define a set of $M$ target revenues $R_1 < R_2 < R_3 < \ldots < R_M = \breve{R}$. For each target revenue $R_k$, solve the optimization problem:

$$\mathbf{p}_k = \arg\max_{\mathbf{p}} \sum_i E\big[\Pi_i(p_i)\big]$$

subject to $\sum_i E[R(p_i)] \geq R_k$ plus all other constraints.

Let $\mathbf{p}_k$ be the solution to the $k$th optimization problem thus defined. Then the pairs $(E[R(\mathbf{p}_k)], E[\Pi(\mathbf{p}_k)])$ are points on the efficient frontier.

3. Define a set of $M$ target profits $\Pi_1 < \Pi_2 < \Pi_3 < \dots < \Pi_M = \Pi^*$. For each target revenue $\Pi_k$, solve the optimization problem:

$$\mathbf{p}_k = \arg\max_{\mathbf{p}} \sum_i E\big[R_i(p_i)\big]$$

subject to $\sum_i E\big[\pi_i(p_i)\big] \geq \Pi_k$ and all of the standard constraints.

Let $\mathbf{p}_k$ be the solution to the $k$th optimization problem thus defined. Then the pairs $(E[R(\mathbf{p}_k)], E[\Pi(\mathbf{p}_k)])$ are points on the efficient frontier.

Each of these approaches generates $M$ points on the efficient frontier by solving $M$ optimization problems. Once these $M$ points have been calculated, additional points on the efficient frontier can be estimated by interpolation.

The efficient frontier describes the combinations of revenue and profit (or other any pair of goals) that a lender can achieve through pricing at a particular time. The shape and location of the efficient frontier is determined by, among other things, the total demand and the price sensitivity of customers in each pricing segment. The lender can move the efficient frontier through activities such as advertising or improved product features. In particular, by increasing total demand and/or decreasing customer price sensitivity, a lender can move the efficient frontier upward and to the right. In this case, the new efficient frontier provides the lender opportunities to increase both revenue and profit relative to the previous prices. Speaking broadly, the location of the efficient frontier is determined by a lender's marketing and product position within his markets. Pricing is the "moment of truth" at which the lender can realize the return from these investments. However, a lender needs to choose a set of prices on the efficient frontier to realize the return—otherwise, he is leaving money on the table and squandering some of his investments.[7]

## SUMMARY

- The goal of optimization is to find a price (or set of prices) that best meets a specified business goal such as maximizing expected profit or maximizing expected revenue. In price optimization, the *decision variables* are the prices for each pricing segment, and the *objective function* determines how the goal—usually revenue or profit—depends on the prices.

- For a single loan without price-dependent risk, an unique profit-maximizing price is guaranteed to exist assuming that the price-response function has a continuous increasing failure rate. In this case, the profit-maximizing price is greater than the cost of funds plus the normalized loss rate. A unique revenue-maximizing price is also guaranteed to exist; however, it may not be greater than incremental cost.

- When price-dependent risk is significant, it may be that the profit-maximizing price yields an expected profit that is less than 0, in which case it is unprofitable to lend to this segment at any price. If it is profitable to lend to the segment, the profit-maximizing price that incorporates price-dependent risk will be lower than the profit-maximizing price that does not.

- When a lender wants to find the set of prices that best meets some business goal for more than one pricing segment, he faces a multivariable nonlinear optimization problem. In the absence of constraints, the prices that best meet the overall business goal can be found by calculating the price for each pricing segment individually.

- Lenders apply constraints to price optimization to ensure that the recommended prices meet certain restrictions. Typical constraints include bounds that specify minimum and maximum prices for each pricing segment, structural constraints that ensure that prices follow certain desirable patterns, and business performance constraints that ensure that the prices are consistent with other business needs such as maintaining required levels of new balances in certain segments.

- Once constraints have been applied, nonlinear constrained optimization algorithms need to be employed to find the prices that maximize the objective function subject to the constraints.

- Constraints are often necessary to ensure reasonable prices, but lenders should avoid overconstraining the optimization problem. In the extreme, overconstraining can lead to infeasibility, in which case, the optimization problem has no solution. However, even in the absence of infeasibility, excessive constraints will reduce the amount of profit or revenue that can be achieved.

- A price-optimization problem may have multiple local maxima—only one of which will be the global optimum. Multiple maxima may result from the structure of the objective function or from the constraints imposed (or both). The possibility of multiple maxima cannot be totally eliminated; however, it can be reduced by ensuring that the individual price-optimization problem for each segment is guaranteed to have a unique solution, by setting appropriate bounds on individual prices, and by imposing only constraints that result in a convex feasible region.

- In many cases, lenders seek to pursue two business goals—for example, expected revenue and expected profit. In this case, an efficient frontier is a useful tool for visualizing the trade-offs between the different goals. The efficient frontier shows the combination of business goals that can be achieved using pricing. The efficient frontier can be calculated by running a number of constrained optimization problems to generate points on the frontier.

- The location and shape of a lender's efficient frontier is determined by his brand and product strength within the markets he serves. Actions by the lender that increase demand and/or reduce price sensitivity will move the efficient frontier outward and allow for the possibility of increasing both expected profit and expected revenue.

## NOTES

1. We have shown that $p^*$ satisfies the first-order condition to maximize expected profit. However, this is not sufficient to show that it is a maximizer: the same first-order condition would be satisfied by a price that minimizes expected profit. One way to show that $p^*$ is a maximizer is to take the second derivative of $E[\pi(p)]$ and show that it is less than 0 at $p^*$. However, it is apparent that $E[\pi(p^*)] > E[\pi(c + 1/o)] = 0$, so $p^*$ cannot minimize $E[\pi(p)]$ and $p^*$ must be a maximizer.

2. The topic of learning and earning to derive adaptive pricing policies is a very active area of research. One of the most consistent findings from this research is that periodic price testing is needed to ensure optimality: calculating a single price and then not varying from that price can lead to suboptimal results, even when the observed demand at that price is consistent with expectations. Özer and Phillips (2012) give a short introduction to some of the issues and major findings in this area, and den Boer (2015) provides a review of the literature.

3. This section presumes some familiarity with basic concepts of nonlinear optimization. A good introduction to the topic can be found in Luenberger and Ye (2008) and a deeper treatment in Boyd and Vandenberghe (2004).

4. As noted in Chapter 6, all else being equal, high-risk customers tend to be less price sensitive than low-risk customers, and customers applying for a large loan tend to be more price sensitive than those applying for a smaller loan. Thus, in the absence of constraints, we would expect profit-maximizing loan prices to increase with risk and decrease with loan size, which is the desired pattern. However, once other constraints are added, these patterns may no longer hold and additional constraints may be required to ensure that they still hold.

5. The fact that certain price endings such as 5 and 9 can stimulate demand is well established in retail—see Özer and Zheng (2012) for an overview of the research.

6. It is theoretically possible that $\Pi^* = \Pi$ and $R = R^*$. In this case, there is no conflict between the objectives because a single set of prices maximizes both expected profit and expected revenue. In this case, the efficient frontier is a single point. This is unlikely to occur in the real world.

7. The efficient frontier was introduced by Markowitz (1959) to explain the trade-off between risk and return in a portfolio of securities. The idea of using the efficient frontier to represent achievable combinations of two different objectives is widely used in many fields. Phillips (2012b) gives a fuller discussion of the use of efficient frontiers in pricing.

# 8 BEHAVIORAL ECONOMICS AND CREDIT PRICING

One of the tenets of neoclassical economics is that consumers are rational. In choosing among alternatives, a rational consumer uses all the information available to her, systematically evaluates her alternatives, and chooses the one that maximizes the net present value of her utility. A rational consumer always has a willingness to pay (which may be less than or equal to zero) for every loan being offered to her by every lender. If her willingness to pay is less than the prices of all loans on offer, she will not borrow. Otherwise, she will choose the loan such that the difference between the price of the loan and her willingness to pay is maximized. Variation in this willingness to pay among consumers generates a price-response function across a population.

The assumption of consumer rationality provides an intuitive and compelling basis for the intellectual structure underlying price optimization. As discussed in Appendix C, the idea of rationality is based on a handful of plausible axioms about how consumers behave. However, it has been known to merchants and lenders for ages that consumers do not always behave rationally. To take two simple examples:

- Consumers are more likely to buy an item if it is presented to them as "10% Off! Normally $10" than if $9 is simply listed as the price.
- Diners at restaurants will order more expensive items if the prices are presented as numbers without dollar signs than if prices are listed with dollar signs next to them.[1]

Both of these examples are inconsistent with consumer rationality. A rational consumer's purchase decision would not depend on whether or not $9 was the list price or a sale price. Similarly, a rational restaurant patron would order the item on the menu that maximized expected surplus (expected utility minus price). Her order would not be influenced by whether or not the prices are accompanied by dollar signs. But, in both of these situations—and many others—real-world consumer behavior deviates from rationality.

The rational consumer of economic textbooks—sometimes called *Homo economicus*—is a sort of utility-maximizing computer with the ability to reliably calculate the implications of complex decisions. In the words of the economists Cass Sunstein and Richard

Thaler, "Homo economicus can think like Albert Einstein, store as much memory as IBM's Big Blue, and exercise the willpower of Mahatma Gandhi" (Thaler and Sunstein 2009, 6). Real humans—*Homo sapiens* rather than *Homo economicus*—are often unable or unwilling to expend the mental energy needed to make the rational decision in complex situations. When it comes to financial decisions such as how much to borrow, under which terms, from which lenders, and when to pay back existing debt, most people, most of the time, do not make the "rational" decision.

This chapter discusses the implications of subrational consumer decision making for loan pricing. In the extreme, if massive deviations from rationality are the norm, then the idea of a willingness to pay for a loan (or anything else) may not be realistic. Consumers could react to prices inconsistently and unpredictably. In this case, price optimization might require calculations very different from those described in this book. In the extreme case, if consumers were completely unpredictable, price optimization would be impossible. Even if consumers are generally rational, it could be the case that lenders could benefit by pricing in a way that takes advantage of systematic deviations from rationality. Finally, if consumers are systematically making subrational financial decisions, it could justify government intervention to "save consumers from themselves." These are some of the issues that we explore in this chapter. We begin by identifying several categories of subrational behavior that influence financial choices made by consumers. We then discuss the implications of these deviations for both lenders and regulators.

## HOW DO CONSUMERS DEVIATE FROM RATIONALITY?

Appendix C provides an overview of the classical model of consumer choice. For our purposes, the most important features of this model are the following:

- At any time a rational consumer has a set of preferences among possible consumption bundles. These preferences possess certain intuitive properties such as completeness, reflexivity, and transitivity.

- A rational consumer's preferences can be represented by a utility function that assigns a number to every consumption bundle such that the consumer prefers a bundle with a higher utility to a bundle with a lower utility.

- In a static world, a rational consumer would choose the consumption bundle that maximizes her utility subject to her budget constraint.

- A rational consumer facing a budget constraint will have a maximum willingness to pay for every item available, including loans. Her willingness to pay for an item is not simply a function of her utility for that item, it is also a function of her budget as well as what other items are available, her utilities for those items, and their prices.

- For purchases that have uncertain utility at the time of purchase, the consumer bases her decision on her expected risk-weighted utility. A risk-neutral consumer will compare alternatives on the basis of their expected values, while a risk-averse consumer may prefer an alternative with a lower expected value if the risk (potential downside) is lower.

- The static consumer choice model can be extended to decisions over time by assuming that the consumer has a discount rate that she uses to discount future outcomes back to the present time. Using this discounted utility model, a consumer evaluates alternatives with payoffs over time by comparing the net present value of the expected risk-weighted utilities over time calculated using her discount rate.

Consumer choices that are in accordance with the classical model of consumer choice are termed *rational*, whereas decisions or patterns of decisions that cannot be reconciled with the classical model are termed *subrational*.

As noted in Chapter 4, it is important to recognize that the classical model allows for consumers to have preferences not only on loans but also on lenders. As shown in Example 4.1, consumers may have a higher utility for a loan under identical terms from Lender A than Lender B, in which case Lender A can charge a higher price for the same loan than Lender B and still attract business. Furthermore, if consumers put a value on their own time (as they generally do), it follows that they will usually not research all possible alternatives before making a decision. This can be rational if the cost (in time and effort) of further research exceeds the expected gain from finding a lower price. Thus, it should not be surprising that consumer-lending markets typically support a wide range of prices such as that shown in Table 1.5. A key point is that, even if customers are entirely rational, markets can still display a wide range of price variation.

In fact, the assumption of consumer rationality is quite flexible and can account for a wide range of behavior that might at first glance seem to be subrational. For example, rational consumers can have preferences that change over time: I can prefer scrambled eggs to spaghetti for breakfast but prefer spaghetti to scrambled eggs for dinner without violating transitivity. Furthermore, the fact that consumers are not always rational does not mean that they are completely capricious: in fact, consumer decisions deviate from the optimal decisions in predictable ways. Back in the late 1950s Daniel Kahnemann and Amos Tversky identified a number of the ways in which human decisions deviate from rationality. They are credited with first noting that these deviations from the classical model could have significant implications for economics. In the past 20 years or so, there has been an explosion of interest in how human beings actually make decisions, how these decisions deviate from predictions based on the assumption of consumer rationality, and the implications of these deviations for business and government policy. This is the field called *behavioral economics*, and behavioral economists have identified a number of ways in which customers systematically deviate from rationality in making decisions.[2] In this section, we describe four of these deviations from rationality—decision heuristics and mental accounting, numeracy, framing, and dynamic inconsistency—with implications for loan pricing.

## Decision Heuristics and Mental Accounting

Household financial decisions can be extremely complex. For example, mortgages in the United States come in a bewildering variety of combinations of fixed-rate, variable, and hybrid mortgages; with or without points; with or without prepayment penalties; and so on. For a rational consumer to choose the best mortgage among the choices she has available to her, she must forecast her future income and how long she plans to keep the house, along with forecasting future inflation, housing price trends, and tax rates. Even given this information, determining which mortgage would minimize her expected net present value of future payments would require sophisticated mathematical calculations. For example, one academic paper calculated that a household should refinance when the interest rate for a new mortgage falls below the rate that they are currently paying by at least

$$\frac{1}{\psi}\left[\phi + W\left(-e^{-\phi}\right)\right],$$

with

$$\psi = \frac{\sqrt{2(\rho+\lambda)}}{\delta},$$

$$\phi = 1 + \frac{\Psi(\rho+\lambda)k}{M(1-\tau)},$$

where $W$ is the Lambert W function, "$\rho$ is the real discount rate, $\lambda$ is the expected real rate of exogenous mortgage repayment, $\delta$ is the standard deviation of the mortgage rate, $\kappa/M$ is the ratio of the tax-adjusted refinancing cost to the remaining mortgage value, and $\tau$ is the marginal tax rate" (Agarwal, Driscoll, and Laibson 2013, 591). It seems unlikely that many (if any) households actually make their refinancing decisions in strict conformance with this rule or any other rule of comparable complexity. Yet this is exactly what the assumption of consumer rationality requires.[3]

When a decision is difficult or requires intense mental effort, most people fall back on *heuristics*, or rules of thumb. As Daniel Kahnemann (2011) points out in his book *Thinking, Fast and Slow*, this makes sense. We make thousands of decisions every day, but we have the time and mental energy to subject only a handful of those decisions to rigorous analysis. In many cases, making a "good enough" decision quickly is more important than taking the time to calculate the "optimal" decision. This bias toward action over analysis may even have an evolutionary basis—when our ancestor saw a lion approaching, it was more important to follow the simple heuristic "run as fast as you can in the opposite direction," than it was to take the time to calculate the optimal escape route.

According to bankers and mortgage brokers, two simple rules that are commonly used by mortgage shoppers are "I won't consider any mortgage that includes points" and "I want the mortgage with the shortest term that has a payment that fits within my monthly budget." Both of these rules simplify the exceptionally complicated problem of mortgage selection. However, either one can lead to a consumer rejecting the mortgage that would minimize the expected net present value of her future payments. The use of heuristics can skew customers' borrowing decisions whenever comparing alternatives is difficult.

*Mental accounting* is another heuristic that can influence financial decision making.[4] According to economic theory, the source of current or expected future income should not influence household spending or savings decisions: an unanticipated additional $1,000 increase in disposable income should be the treated the same if it comes from a windfall bonus, an unexpected gain in the value of a pension fund, or a raise. Yet consumers react very differently to these happy events. One study estimated that consumers tend to spend (rather than save or invest) almost 100% of any increase in current income, from 40% to 60% of an asset increase, and virtually nothing from an increase in future income. Another study showed that consumers spend about 59% of an unanticipated bonus compared to 83% of an equivalent increase in current income, but only about 3% of an increase in the value of their retirement portfolio. A rational consumer would treat all increases in after-tax wealth the same, regardless of the source. In contrast, mental accounting posits that consumers unconsciously file gains and losses into different accounts depending on the source, and they respond differently to changes in the values of these different accounts.

Mental accounting is likely to be one reason that households with a portfolio of debt accounts do not manage them in the most logical fashion. For example, some households continue to pay high interest on revolving debt (e.g., credit cards) while maintaining substantial balances in savings accounts at very low interest rates. Mental accounting would suggest that credit card debt is mentally filed in the "current consumption" account while savings is filed in the "savings for the future" account, and some consumers do not see a conflict from simultaneously holding high-cost debt and low-return savings. However, mental accounting does not explain a related phenomenon—that many consumers holding debt in different accounts with different associated APRs do not pay down the debt in a way that minimizes total interest payments. A survey asked consumers to imagine that they held two credit cards: a MasterCard with a balance of $100 and a 10% APR and a Visa card with a balance of $1,000 and a 15% APR. The consumers were all told that they had just received a government stimulus check that they were to use to pay down their credit card debt. Some of the consumers were told that the size of the check was $1,000, and others were told that it was $100. Regardless of the size of the check, the optimal decision is to use the entire amount to pay down the high-APR Visa account. Nonetheless, the survey participants repaid significantly more money on the low-APR MasterCard account when the rebate check was $100 than when the rebate was $1,000. In fact, many of those who "received" the $100 rebate check chose to completely pay off the low-APR MasterCard account and made no payment on the high-APR Visa card.

To determine whether similar effects behavior occurred in a more realistic setting, the same researchers enlisted a number of undergraduates to play a debt management game in which participants were initially saddled with debt in six different accounts, each with a different APR, as shown in Table 8.1. The game was played for 25 rounds. In each round participants were given a $5,000 payment that they could allocate any way they wished among the six accounts with positive balances. Each participant also received payments of $20,000 in round 6, $15,000 in round 12, and $40,000 in round 19. Participants received a bonus after the last round depending on the amount of debt they had remaining, with lower debt resulting in a higher payment. The optimal policy is to use all the money received to pay down current debt in descending order of APR. A player who followed this strategy would have three accounts still open and $29,428 in total debt at the end of the game. When the game was played by 162 Duke undergraduates, the average ending debt was $38,371. In other words, the average player paid $8,943 in additional interest simply as a result of poor allocation decisions. Furthermore, not a single one of the 162 players optimally allocated money in each round, and in every round of the game, between 40% and 60% of the money was allocated incorrectly.[5]

TABLE 8.1
*APRs and initial balances for each account in
the debt management game*

| Account | APR (%) | Initial amount ($) |
|---------|---------|---------------------|
| 1 | 2.50 | 3,000 |
| 2 | 3.00 | 8,000 |
| 3 | 3.50 | 11,000 |
| 4 | 3.25 | 13,000 |
| 5 | 3.75 | 52,000 |
| 6 | 4.00 | 60,000 |

SOURCE: Amar et al. 2011.

In a variation of the game, the participants were given the option to invest some of their money in a savings account with a 2% interest rate in each period. They could withdraw this money (with interest) at any point later in the game and use it to repay debt. Under the terms of the game, a rational player would never put money into the savings account; however, when given the option, many of the players did so. As a result, the additional interest paid by players with the savings account option was $15,105. The addition of an irrelevant alternative led to worse decisions.

The somewhat depressing results of the debt management game were attributed by the researchers to *debt account aversion*: players preferred closing an account to making a partial payment on a larger account, even when it did not make financial sense. Many players paid down their debt to minimize the number of open accounts: a heuristic that is—to paraphrase H. L. Mencken—simple, elegant, and wrong.

If extended to the real world, the implications of the debt management game are somewhat staggering. A player playing the optimal strategy in the financial management game would pay total interest of $82,428 over the course of the game. This is equal to the total income they received of $200,000, plus the optimal final balance of $29,428 minus the starting principal of $147,000. But, on average, players paid between $91,371 and $97,533 in interest (depending on whether they had the savings account option available), which means that between 9.9% and 15.5% of their interest payments were wasted as a result of suboptimal decision making. If these numbers were applied to the credit card industry as a whole, then it would imply that every year about $16 billion in credit card interest payments are wasted due to debt account aversion alone.

The debt management game can be criticized as stylized and unrealistic. However, it is actually far simpler than the financial decisions faced by households in the real world. In the game, income is predictable and the sole goal is to reduce existing debt—players cannot accumulate additional debt. Also, repayment decisions are made simultaneously in each round. In the real world, income may be uncertain, and both income and debt payments can occur at different times, adding a dynamic planning element that is not present in the experiment. Furthermore, in the real world, people must determine how much of their income to allocate to purchases and investments as well as to debt repayment. Real-world financial problems faced by consumers are far more difficult and complex than those faced by players of the debt management game, which would suggest that the frequency of suboptimal decisions in the real world is high. This has been verified empirically. A study of the financial decisions made by 917 households in the United States found that many households paid a significant amount in avoidable fees and interest: "For those who do pay significant fees and credit card interest, a large share of costs could be avoided relatively easily. At the median, almost half of credit card interest could be avoided by a combination of reallocating from high- to low-rate cards, and repaying debt using available 2 checking balances" (Stango and Zinman 2009, 425).

## Framing

A rational consumer would not care if an item was "on sale" or not—only about the price. However, merchants have known for hundreds, if not thousands, of years that a sale sign will help move merchandise. Online retailers have become adept at exploiting this fact. As reported in the *New York Times*:

> Le Creuset's iron-handled skillet, 11 3/4 inches wide and cherry in color. Amazon said late last week that it would knock $60 off the $260 list price to sell the skillet for $200. . . . The suggested price for the skillet at Williams-Sonoma.com is $285 but customers can buy it for $200. At AllModern.com, the list price is $250 but its sales price is $200. At Cutleryand-More.com, the list price is $285 and the sales price is $200. An additional 15 or so on-line retailers—some hosted by Amazon, others on Google Shopping—charge $200. On Le Creuset's own site, it sells the pan at $200. (Streitfeld 2016, 1)

Clearly, online retailers feel that presenting the $200 price as a discount will sell more units than presenting it as the list price—to the extent that they appear to be establishing arbitrary list prices solely to make the $200 price seem like a bargain. This is an example of *framing*: the way a price is presented, or framed, influences demand beyond the value of the price itself.[6]

The power of price promotions to drive sales has been explained in terms of *prospect theory*, which posits that humans feel the pain of a loss more strongly than the pleasure of an equivalent gain. The list price is used by consumers as a baseline (or reference price) and the savings associated with the promoted price is viewed as a gain relative to the baseline. This implies that consumers have a different sensitivity to list prices and discounts: demand for a loan with a list price of $p$ but sold with an advertised discount of $\delta$ would be greater than demand for a loan with a list price of $p - \delta$. This phenomenon has long been recognized in marketing a wide range of consumer goods, so it is not surprising that it is also present in consumer lending: Nomis Solutions research has found that *promotional elasticities* tend to be approximately 20% to 40% higher than list-price elasticities for loans. This effect can be incorporated in estimating price sensitivity by including separate variables for the list price and the promotion discount amount. The coefficient associated with the discount amount reflects the greater sensitivity to the promotional amount than to a drop in the list price.

## Time-Preference Inconsistencies

Assume that a customer with a discount rate of $r_d$ has been approved for $m$ different loan options, with each option having an initial amount borrowed $B$, term $T_k$, and stream of monthly payments $\mathbf{p}_k = (p_{k1}, p_{k2}, \ldots p_{kT_k})$ for $k = 1, 2, \ldots, m$. Assume further that the customer is indifferent among lenders. The classical model of time preference described in Appendix C posits that her first step in choosing a loan would be to calculate the net present value of each alternative $k$:

$$NPV(B, T_k, \mathbf{p}_k) = B - \sum_{t=1}^{T_k} \delta_t(r_d) p_{kt},$$  (8.1)

where

$$\delta_t(r_d) = 1 / (1 + r_d)^t$$  (8.2)

is her discount factor.[7] If all the loans have $NPV < 0$ she will not borrow; if one or more has an $NPV > 0$, she will choose the loan with the highest NPV.

It has been known for a long time that the discounted utility model is not a particularly good representation of the way that consumers actually make choices. Even Paul Samuelson, the economist who originally proposed the model, did not claim that it was realistic—"It is completely arbitrary to assume that the individual behaves so as to maximize an integral of the form envisaged" (Samuelson 1937, 161). Indeed, over time, both experience and experiments have revealed many differences between the predictions of the discounted utility model and the ways in which people actually behave. Two of the key discrepancies are the following:

1. *Preference reversals.* Would you prefer chocolate mousse or fruit for dessert at dinner tonight? What about next week? In a study, 70% of the people chose chocolate for today while 74% chose fruit for next week. It is unlikely that many of the respondents felt that their preferences for fruit and chocolate were going to switch over the course of the week. The more likely explanation is that some of the respondents valued immediate outcomes relative to future outcomes more strongly than predicted by the discounted utility model.[8]

2. *Time inconsistency.* The discounted utility model predicts that a consumer's preference for outcomes that occur at different times should depend only on the time interval between them, not on the timing of the first outcome. For example, given the choice between $1,000 today or $1,100 in two weeks, a significant number of people would choose the smaller amount today. However, given the choice between $1,000 in a year or $1,100 in 54 weeks, many of the same people would choose the larger sum later. This pattern of choices is inconsistent with the discounted utility model.

Observations of consumer behavior and experiments have shown that many people act as if they have discount rates that increase as an event gets closer in time. In one study, subjects were asked to specify the amount of money that they would require in 1 month, 1 year, and 10 years to make them indifferent to receiving $15 right now. The median responses of $20, $50, and $100, respectively, imply an average annual discount rate of 345% over 1 month, 120% over 1 year, and 19% over 10 years.[9] One model designed to represent this effect is called *hyperbolic discounting*. In hyperbolic discounting, delay from now to a time $t$ periods from now is discounted by a factor of $\hat{\delta}_t(r_d) = 1 / (1 + r_d)^t$. Example 8.1 illustrates how hyperbolic discounting can account for preference reversals.

**Example 8.1: Hyperbolic Discounting and Preference Reversal.** Assume that a customer has a choice between a payoff of $1,000 in 60 months or $800 in 48 months and that she compares future outcomes using hyperbolic discounting with a rate of 3% per month; that is, she weights an outcome with value $V$ that occurs $t$ months in the future by an amount equal to $V/(1 + .03t)$. In this case, she values the $1,000 outcome at $1,000/(1 + .03 \times 60)$ = $357 and the $800 outcome at $800/(1 + .03 \times 48)$ = $328, and she would choose the later $1,000 payoff. In 42 months, the $800 payoff is now 6 months in the future, whereas the $1,000 payoff is 18 months in the future. Her present value of the two outcomes is now $800/(1 + .03 \times 6)$ = $678 and $1,000/(1 + .03 \times 18)$ = $649. Her preferences have reversed: she now prefers the $800 sooner to waiting for the $1,000. Her preferences over time for the two alternatives are shown in Figure 8.1.

While hyperbolic discounting can account for preference reversals, it does not account for the fact that many people seem to weight immediate outcomes (either good or bad) much more strongly than future outcomes. This phenomenon is called *present bias*, and it implies that a delay of a single period is felt much more strongly than subsequent delays. *Quasi-hyperbolic discounting* accounts for present bias by positing that consumers use a discontinuous discount factor of the form:

$$\overline{\delta}_t(r_d) = \begin{cases} 1 & \text{for } t = 0, \\ \beta/(1 + r_d)^t & \text{for } t > 0. \end{cases} \tag{8.3}$$

Here, $0 \le \beta \le 1$ is a factor by which outcomes are discounted for any delay. A value of $\beta = 1$ corresponds to an individual who is not present biased and uses the standard discount factor in Equation 8.2. Smaller values of $\beta$ correspond to greater levels of present bias. In the extreme, a value of $\beta = 0$ would represent someone who completely lived for the moment and gave no weight to future outcomes.[10]

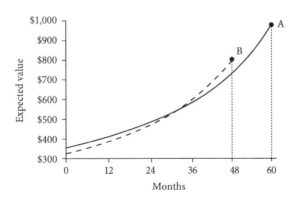

**Figure 8.1**   Hyperbolic discounting and preference reversal

N O T E : Outcome A is a payment of $1,000 in 60 months and Outcome B is a payment of $800 in 48 months. The solid curve shows the present value of Outcome A evaluated by a customer using hyperbolic discounting with a discount rate of .03 and the dashed curve shows the present value of Outcome B evaluated by the same customer. Her preferences reverse at month 33. More details are given in Example 8.1.

There is strong evidence that many people are present biased and that present bias is associated with poor financial decisions. A survey of people who were taking advantage of a volunteer income-tax assistance program found that about 36% of the participants were present biased. The present-biased participants were about 15%–20% more likely to hold credit card debt. They also had about $400 to $500 more debt per person than their counterparts who were not present biased. Another study showed that individuals who displayed significant present bias tend to have higher balances on revolving accounts ($1,565 versus $776), to have lower average credit scores (598 versus 623), and to be more likely to have at least one account in default (54% versus 45%).[11]

Both hyperbolic and quasi-hyperbolic discounting can lead to preference reversals such as the one illustrated in Figure 8.1. Such preference reversals are an example of *time inconsistency*. Time inconsistency raises philosophical questions. Does our existence consist of a series of "selves"? If so, how does our current self account for the well-being of future selves in making decisions? While psychologists and philosophers debate these questions, it does appear that human beings—in common with a number of other animal species—are time inconsistent and demonstrate preference reversals of the sort illustrated in Figure 8.1.

Preference reversals are related to issues of self-control. For example, we may decide that we want to give up our usual Saturday-night dinner of steak and potato to lose weight before summer. In this case, looking good in our swimming suit would correspond to point A in Figure 8.1 and the steak-and-potato dinner to point B. At the beginning of the week, the prospect of the steak-and-potato dinner is sufficiently far off that we can confidently plan to give it up to enjoy the greater (but more distant) reward of losing weight. As Saturday gets closer, our preferences may reverse and we decide to eat steak and potatoes after all. If this happens every week, we will continue to enjoy our regular steak and potato dinners but never achieve the higher utility we would have gained from losing weight.

Differences in weighing future outcomes manifest themselves at an early age. The famous "marshmallow experiment" (sometimes called the "Stanford marshmallow experiment") refers to a series of experiments carried out by the psychologist Walter Mischel and his colleagues to measure the level of self-control in four-year-old children. The experiment typically begins with the experimenter presenting some treats to the child—usually, but not always, marshmallows. In the most common version of the experiment, a single treat—for example, one marshmallow—is set within reach of the child. The experimenter explains that she is going to leave the room and that child can ring the bell to call her back if he wants to eat the marshmallow. However, if the child waits until the experimenter returns without ringing the bell, the child will receive a bigger reward—two marshmallows. The experimenter then leaves the room and the experiment ends either when the child rings the bell or when the experimenter returns on her own accord—usually after about 15 minutes.

Children in the marshmallow experiment demonstrated a wide range of behavior, with some ringing the bell as soon as the experimenter left the room, while others waited patiently until the experimenter returned, and still others managed to wait a few seconds or a few minutes before succumbing to temptation. Children who waited for a few minutes before ringing the bell demonstrated preference reversal—in this case, eating one marshmallow now corresponded to point B in Figure 8.1 and eating two marshmallows later to point A. Evidently, both time inconsistency and differences in time preference manifest themselves at an early age.[12]

The follow-ups to the marshmallow experiment have been in some ways even more intriguing than the original experiments. When a sample of the children was studied 10 years later (at age 14), those who had waited longer were described by their parents as "more verbally fluent and able to express ideas; they used and responded to reasons, were attentive and able to concentrate, to plan, and to think ahead, and were competent and skillful. Likewise they were perceived as able to cope and deal with stress more maturely and seemed more self assured" (Mischel, Shoda, and Rodriguez 1989). Furthermore, seconds of delay time in eating the marshmallow were positively correlated with SAT scores for the children who (much later) applied to college. This suggests not only that differences in time preference manifest themselves at an early age, but that they are persistent over time and associated with later-life outcomes.[13]

## The Role of Numeracy

Consumer financial decisions can be difficult: making the right choices often requires making mathematical calculations, and sometimes—as in the case of choosing the optimal mortgage—quite complex ones. Consumers vary in their so-called *numeracy*—their facility with mathematics and arithmetic. Perhaps not surprisingly, customers with a higher level of numeracy tend to make better financial decisions. For example, a survey was conducted of borrowers who took out subprime mortgages during 2006 and 2007 in Connecticut, Massachusetts, and Rhode Island. Results from the survey were then matched with performance data for the mortgages over the following 5 years. The survey included five questions specifically designed to test numeracy:

1. In a sale, a shop is selling all items at half price. Before the sale, a sofa costs $300. How much will it cost in the sale?

2. If the chance of getting a disease is 10%, how many people out of 1,000 would be expected to get the disease?

3. A secondhand car dealer is selling a car for $6,000. This is two-thirds of what it cost new. How much did the car cost new?

4. If five people all have the winning numbers in the lottery and the prize is $2 million, how much will each person get?

5. Let's say you have $200 in a savings account. The account earns 10% interest per year. How much will you have in the account at the end of 2 years?

On the basis of their answers to these questions, borrowers were categorized into four financial literacy groups, with Group 1 being the least literate and Group 4 being the most literate. The average percentage of time that members of each group had been delinquent on their mortgage and the frequency of mortgages that were in default for each group were calculated. As shown in Figure 8.2, both delinquency and foreclosures decreased as numeracy increased. Notably, delinquencies occurred in the least numerate group at about

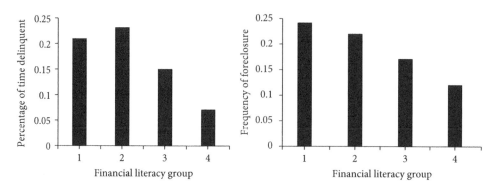

**Figure 8.2**   Fraction of time delinquent and fraction ever foreclosed by financial literacy group from Gerardi, Goette, and Meier (2013)

double the frequency of the most numerate group, and foreclosure was almost four times more likely for the least numerate group than for the most numerate group.

This study provides strong evidence that less numerate borrowers are more likely to default on their mortgage than more numerate borrowers. There are two (not necessarily mutually exclusive) reasons this might be the case: either the less numerate make poorer initial choices of mortgages, or they may make poorer financial decisions after acquiring a mortgage. At any rate, numeracy appears to vary widely in the populations of developed countries, and only a small percentage of individuals qualify as highly numerate. A 2007 study of "early baby boomers" (those born in 1951 through 1956) in the United States found that only 18% could correctly answer the question: "Let's say you have $200 in a savings account. The account earns 20% interest per year. How much would you have in the account at the end of two years?"[14]

Studies have shown that lack of numeracy is particularly concentrated among certain groups, notably the elderly, women, and people with lower educational attainment. Furthermore, increasing levels of financial literacy are correlated with higher financial readiness for retirement among adults. Taken together, the influence of numeracy on the quality of financial decisions and the unequal distribution of numeracy among different groups has implications for both lenders and regulators.

### Fairness and Social Effects

Fairness is one of the most powerful and least understood aspects of pricing. Pricing that is perceived as unfair can trigger strong negative reactions in customers. Here are two examples from outside the world of lending:

1. Cruise lines typically lower prices when a sailing is not booking up according to expectations. Unfortunately for the cruise lines, the nature of the business makes it unlikely that such differential pricing will escape detection. Cruise passengers dine together and the conversation often turns to pricing: "Mr. Smith mentions that his travel agent got a great deal for him and Mrs. Smith—an upper deck ocean-side stateroom for only $1,200. Mr. Jones responds that his travel agent got him an

upper deck ocean-side stateroom for $1,000. Mr. Smith's face falls and his cruise experience is suddenly ruined" (Phillips 2005, 215).

To avoid this situation, a number of cruise lines such as Princess Cruises and Holland America Line began to offer a "lowest price guarantee." If the cruise line ever drops the price for the same product (cabin type and departure city) on the same sailing, it will send a refund check to all passengers who booked the same product at the higher price.

2. In 2000, a frequent purchaser of DVDs through Amazon checked the price of a DVD (*Titus*). He was quoted a price of $26.24. Shortly thereafter, he logged on to his son's computer and was quoted a price of $22.74. Given that his son had not purchased DVDs from Amazon, he came to the conclusion that Amazon was charging higher prices to loyal customers. He posted about his experience on the website DVDTalk.com. The response was immediate and highly negative, with many respondents promising not to purchase from Amazon ever again. In response, an Amazon spokesman promised that "Amazon will never [do] dynamic pricing."[15]

Lenders are more fortunate than cruise lines and online retailers in that borrowers are not likely to compare their mortgage rates or credit card APRs with others. And if they do, they are likely to assume that rate differences are based on differences in credit score, loan amount, or timing—all of which consumers generally consider acceptable reasons for price differentiation.

This does not mean that lenders can differentiate prices with total impunity. As noted in Chapter 7, for most lenders—as for most retailers—the most loyal customers are the least price sensitive. This means that charging loyal customers more than new customers makes sense. Indeed, it appears logical to charge the most loyal customers the most and the least familiar (new) customers the least. This tactic is problematic for at least two reasons. First of all, it violates a strongly held belief that it is unfair to punish loyal customers with higher prices: the idea that Amazon was charging loyal customers more than new customers was met with outrage. Second, if every provider charged loyal customers more, it would result in increased churn as customers loyal to one bank would defect to take advantage of the lower introductory rates offered by competitors. This occurred in the early days of cell phone services when service providers offered deep introductory discounts to attract new customers. Millions of customers learned to take advantage of the introductory discount offered by one carrier; then, when the discount had expired, they migrated to a new carrier to take advantage of the new carrier's introductory discount.

## IMPLICATIONS FOR LENDERS

Most lenders (like most retailers) are aware not only that consumers are not always rational but also that they deviate from rationality in predictable ways. Some companies have begun to design products in a way that helps consumers make the "right" financial decisions. One well-known example is making "opt in" the default choice for employee 401(k) enrollment. One study found that changing the default option from "opt out" to "opt in" increased the enrollment rate in a corporate 401(k) plan from 20% to 98% for new employees. As another example, in August 2017, Walmart introduced a prepaid debit card that rewarded customers who saved money on the card by entering them in a monthly lottery that paid prizes up to $1,000. The idea is to overcome present bias by providing the prospect of an immediate reward for savings behavior that will yield longer-run benefits for the consumer.[16]

In this section, we discuss some of the ways in which pricing is influenced by subrational behavior. Discounts, promotions, and commitment mechanisms are pricing tactics that, if designed carefully, can benefit both lenders and consumers. We finally discuss some of the regulatory implications of subrational consumer behavior.

## Discounts and Promotions

Discounts and promotions drive additional business in lending just as they do for all retailers. Lenders who want to increase their volume of loans can do so by advertising attractive time-bound price promotions. Because promotional elasticities are typically higher than list-price elasticities, the revenue lift from a well-designed promotion will be greater than the lift from an equivalent price reduction. However, several cautions are in order. First of all, new customers attracted by a promotion are—not surprisingly—highly price sensitive. This means that they are the most likely to defect to a competitor who offers a deeper promotion later. Studies on a variety of retail products have shown that, although the short-term elasticity from a promotion is high, the longer-term elasticity from the promotion can be quite low: a successful promotion can attract new customers, but these newcomers are less likely to be loyal in the future. In addition, frequent promotions can train consumers to "wait for the sale"—that is, they become less likely to pay full price and will wait until a promotion arrives. This behavior has become commonplace in retail—for example, more than 75% of fashion goods sold in stores are sold at a discount to the list price. The situation can become even more severe when all the participants in a market begin to compete primarily on promotions.

Field discretion enables local staff to offer discounts that incorporate knowledge of local competitive conditions and individual price sensitivity. Proprietary Nomis Solutions research has shown that customers have a higher elasticity to the discount than they do to a price reduction of the same magnitude. Short-run demand for a loan with a current APR of 10% with an advertised promotion of 9% will be greater than the short-run demand seen from simply dropping the rate to 9%. Demand may be further enhanced if sales staff are given the discretion to offer the 9% discount to selected customers and are trained how to do this correctly. However, as discussed in Chapter 5, discretion needs to be combined with appropriate incentives to avoid overdiscounting by sales staff to drive volume.

One limit to the use of promotions is that, by law, advertised list prices typically need to be "real" in the sense that some customers must actually pay them. In the United States, the Code of Federal Regulations states that "to the extent that list or suggested retail prices do not in fact correspond to prices at which a substantial number of sales of the article in question are made, the advertisement of a reduction may mislead the consumer." In 2005 Overstock.com, an online retailer, was fined $6.8 million for violating this principle by posting meaningless list prices. A lender who is extensively using promotions should take care to ensure that they maintain list price integrity—that is, that at least some customers actually pay the list price.

## Commitment Mechanisms

As shown in Example 8.2, a customer with time-inconsistent preferences can be exploited to make money without risk.

---

**Example 8.2: Intertemporal Arbitrage.** A customer evaluates future prospects using hyperbolic discounting with a discount rate of .03 as in Example 8.1. Assume that she initially holds an investment that pays off $800 in 48 months. This is Outcome B in Figure 8.1. She would be willing to pay up to $357 − $328 = $29 to immediately switch to an investment that pays off $1,000 in 60 months—Outcome A in the figure. However, after about 33 months, her preferences switch. After 42 months, she would prefer to have the $800 payment sooner rather than the $1,000 payment later and would be willing to pay $678 − $649 = $29 to switch back. A third party who understood her preferences could make a risk-free $58 through intertemporal arbitrage.

---

An implication of time-inconsistent preferences is that a consumer may act differently in the future than her current self would wish her future self to act. If a consumer is sufficiently sophisticated to realize that her preferences will reverse at some point in the future, she may be willing to enter into a contract or agreement now that constrains her future behavior. Such an agreement is called a *commitment mechanism*.

Commitment mechanisms might have the potential to provide benefit to both consumers and financial service companies. Automated withdrawal of loan repayments serves as a mild form of commitment mechanism—it forces a consumer to take an action if she decides to miss a payment. In this sense it is similar to scheduling a weekly appointment with a personal trainer—it takes effort to postpone or cancel the appointment. With respect to the loan payment, the knowledge that the amount will automatically be withdrawn focuses the consumer's attention on ensuring that she has enough money in her account to make the payment rather than contemplating the possibility of not making the payment.

Perhaps the best-known commitment mechanisms in financial services are Christmas clubs, which help consumers save money to purchase Christmas presents. A consumer can deposit money in a Christmas club any time during the year but cannot withdraw the money before December 1 without paying a penalty. Christmas club accounts would seem to be inferior to other savings products offered by the bank, which often offer higher rates and are fully liquid. However, for a consumer participating in a Christmas club, the lack of liquidity is the whole point: the inability to withdraw without a penalty "creates structure and discipline" for the customer, in the words of a spokesperson for Atlantic Coast Bank.[17] For a participant, spending the money now is the tempting near-term alternative represented by point A in Figure 8.1, and having money to buy Christmas presents is the long-term alternative represented by point B. Christmas Club members are willing to accept reduced interest to guarantee that they do not succumb to temptation but achieve the more desired long-term alternative. Subjects in experimental settings have been willing to commit a significant amount of their savings to illiquid savings accounts even when the rate on the illiquid account is equal to or even less than a fully liquid account.[18]

It is interesting to consider whether there is a commitment mechanism in lending that might provide benefits to both lenders and consumers. Automatic withdrawal of loan payments may serve as a weak commitment mechanism. However, a strong commitment mechanism would be one that prevented (or discouraged) borrowing that a consumer would later regret. Such a mechanism could conceivably break or avoid the cycle of dependency that payday lenders are often accused of creating.

## Regulatory Issues

The financial services industry is among the most regulated—if not *the* most regulated—sector in most industrialized countries. Lenders are generally (and rightly) subject to the same regulations against fraud, misrepresentation, and bait-and-switch pricing as other retailers. However, even more stringent regulations are usually imposed on lenders regulating the types of products they can offer, who they can offer them to, and how they can be priced. Regulators and consumer advocates argue that stringent regulation of consumer lending is needed because lending products are complex and many customers find them confusing, which suggests that regulation is required to make sure that options are presented to customers in a clear and consistent fashion to facilitate choice. A related concern is that bad financial decisions may have devastating consequences for a household. Finally, bad financial decisions by a large number of households can have broader economic consequences. A key cause of the 2008–2009 financial crises was that too many consumers took on too much debt, which they were later unable to repay. This implies that there is a public interest in making sure that consumers make good financial decisions.

Given the intensity of regulatory scrutiny, the fact that customers do not always behave rationally poses both opportunities and pitfalls for lenders. The main opportunity is that, by understanding patterns in how customers make decisions, lenders can craft and present products that are both good for the customer and good for the lender. A pitfall is that some lenders might exploit the fact that consumers do not always make rational decisions and create products that are bad for the customer but good for the lender. It is doubtful that regulators and consumer advocates would allow a lender to persist in offering such a product for long. The most dangerous pitfall is that lenders might act in a way that is good (or at least neutral) for customers and good for lenders but still get in trouble with regulators. This pitfall can be avoided only by establishing clear lines of authority and responsibility for pricing, being clear about what data and algorithms are being used to set prices, and being able to demonstrate that all aspects of the price-setting and price-quoting processes are aligned with the pursuit of legitimate business goals.

## Subrationality and the Limits of Modeling

One of the implications of subrational customer behavior is that at some point, it may become impossible to improve predictions of how customers will respond to prices by collecting more data or using more sophisticated "machine learning" approaches. Consider the question of how demand for a particular mortgage would change if a lender increased the price by 25 basis points. In a world of rational customers, a lender possessing all the relevant financial data on customers, along with their individual discount rates and available alternatives, could, in theory, calculate the willingness to pay for a loan on the part of each customer. Armed with this knowledge, the lender could precisely calculate the price-response curve that he faced for the loan and could determine the price that maximized his expected profitability using the approaches described in Chapter 7. Even better—at least from the point of view of the lender—he could segment customers exactly according to their willingness to pay and would be limited only by regulation from extracting all the available surplus using market-of-one pricing.

The idea that a lender could obtain enough information to determine every customer's exact willingness to pay for his loan is not realistic—at least not yet. However, it is certainly becoming more plausible in this era of big data. Even if full information is not available, as long as customers are rational, obtaining additional information will always enable lenders to making better segmentation and pricing decisions. However, if consumers are not rational, this isn't necessarily the case. There comes a point at which knowing more about customers does not necessarily lead to better prices because the decisions of a subrational customer have an irreducible random component—or they are at least based on psychological processes that are not directly observable or possible to model. In this case, even full knowledge of a consumer's financial situation and the decisions she made in the past may not enable a lender to predict her future decisions.

Lenders are very far from the point at which additional data and better modeling will not help them make better decisions. On the contrary, additional data and more sophisticated models have enabled increasingly accurate predictions of fraud, default, and price sensitivity, and they will continue to do so for the foreseeable future. However, the use of analytics needs to be coupled with insights into customer behavior and common sense. An inferior product at an inferior price may outsell a superior product at a better price if the superior product is presented poorly or if its price is not properly framed. It is incumbent on lenders not only to ensure that they are offering the right products at the right prices to the right customers at the right time but also that they are designing and presenting their products in a way that helps real customers—*Homo sapiens* not *Homo economicus*—find and choose the ones that best fit their needs.

## SUMMARY

- Consumers do not always behave in accordance with the assumption of rational customer behavior as postulated by classical economic theory. Instead, they commonly demonstrate subrational behavior. Deviations from rationality have been found both in controlled experiments and in the real world. These deviations are the primary topic of the field of behavioral economics.

- Consumers demonstrate subrational behavioral by using heuristics to choose among complex alternatives. Using heuristics allows consumers to simplify decisions but may result in suboptimal choices—for example, choosing a mortgage with a higher expected net present value of payments.

- Mental accounting is an example of a heuristic in which consumers classify income and loss into different accounts depending on the source. For example, consumers show a greater propensity to spend a bonus than an unanticipated gain in investment value, even though the two events have an equivalent effect on household wealth.

- Consumers are sensitive to the way that prices are framed: a price presented as a discount is likely to drive more demand than the same price presented as the list price.

- Some people demonstrate inconsistency in choosing among options with outcomes in the future. In this situation, consumer choices can demonstrate both preference reversals and present bias. Hyperbolic and quasi-hyperbolic discounting are mathematical models of intertemporal choice that have been formulated to represent these deviations from the predictions of the discounted utility model.

- Numeracy—the ability to make arithmetic calculations—also plays a role in financial decision making. Consumers who are more numerate tend to make better financial decisions than consumers who are less numerate. As a result, all else being equal, less-numerate consumers have higher delinquency and foreclosure rates.

- Deviations from rationality present both an opportunity and a challenge for lenders. At one level, such deviations are an opportunity to develop products and pricing strategies that are win-win in the sense that they are good for customers and profitable for lenders. On another level, deviations from rationality provide a rationale for regulators to intervene to prevent consumers from being exploited by lenders.

- The use of promotions can be effective in driving business—however, lenders need to make sure that they avoid high levels of churn associated with extremely price-sensitive customers who are the ones most likely to respond to promotions.

- Introductory discounts can be used to drive new business. To appear fair, such discounts need to be positioned as a benefit to new customers, not a penalty for loyal customers.

- Commitment mechanisms may be a way to enable customers to make better financial decisions by avoiding the preference reversals associated with time-inconsistent preferences.

- The fact that customers do not always make rational decisions raises the potential for regulatory scrutiny of even innocuous or beneficial innovations. Lenders need to be able to explain to regulators why a particular scheme is either neutral or beneficial for customers and is not exploiting them.

## NOTES

1. The restaurant-pricing example is from Kimes, Phillips, and Summa (2012).
2. Some good popular treatments of behavioral economics are *Predictably Irrational*, by Ariely (2010); *Thinking, Fast and Slow*, by Daniel Kahnemann (2011); and *Nudge*, by Thaler and Sunstein (2009). A popular treatment of the origins of behavioral econom-

ics through the work of Daniel Kahnemann and Amos Tversky is *The Undoing Project: A Friendship That Changed Our* Minds, by Michael Lewis (2016). Surveys of subrational consumer behavior as it applies specifically to pricing can be found in Özer and Zheng (2012) and Hinterhuber (2015).

3. For a definition of mortgage points, see Chapter 1. Three papers presenting detailed analytic methodologies for choosing among mortgage alternatives are Agarwal, Driscoll, and Laibson (2013); Campbell and Cocco (2003); and Kalotay and Qian (2007). The latter uses a Black-Sierpinski model for future interest movements. All the approaches detailed in these papers are well beyond the mathematical capabilities of a typical household.

4. The phenomenon of mental accounting was initially identified and studied in household finance decisions by Richard Thaler (1990).

5. The survey and debt management game results are reported in Amar et al. (2011).

6. The "irrational" influence of a promotion in inducing additional demand needs to be separated from the rational phenomenon of *pull forward*, in which a temporary price promotion induces some consumers to purchase now who would have purchased later. More information on promotion elasticity and how it can be separated from pull-forward effects and estimated can be found in Blattberg and Briesch (2012).

7. As implied by the name and discussed in more detail in Appendix C, the discounted utility model assumes that consumers maximize the net present value of future *utility*. For simplicity, Equation 8.1 assumes that they maximize the net present value of *cash flows*. This simplification does not change the basic idea.

8. The fruit and chocolate example is from Read and van Leeuwen (1998). Additional examples of consumer behaviors that violate the expected utility model and discussions of alternative approaches can be found in the excellent overview by Frederick, Loewenstein, and O'Donoghue (2002).

9. The time value of money experiments were done by Thaler (1981).

10. The quasi-hyperbolic discounting model was proposed by Daniel Laibson (1997).

11. The studies on the influence of present bias and time preference on credit card debt and financial conditions are by Meier and Sprenger (2010). The fact that the study participants had chosen to take advantage of a free tax-assistance program means that they are not necessarily representative of the population as a whole.

12. The experiment described is one of many different variations that were performed by Walter Mischel and his colleagues at Stanford and Columbia Universities as well as by many other researchers. A summary of some of their experiments can be found in Mischel, Shoda, and Rodriguez (1989).

13. The link between time preference at an early age and outcomes later in life has been confirmed in a number of studies. For example, Golsteyn, Grönquist, and Lindahl (2014, F621) find a strong association between a high discount rate as measured in 13-year old children in Sweden and life outcomes: "A higher discount rate is linked to weaker performance in both compulsory and secondary school, lower educational attainment, and lower scores on military achievement tests at age 19."

14. The results on foreclosure and delinquency by financial literacy group are from Gerardi, Goette, and Meier (2013). The five questions used to classify customers were taken from an earlier study by Banks and Oldfield (2007). The study on the financial literacy of early baby boomers was by Lusardi and Mitchell (2007). On the connection

between numeracy on readiness for retirement, see Lusardi and Mitchell (2011). A good survey on numeracy and financial decision making is Lusardi (2012).

15. The two examples of perceived pricing unfairness are from Phillips (2005). The money-back policy for cruise lines is described in Lieberman (2012).

16. A 401(k) plan is a scheme by which an employee may elect to have a percentage of his income deposited in an account such that taxes are not levied until the money is withdrawn. In many cases, part of the employee's contribution might be matched by their employer. The results on improved participation from changing the default from "opt-out" to "opt-in" are from Madrian and Shea (2001). The results from additional "opt in, opt out" experiments are discussed in Thaler and Sunstein (2009). The Walmart debit card is described in Walker (2017).

17. The quote is from Conte (2011).

18. The experimental results on commitment mechanisms are described in Beshears et al. (2011).

# APPENDIX A: BASIC FORMULAS

In this appendix we review some basic results regarding discounting and mathematical series that are used in the text.

## DISCOUNT RATES AND DISCOUNTING

Consider a stream of $T + 1$ risk-free (i.e., certain) cash flows: $c_0, c_1, c_2, \ldots c_T$. We assume that $c_0$ occurs now and that each of the subsequent cash flows occurs at the end of each of $T$ subsequent periods of equal length. Assume a constant discount rate $r$ per period. Then, the net present value (NPV) of the stream of cash flows is the following:

$$NPV(r; c_0, c_1, c_2, \ldots c_T) = c_0 + \frac{c_1}{(1+r)} + \frac{c_2}{(1+r)^2} + \cdots + \frac{c_T}{(1+r)^T}$$

$$= \sum_{t=0}^{T} \frac{c_t}{(1+r)^t}. \tag{A.1}$$

**Example A.1: Net Present Value.** A proposed investment requires that $25 million is spent now. It will return $8 million in 1 year, $12 million in 2 years, $10 million in 3 years, and nothing thereafter. The net present value of the investment evaluated at an annual discount rate of 10% (in millions of dollars) is

$$-\$25 + \frac{\$8}{(1.1)} + \frac{\$12}{(1.1)^2} + \frac{\$10}{(1.1)^3} = -\$.297.$$

Evaluated at a 10% discount rate, the investment has a negative NPV and would be considered unprofitable. However, at a 5% discount rate, the project would have an NPV of $2.14 million and might be considered very profitable. This shows that the choice of discount rate can strongly influence both the magnitude and the sign of the net present value of a cash stream.[1]

Equation A.1 holds for all values of $r > -1$, and in fact, negative discount rates can be relevant for lenders in a deflationary environment. However, Equation A.1 is not meaningful for interest rates less than $-100\%$; that is, $r \leq -1$.

We can also write Equation A.1 as

$$NPV = \sum_{t=0}^{T} \delta_t(r) c_t,$$  (A.2)

where $\delta_t(r) = 1/(1 + r)^t$ is the discount factor for period $t$. Specifying a discount factor rather than a discount rate is useful in comparing alternative approaches to discounting such as those discussed in Chapter 8.

The timing of cash flows is an important consideration in calculating net present value: in particular, cash flows need to be discounted at the rate consistent with their period. Equation A.1 assumes that cash flows occur at the end of each year with a corresponding annual discount rate. Monthly payments need to be discounted at a monthly discount rate, weekly payments at a weekly discount rate, and so on. To calculate the NPV of a periodic cash flow that occurs more frequently than annually, we sometimes need to convert the annual rate into an equivalent monthly or weekly rate. Assume that cash flows occur at a regular period of $n$ times per year and that the annual discount rate is $r_A$, where the subscript $A$ denotes "Annual." If cash flows occur weekly, then $n = 52$; if they occur monthly, $n = 12$. For a given period, we want to find the rate $r$ such that $\$1/(1 + r)^n = \$1/(1 + r_A)$, which, after applying some algebra, gives us the following:

$$r = (1 + r_A)^{(1/n)} - 1.$$  (A.3)

---

**Example A.2: Converting Annual to Monthly and Weekly Discount Rate.** A consumer has an annual discount rate of 7.5%. Her corresponding monthly discount rate is $(1.075)^{(1/12)} - 1$ $= .6045\%$ and her corresponding weekly rate is $(1.075)^{(1/52)} - 1 = .1392\%$.

---

## COMPOUNDING AND CONTINUOUS DISCOUNTING

Equation A.1 assumes that compounding occurs once per period. Thus, if a customer borrowed \$1,000 at a rate of 5.0% for 1 year, at the end of the year she would owe \$1,050. However, the lender could also charge *compound interest*. If, for example, the lender charged an annual percentage rate (APR) of 5.0% but compounded the interest every 6 months, then the amount due at the end of the year would be given by $1.025 \times 1.025 \times \$1,000 = \$1,050.63$. In other words, the lender has applied an interest rate of 2.5% twice during the year. Specifically, if the bank compounded the interest $n$ times over a period, at the end of the period the borrower would owe an amount equal to

$$P(B, r, n) = B(1 + r/n)^n$$  (A.4)

where $B$ is the amount borrowed, and $r$ is the APR.

Example A.3: Compounding. The APR for a $100,000 loan is 6.0% compounded monthly. With no payments, the balance of the loan at the end of the year would be $100,000 × $(1+.06/12)^{12} = \$106,167.78$.

For a given APR, the more frequently that interest is compounded during a period, the larger the amount owed at the end of the period. The logical extreme is continuous compounding. In this case, the amount owed after a year can be computed by taking the limit of Equation A.4 as $n$ approaches infinity:

$$\lim_{n \to \infty} B(1+r/n)^n = Be^r. \tag{A.5}$$

Here, $e$ is the mathematical constant $e = 2.178$. (In Excel, $e^r$ is calculated by the function $EXP(r)$.)

Example A.4: Continuous Compounding. The APR for a $100,000 loan is 6.0% compounded continuously. With no intermediate payments, the balance of the loan at the end of the year would be $100,000 \times e^{.06} = \$106,183.65$.

Under continuous discounting, the discount factor to be applied over a period $t$ is equal to $1/e^{rt}$, where $t$ is number of years. Thus, for a rate of 6.0%, the continuous discount factor to be applied for 6 months would be $1/e^{.03} = .97$ and the continuous discount factor to be applied to 2 years is $1/e^{.12} = .887$.

## SERIES

In many cases, we are interested in calculating the net present value of a stream of periodic cash flows of equal magnitude. Two mathematical identities for the closed-form solution of series are quite useful:

$$\sum_{t=0}^{T} \alpha^i = \frac{(1-\alpha^{T+1})}{(1-\alpha)}, \text{ and} \tag{A.6}$$

$$\sum_{t=1}^{T} \alpha^i = \alpha \frac{(1-\alpha^T)}{(1-\alpha)} \tag{A.7}$$

Both of these identities are valid when $0 \le \alpha < 1$ but may break down for $\alpha < 0$ or $\alpha \ge 1$. Equation A.7 is particularly useful in evaluating the net present value of a constant stream of revenues or costs over a fixed life. In particular, if the periodic interest rate is $r$ and there is a fixed future stream of income with a value of $v$ that will be received in each period from period 1 through period $T$, then the net present value of this income stream can be found by setting $\alpha = 1/(1 + r)$ and rearranging Equation A.7 to obtain

$$NPV = \frac{\upsilon \left[ (1 + r)^T - 1 \right]}{r(1 + r)^T} \tag{A.8}$$

**Example A.5: Net Present Value of a Constant Cash Flow.** The net present value of $50 per month for 5 years at a monthly interest rate of .1% is given by the following:

$$NPV = \frac{\$50 \times \left[ (1.001)^{60} - 1 \right]}{.001 \times (1.001)^{60}} = \$2,910.36.$$

Equation A.8 is only valid if $r > 0$: it is not valid for negative discount rates.

**NOTE**

1. Net present value can be calculated using the Excel function $NPV(r, c_1, c_2, \ldots, c_T)$, where $r$ is the discount rate and $c_1, c_2, \ldots, c_T$ are the future cash flows. Note that the first element of the cash flow in the Excel NPV function is $c_1$, not $c_0$, which means that if there is a cash flow in the current period, it needs to be explicitly added. The net present value in Example A.1 can be calculated by $-25 + NPV(.1, 8, 12, 10)$.

# APPENDIX B: THE MATHEMATICS
# OF A SIMPLE LOAN

---

In this appendix we derive the equations for the periodic payments and net interest income (NII) for a riskless simple loan. We also derive useful linear approximations for the periodic payments and net interest income from a riskless simple loan.

## PERIODIC INTEREST

Consider a simple loan with initial balance $B$ to be repaid in $T$ periodic installments with periodic rate $r \geq 0$. In each period, the borrower makes a payment of $P$. Part of each payment goes toward paying the interest, and the remainder is applied to reduce the balance. We want to find the value of $P$ such that the last payment at time $T$ exactly pays off the remaining interest and balance. Let $B(t)$ be the balance remaining immediately after payment $t$. Then $B(0) = B$ and $B(1) = (1 + r)B - P$. That is, immediately after payment 1, the remaining balance is the initial balance plus one period's accrued interest minus the payment. Moving forward in time, we can write:

$$B(1) = (1+r)B - P$$
$$B(2) = (1+r)B(1) - P = (1+r)^2 B - (1+r)P - P$$
$$B(3) = (1+r)B(2) - P = (1+r)^3 B - (1+r)^2 P - (1+r)P - P$$
$$\vdots \qquad \vdots \qquad\qquad \vdots$$
$$B(t) = (1+r)B(t-1) - P = (1+r)^t B - \sum_{i=0}^{t-1}(1+r)^i P. \qquad (B.1)$$

Here, we define $B(0) = B$ for convenience. We can use Equation A.6 to simplify:

$$\sum_{i=0}^{t-1}(1+r)^i = \frac{(1+r)^t - 1}{r}.$$

Substituting this equation into Equation B.1 gives us

$$B(t) = (1+r)^t B - \frac{[(1+r)^t - 1]P}{r}. \qquad (B.2)$$

Because the balance immediately after payment $T$ needs to be 0, we set

$$B(T) = (1 + r)^T B - \frac{[(1 + r)^T - 1]P}{r} = 0.$$

We can solve this equation for $P$ to obtain

$$P = \left[ \frac{r(1 + r)^T}{(1 + r)^T - 1} \right] B. \tag{B.3}$$

The lending interest from a riskless simple loan is the sum of all of the payments minus the balance. That is:

$$LI = TP - B = \left[ \frac{(rT - 1)(1 + r)^T + 1}{(1 + r)^T - 1} \right] B. \tag{B.4}$$

---

**Example B.1: Periodic Payments and Lending Interest for a Riskless Simple Loan.** A riskless simple loan with a 1-year term has a starting balance of $B = \$5,000$ at an APR of 5% and monthly payments. The corresponding monthly rate is $.05/12 = .0042$. The monthly payment is $.0042 \times (1 + .0042)^{12} \times \$5,000 / [(1 + .0042)^{12} - 1] = \$428.04$. The lending interest is $LI = 12 \times \$428.04 - \$5,000.00 = \$136.48$.

---

## LINEAR APPROXIMATIONS

Denote the periodic payment on a simple loan with initial balance $B$, rate $r$, and $T$ by $P(r, T, B)$. As shown in Equation B.3, $P(r, T, B)$ is a nonlinear function of $r$, which makes it somewhat cumbersome to deal with. However, for low interest rates and shorter-term loans, the monthly payment for a loan is an "almost linear" function of $r$. In particular, we can approximate the periodic interest payment for such loans by the linear function:

$$\tilde{P}(r, T, B) \approx \frac{B}{T} + r \left[ \frac{B(T+1)}{2T} \right] \tag{B.5}$$

where $\tilde{P}(r, T, B)$ is a linear approximation of the true value $P(r, T, B)$.[1] The approximation in Equation B.5 is intuitive. It says that the periodic payment on a simple loan with interest rate $r$ is approximately equal to the zero-rate payment $B/T$ plus the interest payment on approximately half of the initial balance.

Table B.1 shows the actual monthly payment $P(r, T, B)$, the approximate monthly payment $\tilde{P}(r, T, B)$ calculated using Equation B.5 and the error calculated as $100 \times [\tilde{P}(r, T, B) - P(r, T, B)] / P(r, T, B)$. For shorter-term loans and for low interest rates, the approximation works remarkably well. However, for longer terms and higher interest rates, it begins to break down and may substantially underestimate the payment.

The lending income from a simple loan is the total of all payments minus the amount borrowed. This suggests that an approximation for the lending interest from a riskless simple loan can be derived from B.5:

Actual monthly payments and monthly payments estimated using the linear approximation
in Equation B.5 for a $10,000 loan with different annual rates and terms

| Annual rate (%) | | TERM (MONTHS) | | | | |
|---|---|---|---|---|---|---|
| | | 12 | 24 | 60 | 120 | 360 |
| 2 | Actual | $842.31 | $425.32 | $175.20 | $91.93 | $36.87 |
| | Approx. | 842.28 | 425.27 | 175.06 | 91.66 | 36.06 |
| | % error | −0.00% | −0.01% | −0.08% | −0.30% | −2.20% |
| 5 | Actual | 855.57 | 438.22 | 188.20 | 105.52 | 53.01 |
| | Approx. | 855.40 | 437.89 | 187.38 | 103.87 | 48.20 |
| | % error | −0.02% | −0.08% | −0.44% | −1.56% | **−9.06%** |
| 10 | Actual | 877.16 | 459.46 | 210.36 | 129.78 | 84.59 |
| | Approx. | 876.53 | 458.20 | 207.20 | 123.54 | 67.76 |
| | % error | −0.07% | −0.28% | −1.50% | −4.81% | **−19.90%** |
| 15 | Actual | 898.14 | 480.40 | 232.98 | 155.61 | 118.95 |
| | Approx. | 896.79 | 477.68 | 226.22 | 142.40 | 86.52 |
| | % error | −0.15% | −0.57% | −2.90% | **−8.49%** | **−27.27%** |
| 20 | Actual | 918.57 | 501.04 | 255.96 | 182.52 | 153.74 |
| | Approx. | 916.26 | 496.40 | 244.49 | 160.52 | 104.4 |
| | % error | −0.25% | −0.92% | −4.48% | **−12.08%** | **−32.00%** |

NOTE: The error percentage is calculated as $100 \times$ (approx. − actual)/actual. Errors with absolute magnitude
greater than 5.0% are shown in **bold**.

$$\tilde{LT}(r, T, B) = T \times \tilde{P}(r, T, B) - B$$
$$= \frac{rB(T+1)}{2}.$$

(B.6)

## NOTE

1. The approximation in Equation B.5 can be derived using a Taylor series approximation. In particular, for small values of $r$ we can write

$$P(r, T, B) \approx P(0, T, B) + r[dP(r, T, B)/dr]\big|_{r=0}.$$

Setting $P(0, T, B) = B/T$, evaluating the derivative of $P(r, T, B)$ with respect to $r$ at
$r = 0$ and simplifying gives the approximation in Equation B.5.

# APPENDIX C: AN OVERVIEW OF BASIC CONSUMER THEORY

Classical economic theory assumes that consumers are rational in a specific sense: they possess preferences over different consumption bundles and these preferences possess certain properties. If those properties hold, then it can be shown that every consumer will have a willingness to pay for every loan offered by every lender in the market, and the distribution of that willingness to pay across customers will give rise to a price-sensitivity function as described in Chapter 4. This appendix describes the assumptions underlying "rational" consumer behavior and how these assumptions imply the existence of a maximum consumer willingness to pay. If these assumptions do not hold, customers may demonstrate the types of subrational behavior described in Chapter 8.

## A STATIC MODEL OF CONSUMER BEHAVIOR

Consider a static world in which consumers consider only the current period when they make decisions. How would consumers choose what to purchase in such a world? Assume that there are $n$ goods available, and let $x_i$ be the amount of good $i$ that the consumer decides to purchase. Thus, $x_1$ might denote gallons of gasoline, $x_2$ might denote loaves of bread, and so on. For convenience we assume that $x_i \geq 0$, which means that each consumer is a (potential) buyer rather than seller of each good. Then, any vector $\mathbf{x} = (x_1, x_2, \ldots, x_n)$, where each $x_i \geq 0$, denotes a *consumption bundle*. Let $\mathbf{x}_A$ and $\mathbf{x}_B$ denote two different consumption bundles. We assume that, for any two such bundles, each consumer either prefers bundle A to bundle B or is indifferent between them. If the consumer strictly prefers $\mathbf{x}_A$ to $\mathbf{x}_B$, we write $\mathbf{x}_A \succ \mathbf{x}_B$. If the consumer is indifferent between the two bundles, we write $\mathbf{x}_A \sim \mathbf{x}_B$. If the consumer is either indifferent or prefers $\mathbf{x}_A$ to $\mathbf{x}_B$, we write $\mathbf{x}_A \succeq \mathbf{x}_B$.

Rational consumer behavior obeys the following four axioms:

1. *Completeness.* For any two bundles, $\mathbf{x}_A$ and $\mathbf{x}_B$, either $\mathbf{x}_A \succ \mathbf{x}_B$, $\mathbf{x}_B \succ \mathbf{x}_A$, or $\mathbf{x}_A \sim \mathbf{x}_B$.

2. *Reflexivity.* $\mathbf{x}_A \succeq \mathbf{x}_A$.

3. *Transitivity.* If $\mathbf{x}_A \succeq \mathbf{x}_B$ and $\mathbf{x}_B \succeq \mathbf{x}_C$, then $\mathbf{x}_A \succeq \mathbf{x}_C$.

4. *Nonsatiation.* Assume that $\epsilon$ is a vector with each component greater than or equal to 0. Then, for any bundle $\mathbf{x}$, $\mathbf{x} + \epsilon \succeq \mathbf{x}$.[1]

The completeness axiom states that, for any two bundles, a consumer either prefers one bundle to the other or is indifferent between them. Reflexivity requires that a bundle is not strictly preferred to itself. Both of these axioms are intuitive.

Transitivity says that if a consumer prefers bundle A to bundle B and bundle B to bundle C, then she must prefer bundle A to bundle C. Transitivity may not seem obvious, but it is required to avoid a "money pump." If a consumer holds bundle A but prefers bundle B, she would be willing to pay something to exchange A for B. If she prefers bundle C to bundle B, she would be willing to pay something more to exchange B for C. But if she prefers A to C, she would be willing to pay to exchange C for A. She is now back where she started, and we can start the cycle again, extracting money from her for every exchange. Because such money pumps do not exist, transitivity is usually considered a reasonable assumption.

Nonsatiation is probably the least intuitive of the four axioms: it requires that more of each item is always more desirable than less. Nonsatiation is clearly violated by goods where "enough is enough" and acquiring beyond a point actually reduces utility: I might prefer owning two cats to owning one cat, but this does not mean that I prefer owning ten cats to owning two cats. The primary argument for the reasonability of the nonsatiation assumption is that consumers generally operate in the nonsatiation range for goods of interest.

Given these four axioms, it is a straightforward mathematical exercise to show that there exists a *utility function* $u(\mathbf{x})$ for each consumer that assigns a positive number to each possible consumption bundle such that, for any two bundles $\mathbf{x}_A$ and $\mathbf{x}_B$, $u(\mathbf{x}_A) > u(\mathbf{x}_B)$ implies that $\mathbf{x}_A \succ \mathbf{x}_B$, and $u(\mathbf{x}_A) = u(\mathbf{x}_B)$ implies that $\mathbf{x}_A \sim \mathbf{x}_B$.[2]

Economic theory posits that a consumer chooses the consumption bundle that maximizes her utility subject to her budget constraint. That is, she chooses the value of $\mathbf{x}$ that solves the optimization problem

$$\max \, u(x_1, x_2, \ldots, x_n) \tag{C.1}$$

$$\text{subject to:} \quad \sum_{i=1}^{n} p_i x_i \leq I$$

$$x_i \geq 0$$

where $x_i$ is consumption of good $i$, $p_i > 0$ is the price of good $i$, and $I$ is the consumer's budget. The solution to Problem C.1 is the consumption vector $\mathbf{x}^* = (x_1^*, x_2^*, \ldots, x_n^*)$ that the consumer would choose given current prices.

To determine how a customer would respond to changes in the price of a particular good—say, good $i$—we can solve Problem C.1 for different values of $p_i$ and record the corresponding value of $x_i$. Under the axioms of consumer behavior listed earlier and a few additional technical assumptions, consumer demand will obey the law of demand: the amount purchased of any good will be a nonincreasing function of its price.[3]

The discussion so far has assumed that goods are continuous—that is, a consumer can decide to purchase any amount of a good. However, the same results hold if one or more of the goods are discrete and the consumer's decision is whether or not to purchase one unit of the good at the current price. This is the case with many lending products such as mortgages and credit cards. In this case, there will be a value for each good $v_i$ such that the consumer will purchase the good if it priced less than $v_i$ and will not purchase if the price is greater than $v_i$. It could be the case that $v_i \leq 0$, in which case the consumer would not purchase the good at any price. We refer to $v_i$ as the consumer's *willingness to pay* for good $i$. We note that $v_i$ for a particular consumer depends on her utility for all available goods and on the prices of all other goods in the marketplace and on her budget. This means that if the good in question is a specific loan from a specific lender, the consumer's willingness to pay may depend upon the prices offered by competing lenders for the same or similar loans. Thus, the willingness to pay of each customer incorporates the current prices for competing goods.

## CONSUMER BEHAVIOR WITH INTERTEMPORAL CHOICE

The static problem in C.1 cannot accommodate borrowing or saving: to derive demand for borrowing we need a multiperiod model. Consider a consumer who makes decisions in two periods—the current period and a single future period. For simplicity, assume that she is starting with zero wealth, has certain income of $I$ in both periods, and has the same utility function and consumption opportunities in both periods. If she has no opportunity to borrow or save money, then her optimal (utility-maximizing decision) is to spend all her income in each period. In this case, she would solve Problem C.1 independently in each period.

Assume that the consumer has the ability to borrow money in the first period at a rate $r > 0$. If she borrows an amount $B$ in the first period, she needs to pay back $(1 + r)B$ in the second period. Under which conditions would she borrow and how much would she borrow? Let $Y_t$ be her total expenditure in periods $t = 1, 2$. Then, we can calculate her utility in each period for any values of $Y_t$ by solving Problem C.1 with the budget constraint $\sum_{i=1}^{n} p_i x_{it} \leq Y_t$ in each period, where $x_{it}$ is the consumption of good $i$ in period $t$. For any value of $Y_t$ she will achieve a level of utility that we denote by $U(Y_t)$. Consumer theory specifies that, under most conditions, $U(Y)$ is concave—that is, the utility of additional expenditure decreases with total expenditure. This assumption of *decreasing marginal utility of consumption* implies that the utility function $U(Y)$ has the form shown in Figure C.1. It is also reasonable to assume that a consumer values current consumption more than future consumption: "Jam today is better than jam tomorrow." This preference can be quantified using a personal discount rate $r_d \geq 0$ such that the total utility today from consuming $Y_1$ now and $Y_2$ in the next period is the present value $U(Y_1) + U(Y_2)/(1 + r_d)$. Assume that a consumer is deciding how much money (if any) she wants to borrow in the first period, and let $B \geq 0$ be the amount that she borrows. Then her decision can be written as a constrained optimization problem:

$$\max_{B} U[I + B] + U[I - (1 + r)B]/(1 + r_d) \qquad (C.2)$$

subject to:   $B \leq I/(1 + r)$

$B \geq 0$

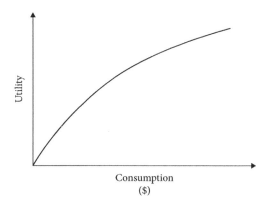

**Figure C.1**   Example utility function demonstrating decreasing marginal utility of consumption

In the first period, the consumer spends her income plus whatever she borrows. In the second period, she spends her income minus the amount she borrowed and the accrued interest. The first constraint states that she cannot borrow more in the first period than she can pay back in the second period. The second constraint specifies that she can only borrow a non-negative amount.

Looking at the objective function in Equation C.2, the consumer will borrow if the marginal utility from an additional dollar in the first period is greater than the discounted marginal utility lost in the second period from needing to repay the additional dollar plus interest. In particular, she will borrow if there is some $B > 0$ such that

$$U'[I + B] > U'[I - (1 + r)B](1 + r) / (1 + r_d).$$

Because of decreasing marginal utility, it must be the case that $U'[I + B] \leq U'[I - (1+r)B]$. Therefore, she would be willing to borrow if and only if $r < r_d$, that is, if the interest rate on the loan is less than her discount rate. In this case, she would borrow up to the point at which the marginal utility gained from spending the funds in the first period is exactly equal to the discounted marginal utility lost from not having the funds available to spend in the second period. In other words, she would choose $B^*$ so that

$$U'[I + B^*] = \left[\frac{1 + r}{1 + r_d}\right] U'[I - (1 + r)B^*]. \tag{C.3}$$

Because $U'[I + B] \leq U'[I - (1+r)B]$ for any $r > 0$, $B > 0$, the condition in Equation C.3 has no solution with $B > 0$ if $r > r_d$, which means that the consumer would not borrow. If $r < r_d$, she would borrow an amount equal to the value of $B^*$ that solves Equation C.3. If this value is more than she can pay back in the second period, then she would borrow the total amount she could pay back, that is $B^* = I/(1 + r)$. The amount she borrows is a decreasing function of $r$, dropping to 0 when $r = r_d$.

This model is simplistic, but it captures the essence of price response when consumers have the option of borrowing from future income to pay for current consumption. It illustrates the fact that, for a given interest rate, only individuals whose personal discount rate is greater than the lending rate will borrow. Furthermore, the amount that they borrow increases as the cost of borrowing decreases.

The two-period model can easily be extended to the case in which consumers have the additional option of saving at a rate $r_s < r$. In this case, consumers with $r_d < r_s$ would save and consumers with $r_d > r$ would borrow. As the savings rate is increased, more consumers will save, and those who do save will save more. As the lending rate $r$ is increased, fewer consumers will borrow, and those who borrow will borrow less. It must always be the case that $r_s < r$; otherwise, consumers would borrow all the money they could at $r$ and then save it at the higher rate $r_s$, giving them an amount $(r_s - r)B$ of "free" money to spend in the second period. This would be a case of intertemporal arbitrage. In reality, the difference between the borrowing rate and the savings rate would include both transaction costs and the risk of default as well as the return from a risk-free alternative investment such as US government bonds. In a two-period economy consisting of consumers with different levels of income, different utility functions, and different discount rates, $r_s$ and $r$ would equilibrate at the values for which the demand for borrowing equaled the demand for savings.

The two-period model can be extended to multiple periods using the *discounted utility model* in which each consumer uses a discount rate to weight future outcomes. In this case, each consumer chooses the set of future consumption bundles—including the amount to borrow and save—that maximizes $U_0(\mathbf{x}_0) + U_1(\mathbf{x}_1)/(1 + r_d) + U_2(\mathbf{x}_2)/(1 + r_d)^2 + \ldots$, where $U_t(\mathbf{x}_t)$ is the consumer's anticipated utility function at time $t$ for consumption bundle $\mathbf{x}_t$. The discounted utility model assumes consumers make decisions involving both current and future income and costs in the same fashion that companies choose among competing projects based on the net present value of cash flows.[4] In the discounted utility model it can be shown that, in each period, a consumer will borrow if her discount rate is greater than the interest rate for loans and will save if her discount rate is less than the market interest rate on savings.

The discounted utility model of consumer decision making is widely used and has several virtues. In addition to simplicity, it is consistent in the sense that it assumes that the consumer's "future selves" will evaluate trade-offs between current and future consumption in the same fashion as the consumer's current self. It also mirrors the interest payment structure on a simple loan at a fixed interest rate, which makes the consumer's decision of whether to borrow and/or save easy to characterize. For these and other reasons, the discounted utility model has been the dominant approach to analyzing intertemporal consumer decisions. However, we should note that the discounted utility model is not the only model consistent with the axioms of consumer behavior. Furthermore, there is extensive evidence that many—perhaps even most—consumers do not make decisions in a fashion consistent with the discounted utility model. We discuss the implications of this fact and some alternatives to the discounted utility model for characterizing intertemporal consumer choice in Chapter 8.

## NOTES

1. We assume that every item is a "good" in the sense that obtaining a small additional amount of that item increases—or at least does not decrease—utility. If owning more of an item would reduce a customer's utility, then the item is a "bad." In this case, we can

leave the item out of consideration or, sometimes, convert it into a good by changing the sign—for example, considering garbage removal as a good rather than garbage as a bad.

2. The utility function representing a particular consumer's preferences is not unique. If $u(\mathbf{x})$ is a utility function representing the preferences of a given consumer, then the utility function $\breve{u}(\mathbf{x}) = au(\mathbf{x}) + b$ with $a > 0$, $b \geq 0$ is also a valid utility function for that consumer. This means that the utility function for a consumer is ordinal but not cardinal—that is, the utilities associated with two different bundles can tell you only which of the bundles the consumer would prefer (or that she is indifferent between them). The relative magnitudes of utilities convey no information: it is meaningless to say that one bundle has "twice as much utility" as another.

3. There are three important cases recognized by economists in which the basic law of demand does not hold and demand for a good may increase with price: First, *Giffen goods* have the property that, as the price of a Giffen good rises, consumers are unable to afford a more expensive superior substitute and thus purchase more of the Giffen good. The classic example is a student on a limited budget who eats ramen six times a week for dinner and splurges on a steak one night a week. If the price of ramen goes up, instead of buying less ramen, the student may be forced to give up her weekly steak and eat ramen seven times a week. In this case, a rise in the price of ramen leads to an increase in demand. The second case occurs when *price is a signal of quality*. When faced with many alternatives, consumers may have insufficient information on the underlying quality of each alternative and may use price as an indicator of quality. A classic example is wine—faced with a plethora of chardonnays priced between $4 and $120 per bottle, a consumer may decide to purchase a bottle in the $20 range because she has previously enjoyed chardonnays around that price and $20 is "not too much to pay." If this approach is used by a sufficiently large fraction of consumers, then a vintner who repriced his chardonnay from $15 to $20 might actually see increased demand. The third case is *prestige goods*. Certain luxury goods such as high-end automobiles and fashion goods may be valued by consumers not only because of their attributes but also because they signal that their owner is able to afford such expensive items—in other words, conspicuous consumption.

In each of these three cases, raising the price of a good may increase demand and lowering its price may reduce demand. However, consumer lending does not appear to fall into any of these categories. Specifically, the conditions for a Giffen good are, at best, extremely rare, and it is difficult to see these conditions applying to a consumer loan. In the same vein, it is unlikely that consumers use the APR of a loan as a signal of its quality or that they brag about the high rate that they are paying on their mortgage to impress others. For these reasons, it is safe to say that consumer loans obey the law of demand and that the demand for a loan will decrease with its price.

4. The discounted utility model was first proposed by Paul Samuelson (1937). Tjalling Koopmans (1960) showed that the discounted utility model could be derived by imposing some additional plausible axioms on intertemporal decision making.

# BIBLIOGRAPHY

Ackroyd, Peter. 1991. *Dickens*. HarperCollins, New York.

Adams, William, Liran Einav, Jonathan Levin. 2009. Liquidity constraints and imperfect information in subprime lending. *American Economic Review* 99(1): 49–84.

Agarwal, Sumit, Souphala Chomsisengphet, Chunlin Liu. 2010. The importance of adverse selection in the credit card market: Evidence from randomized trials of credit card solicitations. *Journal of Money, Credit and Banking* 42(4): 743–754.

Agarwal, Sumit, John C. Driscoll, David I. Laibson. 2013. Optimal mortgage refinancing: A closed-form solution. *Journal of Money, Credit and Banking* 45(4): 591–622.

Amar, M., D. Ariely, S. Ayal, C. E. Cryder, S. I. Rick. 2011. Winning the battle but losing the war: The psychology of debt management. *Journal of Marketing Research* 48: 538–550.

Angrist, J. D., J.-S. Pischke. 2009. *Mostly Harmless Econometrics: An Empiricist's Companion*. Princeton University Press, Princeton, NJ.

Ariely, Dan. 2010. *Predictably Irrational: The Hidden Forces That Shape Our Decisions*. Rev. ed. HarperCollins, New York.

Ausubel, Lawrence M. 1999. Adverse selection in the credit card market. Working paper, University of Maryland.

Baig, Suleman, Moorad Choudry. 2013. *The Mechanics of Securitization: A Practical Guide to Structuring and Closing Asset-Backed Security Transactions*. John Wiley & Sons, Hoboken, NJ.

Bajaj, Vikas, Jack Healy. 2008. Stocks drop sharply and credit markets seize up. *New York Times*, November 19, B1.

Banks, J., Z. Oldfield. 2007. Understanding pensions: Cognitive function, numerical ability and retirement saving. *Fiscal Studies* 28(2): 143–170.

Barnes, Brenda A. 2012. Airline pricing. Özalp Özer, Robert L. Phillips, eds., *The Oxford Handbook of Pricing Management*. Oxford University Press, 135–151.

Baughn, W. H., C. E. Walker. 1978. *Bankers' Handbook*. Dow Jones–Irwin, Homewood, IL.

Beddows, Sarah, Mick McAteer. 2014. *Payday Lending: Fixing a Broken Market*. Association of Chartered Certified Accountants (ACCA), London.

Bernerth, J. B., S. G. Taylor, H. J. Walker, D. S. Whitman. 2012. An empirical investigation of dispositional antecedents and performance-related outcomes of credit scores. *Journal of Applied Psychology* 97(2): 469–478.

Beshears, John L., James J. Choi, David Laibson, Brigitte C. Madrian, Jung Sakong. 2011. Self control and liquidity: How to design a commitment contract. RAND Working Paper Series WR-895-SSA.

Bijmolt, T., H. J. Heerde, R. G. Pieters. 2005. New empirical generalizations on the determinants of price elasticity. *Journal of Marketing Research* 42(2): 141–156.

Blake, T., C. Nosko, Steve Tadelis. 2015. Consumer heterogeneity and paid search effectiveness: A large scale field experiment. *Econometrica* 83(1): 155–174.

Blattberg, Robert C., Richard A. Briesch. 2012. Sales promotions. Özalp Özer, Robert L. Phillips, eds., *The Oxford Handbook of Pricing Management*. Oxford University Press, 585–619.

Bodea, Tudor, Mark Ferguson. 2014. *Pricing: Segmentation and Analytics*. Business Expert Press, New York.

Boyd, Stephen, Lieven Vandenberghe. 2004. *Convex Optimization*. Cambridge University Press, Cambridge.

Bretzke, Tamikah. 2016. New software helps lenders negotiate real-time deals. *Mortgage Business*, September 26. https://www.mortgagebusiness.com.au/breaking-news/10302 -new-software-helps-negotiate-real-time-deals.

Calder, Lendol. 1999. *Financing the American Dream: A Cultural History of Consumer Credit*. Princeton University Press, Princeton, NJ.

Campbell, John Y., Joao F. Cocco. 2003. Household risk management and optimal mortgage choice. NBER Working Paper No. 9759.

Caskey, John P. 2010. Payday lending: New research and the big question. Working Paper No. 10-23, Federal Reserve Bank of Philadelphia.

Chen, Le, Alan Mislove, Christo Wilson. 2016. An empirical analysis of algorithmic pricing on Amazon marketplace. *Proceedings of the 25th International Conference on the World Wide Web*. 1339–1349.

Citigroup. 2016. *Digital Disruption: How Fintech Is Forcing Banking to a Tipping Point*. Citi Global Perspectives & Solutions, Washington DC.

Cohen, Peter, Robert Hahn, Jonathan Hall, Steven Levitt, Robert Metcalfe. 2016. Using big data to estimate consumer surplus: The case of Uber. NBER Working Paper No. 222627.

Consumer Financial Protection Bureau. 2012. *CFPB Supervision and Examination Manual*. CFPB, Washington DC.

Consumer Financial Protection Bureau. 2014. *Using Publicly Available Information to Proxy for Unidentified Race and Ethnicity: A Methodology and Assessment*. CFPB, Washington DC.

Conte, Christian. 2011. Christmas club accounts return to North Florida banks and credit unions. *Jacksonville Business Journal*, November 25. https://www.bizjournals.com/jacksonville/print-edition/2011/11/25/christmas-club-accounts-return-to.html.

Crossman, Penny. 2017. Is AI making credit scores better, or more confusing? *American Banker*, February 7. https://www.americanbanker.com/news/is-ai-making-credit -scores-better-or-more-confusing.

Den Boer, Arnoud. 2015. Dynamic pricing and learning: Historical origins, current research, and new directions. *Surveys in Operations Research and Management Science* 20(1): 1–18.

Deneckere, R. J., R. P. McAfee. 1996. Damaged goods. *Journal of Economics and Management Strategy* 5(2): 149–174.

Dermine, J. 2009. *Bank Valuation and Value-Based Management.* McGraw-Hill, New York.

Durand, D. 1941. *Risk Elements in Consumer Installment Financing, Technical Edition.* National Bureau of Economic Research, Washington DC.

Edelberg, Wendy. 2004. Testing for adverse selection and moral hazard in consumer loan markets. Finance and Economics Discussion Paper Series, Board of Governors of the Federal Reserve System.

Einav, Liran, Mark Jenkins, Jonathan Levin. 2013. The impact of credit scoring on consumer lending. *RAND Journal of Economics* 44(2): 249–274.

Federal Financial Institutions Examination Council (FFIEC). 1999. Interagency fair lending examination procedures. http://www/ffiec/gov.

Federal Reserve Bank of New York. 2017. Quarterly report on household debt and credit, May, 2017. Federal Reserve Bank of New York.

Federal Reserve Bank of St. Louis. 2017. Average maturity of new car loans at finance companies. https://fred.stlouisfed.org/series/DTCTLVENMNQ.

Frederick, Shane, George Loewenstein, Ted O'Donoghue. 2002. Time discounting and time preference: A critical review. *Journal of Economic Literature* 40(2): 351–401.

Gallino, S., A. Moreno. 2014. Integration of online and offline channels in retail: The impact of sharing reliable inventory availability information. *Management Science* 60(6): 1434–1451.

Gelber, Steven M. 2008. *Horse Trading in the Age of Cars: Men in the Marketplace.* Johns Hopkins University Press, Baltimore, MD.

Gerardi, Kristoph, Lorenz Goette, Stephan Meier. 2013. Numerical ability predicts mortgage default. *Proceedings of the National Academy of Sciences* 110(28): 11267–11271.

Golsteyn, B. H., H. Grönquist, Lindahl. L. 2014. Adolescent time preferences predict lifetime outcomes. *Economic Journal* 124(580): F739–F761.

Gorin, Thomas, P. Peter Belobaba. 2004. Revenue management performance in a low-fare airline environment: Insights from the passenger origin–destination simulator. *Journal of Revenue and Pricing Management* 3(3): 215–236.

Graeber, James. 2012. *Debt: The First 5,000 Years.* Melville House, New York.

Green, Paul E., V. Srinivasan. 1990. Conjoint analysis in marketing: New developments with implications for research and practice. *Journal of Marketing* 54(4): 3–19.

Hartwig, Robert P., Claire Wilkinson. 2003. The use of credit information in personal lines insurance underwriting. *Insurance Issues Series* 1(2). Insurance Information Institute, New York.

Hastie, Trevor, Robert Tibshirani, Jerome Friedman. 2009. *The Elements of Statistical Learning.* 2nd ed. Springer-Verlag, New York.

Haughwout, Andrew, Donghoon Lee, Joelle Scally, Wilbert van der Klaauw. 2015. Student loan borrowing and repayment trends, 2015. https://www.newyorkfed.org/media library.

Himmelstein, David U., Deborah Throne, Steffie Woolhandler. 2009. Medical bankruptcy in the United States, 2007: Results of a national study. *American Journal of Medicine* 122(8): 741–746.

Hinterhuber, Andreas. 2015. Violations of rational choice principles in pricing decisions. *Industrial Marketing Management* 47: 65–74.

Honigsberg, Colleen, Robert J. Jackson Jr., Richard Squire. 2016. The effects of usury laws on higher-risk borrowers. Columbia Business School Research Paper No. 16-38.

Huckstep, Aaron. 2007. Payday lending: Do outrageous prices necessarily mean outrageous profits? *Fordham Journal of Corporate and Financial Law* 12(1): 203–231.

Israel, S., A. Caspi, D. W. Belsky, H. Harrington, Hogan S., R. Houts, S. Ramrakha, S. Sanders, R. Poulton, T. E. Moffitt. 2014. Credit scores, cardiovascular disease risk, and human capital. *Proceedings of the National Academy of Sciences* 111(48): 17087–17092.

J. D. Power and Associates. 2015. *2015 Primary Mortgage Origination Satisfaction Study.* J. D. Power, Costa Mesa, CA.

James, Gareth, Daniela Witten, Trevor Hastie, Robert Tibshirani. 2013. *An Introduction to Statistical Learning: With Applications in R.* Springer-Verlag, New York.

Kahnemann, Daniel. 2011. *Thinking, Fast and Slow.* Farrar, Straus & Giroux, New York.

Kalotay, A. J., J. Qian. 2007. A pointer on points. *ORMS Today* 34(3): 12–16.

Kimes, Sheryl, Robert Phillips, Lisabet Summa. 2012. Pricing in restaurants. Özalp Özer, Robert L. Phillips, eds., *The Oxford Handbook of Pricing Management.* Oxford University Press, 106–120.

Knuth, D. 1996. Ancient Babylonian algorithms. D. Knuth, ed., *Selected Papers on Computer Science.* Cambridge University Press, 185–204.

Koopmans, Tjalling. 1960. Stationary ordinal utility and impatience. *Econometrica* 28: 287–309.

Krugman, Paul. 2009. *The Return of Depression Economics and the Crisis of 2008.* W. W. Norton, New York.

Kuckuk, Matt, Robert L. Phillips. 2010. Pricing optimization, segmentation and competitive advantage. https://nomissolutions.com.

Laibson, Daniel. 1997. Golden eggs and hyperbolic discounting. *Quarterly Journal of Economics* 112(2): 443–477.

Lariviere, Martin A. 2006. A note on probability distributions with increasing generalized failure rates. *Operations Research* 54(3): 602–604.

LaRosa, John. 2012. *U.S. Pawn Shops: An Industry Analysis.* Marketdata, Tampa.

Lewis, Edward M. 1991. *An Introduction to Credit Scoring.* Fair, Isaac and Co., San Rafael, CA.

Lewis, Michael. 2005. A dynamic programming approach to customer relationship pricing. *Management Science* 51(6): 986–994.

Lewis, Michael. 2016. *The Undoing Project: A Friendship That Changed Our Mind.* W. W. Norton, New York.

Lieberman, Warren. 2012. Cruise line pricing. Özalp Özer, Robert L. Phillips, eds., *The Oxford Handbook of Pricing Management.* Oxford University Press, 199–216.

Luenberger, David, Yinyu Ye. 2008. *Linear and Nonlinear Programming.* 4th ed. Springer, New York.

Lusardi, Annamaria. 2012. Numeracy, financial literacy and financial decision-making. NBER Working Paper No. 17821.

Lusardi, Annamaria, O. S. Mitchell. 2007. Baby boomer retirement security: The role of planning, financial literacy and housing wealth. *Journal of Monetary Economics* 54: 205–224.

Lusardi, Annamaria, Olivia S. Mitchell. 2011. How ordinary consumers make complex economic decisions: Financial literacy and retirement readiness. NBER Working Paper No. 17078.

Madrian, Briggite C., Dennis F. Shea. 2001. The power of suggestion: Inertia in 401(k) participation and savings behavior. *Quarterly Journal of Economics* 116: 1149–1225.

Markowitz, Harry. 1959. *Portfolio Selection: Efficient Diversification of Investment.* John Wiley & Sons, New York.

Martin, Craig. 2016. Don't buy the backlash—Consumers want a digital loan experience. *National Mortgage News.* https://www.nationalmortgagenews.com /opinion /dont-buy -the-backlash-consumers-want-a-digital-loan-experience.

Meier, Stephan, Charles Sprenger. 2010. Present-biased preferences and credit card borrowing. *American Economic Journal: Applied Economics* 2(1): 193–210.

Melzer, Brian. 2011. The real costs of credit access: Evidence from the payday lending market. *Quarterly Journal of Economics* 126(1): 517–555.

Mischel, Walter, Yuici Shoda, Monica L. Rodriguez. 1989. Delay of gratification in children. *Science* 244(4907): 933–938.

Mishkin, Frederic S. 2010. *The Economics of Money, Banking & Financial Markets.* 9th ed. Addison-Wesley, Boston.

Moenninghoff, Sebastian C., Axel Wieandt. 2013. The future of peer-to-peer finance. *Zeitschrift fur Betriebswirtschaftliche Forschung.* August–September: 466–487. Available at SSRN: https://ssrn.com /abstract=239088.

Morgan, Donald P., Michael R. Strain, Ihab Seblani. 2012. How payday credit access affects overdrafts and other outcomes. *Journal of Money, Credit and Banking* 44(2–3): 519–531.

Munnell, A., L. Browne, J. McEneaney, G. Tootell. 1996. Mortgage lending in Boston: Interpreting the HMDA data. *American Economic Review* 86(1): 25–53.

Myers, J. H., E. W. Forgy. 1963. The development of numerical credit evaluation systems. *Journal of the American Statistical Association* 58(303): 799–806.

Orme, Bryan K. 2009. *Getting Started with Conjoint Analysis.* 2nd ed. Research Publishers, London.

Özer, Özalp, Robert L. Phillips. 2012. Current challenges and future prospects for pricing management. Özalp Özer, Robert L. Phillips, eds., *The Oxford Handbook of Pricing Management.* Oxford University Press, 350–367.

Özer, Özalp, Karen Zheng. 2012. Behavioral economics of pricing. Özalp Özer, Robert L. Phillips, eds., *The Oxford Handbook of Pricing Management.* Oxford University Press, 415–464.

Phillips, R. L., R. Raffard. 2011. Price-driven adverse selection in consumer lending. Working Paper No. 2011-3, Center for Pricing and Revenue Management, Columbia University.

Phillips, R. L., A. S. Simson, G. van Ryzin. 2015. The effectiveness of field price discretion: Empirical evidence from auto lending. *Management Science* 61(8): 1741–1759.

Phillips, Robert L. 2005. *Pricing and Revenue Optimization.* Stanford University Press, Stanford, CA.

Phillips, Robert L. 2012a. Customized pricing. Özalp Özer, Robert L. Phillips, eds., *The Oxford Handbook of Pricing Management.* Oxford University Press, 465–491.

Phillips, Robert L. 2012b. Efficient frontiers in revenue management. *Journal of Pricing and Revenue Management* 11(4): 371–385.

Phillips, Robert L. 2014. Should people or algorithms set prices? *European Financial Review* (October–November): 33–35.

Poon, M. 2007. Scorecards as devices for consumer credit: The case of Fair, Isaac & Company Incorporated. M. Callon, Y. Millo, F. Muniesa, eds., *Market Devices.* Blackwell Publishing, New York, 284–306.

Read, Daniel, Barbara van Leuven. 1998. Predicting hunger: The effects of appetite and delay on choice. *Organizational Behavior and Human Decision Processes* 76(2): 189–205.

Rivers, D., Q. H. Vuong. 1988. Limited information estimators and exogeneity tests for simultaneous probit models. *Econometrica* 39(3): 347–366.

Ross, Stephen L., John Yinger. 2002. *The Color of Credit: Mortgage Discrimination, Research Methodology, and Fair-Lending Enforcement.* MIT Press, Cambridge, MA.

Samuelson, Paul. 1937. A note on measurement of utility. *Review of Economic Studies* 4(2): 155–161.

Simkovic, Michael. 2013. Competition and crisis in mortgage securitization. *Indiana Law Review* 88(1): 214–271.

Slovik, Patrick, Boris Cournéde. 2011. Macroeconomic impact of Basel III. OECD Economics Department Working Paper 844. doi: 10.1787/18151973.

Stango, Victor, Jonathan Zinman. 2009. What do consumers really pay on their checking and credit card accounts? Explicit, implicit and avoidable costs. *American Economic Review* 99(2): 424–429.

Stegman, Michael A. 2007. Payday lending. *Journal of Economic Perspectives* 21(1): 169–190.

Stegman, Michael A., Robert Faris. 2003. Payday lending: A business model that encourages chronic borrowing. *Economic Development Quarterly* 17(1): 18–32.

Stiglitz, Joseph E, Andrew Weiss. 1981. Credit rationing in markets with imperfect information. *American Economic Review* 71(3): 393–410.

Streitfeld, David. 2016. An online deal just for you (Oh, and everyone else, too). *New York Times,* March 6, A1.

Terry, Samuel H. 1869. *The Retailer's Manual.* Jennings Brothers, Newark, NJ.

Thaler, Richard. 1981. Some empirical evidence on dynamic inconsistency. *Economics Letters* 8(2): 201–207.

Thaler, Richard. 1990. Anomalies: Saving, fungibility, and mental accounts. *Journal of Economic Perspectives* 4(1): 193–205.

Thaler, Richard H., Cass Sunstein. 2009. *Nudge.* Penguin, New York.

Thomas, Lyn. 2009. *Consumer Credit Models: Pricing, Profit, and Portfolios.* Oxford University Press.

Thomas, Lyn, David B. Edelman, Jonathan. N. Crook. 2004. *Readings in Credit Scoring.* Oxford University Press.

Tsai, Chih-Fong, Ming-Lun Chen. 2010. Credit rating by hybrid machine learning techniques. *Applied Soft Computing* 10(4): 374–380.

van Ryzin, Garrett. 2012. Models of demand. Özalp Özer, Robert L. Phillips, eds., *The Oxford Handbook of Pricing Management.* Oxford University Press, 340–380.

Walker, Rob. 2017. How to trick people into saving money. *The Atlantic.* May, 72–79.

Wilkinson, G., J. Tingay. 2004. The use of affordability data—Does it add real value? Lyn C. Thomas, David B. Edelman, Jonathan N. Crook, eds., *Readings in Credit Scoring*. Oxford University Press, 63–72.

Woolson, Wendy. 2009. *In Hock: Pawning in America from the Revolution to the Great Depression*. University of Chicago Press.

# INDEX

Page numbers followed by "f" or "t" indicate material in figures or tables.

Printed and bound by CPI Group (UK) Ltd, Croydon, CR0 4YY

23/04/2025

14660941-0001